THE BOOK OF REVELATIONS

The Book of Revelations

Women and Their Secrets
from the 1950s to the Present Day

Juliet Nicolson

Chatto & Windus
LONDON

1 3 5 7 9 10 8 6 4 2

Chatto & Windus, an imprint of Vintage, is part of the
Penguin Random House group of companies

Vintage, Penguin Random House UK, One Embassy Gardens,
8 Viaduct Gardens, London SW11 7BW

penguin.co.uk/vintage
global.penguinrandomhouse.com

First published by Chatto & Windus in 2025

Typeset in 11/16pt AGaramondPro Pro by Six Red Marbles UK, Thetford, Norfolk
Printed and bound in Great Britain by Clays Ltd, Elcograf S.p.A.

The authorised representative in the EEA is Penguin Random House Ireland,
Morrison Chambers, 32 Nassau Street, Dublin D02 YH68

A CIP catalogue record for this book is available from the British Library

ISBN 9781784745318

For Clemmie and Flora,
Imo and Gigi,
and for the voices of daughters
and their daughters everywhere.

Content warning: this book contains sensitive content related to sexual assault and abuse.

Contents

Introduction

Secrecy is one of the most essential, and enigmatic, character-istics of human behaviour. It is embedded in the hard drive of our existence: a leading American psychologist estimates that most of us are holding an average of thirteen secrets at any one time. Secrets bind us together and they tear us apart. Secrets can thrill, but they are equally likely to torment; and those which run deepest travel down the generations wrapped up in betrayal, deceit, shame and fear.

Everyone has their unique experience around secrecy, the keeper and the divulger forever balancing on shifting ground. Choosing whether to conceal or reveal a secret may feel autonomous but more often external influences dictate those decisions. The punitive consequences of rule-breaking may be one deterrent, while another is the judgement of a Greek chorus of family, friends, lovers, colleagues, neighbours, complete strangers and increasingly the anonymous power wielded by social media. These conditions are constantly evolving as behaviour and beliefs that were once considered unacceptable, unrepeatable or illegal become decriminalised, accepted, celebrated, reassessed or re-condemned.

Secrets shroud the truth about our relationships and about our beliefs and practices around addiction, class, race, religion and sex. An outer persona often hides the private truth of an inner life, keeping to themselves the million unobserved thoughts, actions and pieces of information that no one else knows about, the desires either consummated or unfulfilled, the moments of solitary weeping when that feels like the only option. We keep secrets for fun, and for the thrill of being the chosen one, for that exhilarating and moving sense of being trusted with an exclusive knowledge. We keep secrets to protect ourselves, to protect others and to keep order. We keep secrets because we observe boundaries of dignity, loyalty and our own privacy. We do not always wish to reveal how often we sleep with someone, how we voted in a referendum or election, what we earn or who we have chosen to remember in our will. We tell our therapists and doctors things we would not tell our romantic partners. If we respect the importance of trust, we do not pass on confidences. Above all, we keep secrets that are associated with feelings of guilt, fear, shame, stigma and taboo. These are the secrets that require hiding parts of ourselves from public view. They are possibly the most common kind, and take the longest to reveal.

Echoing the old saying that 'a problem shared is a problem halved', the charity Age UK recognises that 'opening up and sharing thoughts, fears, and experiences can really help – whatever your age', which means 'none of us has to keep things to ourselves and feel alone'. And yet we take care with choosing who might bring us advice or comfort. We try to avoid sharing things with people for whom the niggle to tell might worm its way under the skin like an unscratched itch until the craving has been satisfied and confidences have been betrayed for the sake of gossip or revenge. But that transient relief, a powerful adrenalin hit, is followed by the devil's punishment – the long-term scarring effect of guilt, and the prospect of our volubility being found out.

Some secrets are never meant to be shared. Others, especially the kind dependent on romance, or the acquisition of a new skill, count on the moment of revelation: the arrival of an unexpected, much loved guest; the evidence of a perfect backstroke after swimming lessons taken in secret; the word-perfect recital of a poem learned as a surprise; the planning of a marriage proposal, a birthday party; a delivery down the chimney on Christmas Eve by a figure whose identity must remain a secret withheld, but only from children, for ever.

My childhood was cobwebbed with secrets, floating invisibly through adult conversations, unexplained but occasionally illuminated by a glancing ray of guesswork. I was an early secret-keeper too. When I was quite small, but old enough to read, I would escape with a book to the beam-ceilinged attic at home, a space that no one else ever bothered to enter. A small table had been left up there many years before, together with a folding chair, positioned in front of a small window under the slope of the eaves. It was the perfect refuge, a place to be unfindable, unaccountable; a place to read, to hide, to think, to exist in secret.

Women are often the gatekeepers of secrets, their reasons for revelation or concealment under constant vigilance, continual review. This is a multi-generational story about women's changing relationship with secrecy – how it has evolved, altered and, on occasion, remained unchanged since the end of the Second World War. The subject is immense, the number and type of possible secrets inexhaustible. My starting point is personal, subjective, limited: the ways in which secrecy touched, guided, harmed, inhibited and sometimes liberated women like my mother, my daughters and myself through the different phases of our upbringing and the changes in our social environment. Because of women's position at the heart of family life, we have often been society's secret-keepers, so our secrets are particularly telling.

As I heard the stories of more and more women, the wider context and significance of secrecy came into fuller focus. And while I knew that personal stories, despite being gathered from women of different ages and backgrounds, could never hope to give a complete picture, or encompass every experience or type of secret, I began to see common denominators in how secrets can reveal some aspects of the way society functions at large: the secrets we hold inside mirroring the ways of the outside world.

During the course of writing this book, I have learned how women of different generations and cultures, bending, shaping and reacting against the shifting pressures of society and the law, have fought to protect themselves – both by keeping silent and by unsilencing themselves. The secrets that pinioned and delighted our grandmothers vary from the secrets that have preoccupied their daughters and granddaughters. I began to see how the narrative arc of women and secrecy has run in parallel with the progression of the campaign for gender equality. Changes in the law, often as a result of the work of feminist activists, advances in technology, gradual societal emancipation, growing intolerance of shame and prejudice and a collective facing-down of fear have all contributed to the transformation of women's relationship with secret-keeping. But what does the future hold? As I reached the end of the first quarter of this century a downwards curve, dipping away from the revealing of truth, became increasingly evident and, in many cases, alarming. I questioned whether a retreat for women back to silence in the face of the incessant glare and judgement of social media is inevitable. And so this is a book not only about the freedom of speech but about the freedom to choose when to speak and when to remain silent – when to keep our secrets secret.

The compulsion and obligation to keep secrets has long inhibited women's freedom and emphasised their subjugation and position as outsiders, existing for so long on the sidelines of society's hierarchy. From the end of the sixteenth century and right up until the Victorian age, women who gossiped, slandered, blasphemed or spoke in inappropriate tones to their husbands were known as 'scolds' or, as Shakespeare termed them, 'shrews'. These women were made to wear a mask known as a 'Scold's Bridle', an iron contraption that fitted over the top of the head, stretched over the nose and finished in a metal gag across the mouth. Attached to the mouth shield was a tongue suppressor, sometimes fitted with spikes, with the whole device held in position by a padlock behind the neck. In the 1950s, when women were returned to a state of pre-war submissiveness, the accompanying suppression of the female voice was more subtle than a metal tongue trap but no less effective. But in the sixties the contraceptive pill, the ultimate game changer, together with women's growing determination to challenge the status quo (and to be heard doing so), formed the basis for that decade's activism. By giving women choice and control over their sexual and reproductive decisions, levels of societal tolerance began to increase, preparing the way for the Second Wave of the feminist movement and its campaign for economic and political equality.

In the 1970s the experience of being the second sex, nurtured and passed down for millennia, had also encouraged the instinct to observe. At last the means of expressing those observations was becoming possible. The setting up of physical refuges for victims of hidden abuse, and the launch of publications such as *Spare Rib* magazine in the UK and *Ms* magazine in America, eased isolation and offered women the chance to write openly about their ideas and concerns and to know they would be read and listened to, at least by other women. In the 1980s and 1990s therapy started to go mainstream and the changing focus of the popular media provided outlets for confiding previously hidden, puzzling or shameful experiences and thoughts. The gradual relaxing of rules around same-sex partners in 1967 and a new transparency over the details of adoption in governmental acts passed in 1958 and 1960 saw a slow tank roll towards the lifting of legal restraints on aspects of life that had been conducted in secret for so long. The Third Wave of the feminist movement, led in the 1990s by Gen X – women born in the mid-1960s and 1970s – set out to broaden and diversify the feminist cause. The new century belonged to those born in the 1980s and early '90s, the Millennials. This latest phase coincided with the dizzying progress of technology, enabling the rapid spread of world-wide secret-sharing and solidarity – as happened with the 2017 #MeToo movement, when outing abusive behaviour by men resulted in an epidemic of truth-telling.

However, the power and freedoms of social media – the very tools that had encouraged such abuse to be brought out of hiding – soon began to curdle. The uncontrollable, largely unmonitored roller coaster of technology brought with it a danger that had not been fully anticipated by consumers. Anonymity licensed a backlash against confessional 'over-sharing' and freely expressed opinion, offering few places to hide. Platforms like Facebook, X (formerly known as Twitter) and Instagram, as well as CCTV, drones and data theft, removed the boundaries of privacy held sacrosanct by earlier generations, leaving users potentially open to relentless criticism and worse. Trolling introduced an element of fear that saw professional women and those in the public eye choosing to retreat from the vulnerability of fame. Terminology to describe the precarious and punitive consequences of over-sharing, over-confiding and daring to speak openly about personal convictions included 'gaslighting', 'cancelling' and 'ghosting' – concepts co-opted from very different arenas. The rise of populism, punitive political regimes and targeted, personal attacks around the world has in some cases discouraged women from speaking out at all, making a return to secrecy feel like the safer option. In other cases, for example under the gender apartheid in Afghanistan, women have been effectively erased from public life. The long and incomplete campaign for gender equality has become so ruptured with uncertainty that Dr Hannah Dawson of King's College, London, editor of *The Penguin Book of Feminist Writing*, wonders, 'Are we waving or drowning?'

In 1977 the poet Audre Lorde expressed the consequences of silence with transcendent eloquence; her recognition of the inbuilt dilemma in speaking out has lost none of its relevance over half a century later. 'Of course, I am afraid,' she wrote, 'because the transformation of silence into language and action is an act of self-revelation and that always seems fraught with danger.'

As a queer Black woman, Lorde acknowledged the wisdom of the advice given to her by her daughter when Lorde was facing her own mortality: 'You're never really a whole person if you remain silent because there's always that little piece inside you that wants to be spoken out and if you keep ignoring it – it gets madder and hotter and hotter and if you don't speak it out one day it will just up and punch you in the mouth from the inside.' Because we know there will be an ultimate ending for us all, it is essential that silence during life is interrupted before the arrival of the final silencing of death.

This story of secrecy has emerged as a kind of mosaic, formed by looking through three interlocking lenses down the decades and generations. The process of unsilencing has taken place at a range of vocal levels – from a roar to a whisper – and the first lens focuses on the women's movement, and the women who, with courage, energy and tenacity, have fought for so long for human and gender rights. The second perspective is more intimate, and comes from conversations with private individuals who agreed to speak to me about the personal tyranny of secret-keeping, and the specific acts of courage required to confront family as well as society's prejudices. Some of these women I had met over the years through work, travel and friendship, others I came across as my research widened from there. These stories and confessions, so generously shared, have often been difficult to hear, and even more often difficult to tell. My family's many secrets have also changed with the times, so my own experiences form the third and autobiographical viewpoint of the book.

As secrets have emerged, slipped, tumbled from attics, cupboards, shelves, and from the deepest recesses of our minds, the act of exposing vulnerabilities, sharing hidden fears and lancing the corrosive, toxic effect of secrecy has confirmed to me that trust is humanity's indispensable force field. Some details and identities in this book have been changed for privacy and protection in agreement with several of those who have told their stories to me.

I have had no wish to include tales that disparage or malign but rather to write about some of the emotional, psychological and societal effects of concealment. Why do we keep secrets? And why do we reveal them? This book, partly in the shape of a memoir, covers seventy or so years of a lifetime defined at times by the political and personal challenges of three generations of women caught up in hiding, sharing, betraying and defying the act of secret-keeping.

PART I

My Mother's Generation

1950–1970

CHAPTER I

Opinions Neither Heard nor Sought

Families safeguard their own secrets, embellishing and validating, protecting the narrative with each passing generation. The writer and potter Edmund de Waal remembered how, when talking to his grandmother Elisabeth, the conversation would be punctuated by 'hesitancies that trembled into silences, silences that marked places of loss'. In her 2003 memoir *Giving Up the Ghost*, Hilary Mantel describes how 'once a family has acquired a habit of secrecy, memories begin to distort because its members confabulate to cover the gaps in the facts'. And then, Mantel cautions, 'Distortions breed distortion', until 'all the memories are laid side by side, at the same depth, like seeds under the soil'.

My husband's Aunt Pam was born in 1916 during the First World War and she and I often talked about her childhood spent during and in the aftermath of that conflict. Maybe because I was only a niece by marriage she felt less inhibited than talking to a closer relation. Pam would invite me to tea in her sunny conservatory and we would talk until darkness fell, unravelling the stigmas of both of our past lives. They were conversations that I looked forward to like no other, as Pam responded to my prompting and uncovered those seeds long-buried beneath the surface of her memory, sharing with me their depth and significance.

'What did you have for lunch on Sundays?' I once asked her.

'Roast chicken,' she replied without hesitation, before adding, 'I always wore my best red dress on Sundays. I hated that dress. The wool scratched my bare legs. But I never complained.'

'Why ever not?'

'Because I didn't dare make my father cross,' the full force of her father's temper evident in her voice as the memory suddenly returned to her.

The second youngest of five siblings, Pam was only three years old when, in 1919, she and her mother Ethel both caught the Spanish flu that decimated millions across the world. Somehow Ethel nursed herself and her daughter back to health, the sensation of reassurance and maternal devotion moving Pam to tears some ninety-five years later. Oh, how she had loved her mother! A woman with huge eyes 'like beautiful blackbirds' eggs, greenish-blue', abused in word and deed by Basil, who rationed his wife's household allowance as much as he rationed marital fidelity. Pam and her sister Stella used to tell their elder brother that he 'must tackle Daddy. He is making Mummy unhappy. You must kill him.'

But the children were all too frightened of their father to confront him and the infidelity as well as the unhappiness continued. After Ethel's early death at the age of fifty-five, Pam found a sealed letter from her mother addressed to Basil, asking for a separation. It had never been posted. While the courage to take control into her own hands had failed Ethel, Pam's own inability to protect her mother had left her with lifelong regret. During our conversations I would watch her strong, handsome profile, her expression registering every passing feeling. Whenever she spoke about her mother she closed her eyes and a smile, transient but transformative, would float across her face. But with the release of the bad memories, the deep secrets, the guilt she felt at betraying her father and in confiding the secret which had been suppressed for so long, her distress was unmissable. What had once seemed like the irrelevant details of a Sunday lunch and a red dress almost lost to memory had triggered the Proustian recall and brought Pam to the point of confession.

The timing of an admission such as Pam's often coincides with the last years of life, especially for those who had survived two world wars. Pam lived through a time when it was considered indecorous to share private emotions when so many were suffering and secret-keeping became second nature. Unsurprisingly, some women of Pam's generation became professional secret-keepers during the Second World War, chosen to work in intelligence at Bletchley Park. Pledging their silence for the security of their country, these code-breakers kept their life-long oath never to divulge information even in old age.

Betty Webb MBE became part of the Bletchley team in 1941 aged eighteen. Her parents had no idea what she was doing except that she wore a uniform and an intelligence badge. In her memoir *No More Secrets*, published in 2023, Webb described how the signing of the Official Secrets Act took place in an office at Bletchley where the presiding army captain spoke to her with 'a gun resting on the corner of the desk'. She was advised that discussing her work outside the department would be considered an act of treason, punishable by death. Thirty-four years later that wartime oath of secrecy was lifted, too late for Webb's deceased parents to learn what their remarkable daughter had done in the war. Released from her vow, twenty more years elapsed before Webb felt able to talk about her experiences.

Others chose to remain silent almost for ever. Pippa Latour was the last of the surviving female agents in the Special Operations Executive (SOE) in the same war. Born in South Africa, the daughter of a French doctor and an English mother, she moved to the UK aged eighteen in 1939. Fluent in French, she joined the Women's Auxiliary Airforce (WAAF) and in 1944 she was parachuted into Normandy. Working under the disguise of 'Genevieve', a French soap seller trading from her bicycle, Latour picked up information from the German soldiers who were her customers. Using Morse code to send her findings back to her HQ in England, she stored the encrypted codes on a piece of silk. Wrapping the silk round a knitting needle, she skewered the information into a flat shoelace, pinning up her hair with the precious but undetected receptacle for her all-important secrets. Forever aware that her information had contributed to the Allied invasion and the resulting death of innocent French civilians, she remained reluctant to talk about her wartime life until a year before her death in 2023. But at the age of 102 Latour decided to tell her story in her memoir *The Last Secret Agent*, co-written with journalist Jude Dobson and published posthumously, revealing for the first time the true extent of Latour's heroism.

Secrecy was endemic in other female members of my family from that wartime generation, too. My first mother-in-law, Elizabeth, and her sister and brother were born in the late 1920s and early 1930s, the children of two British Mosleyites. Diana, Elizabeth's younger sister, remembered being taken to meetings organised by the fascist leader Oswald Mosley and encouraged by her parents to chalk antisemitic phrases including 'Perish the Jews' (sometimes 'Perish Judah') on the town walls of Bognor Regis. When Diana was away at her convent boarding school she nearly fainted when the Mother Superior informed her that her mother Alma had been locked up in Holloway Prison for her fascist sympathies.

One day Diana was taken to Holloway to visit Alma. Her mother, suddenly an almost unrecognisable white-haired figure, 'looked absolutely distraught. She was crying all the time . . . she was not my mother at all. I felt almost repulsion.' Diana finally admitted on BBC radio in 2010 that by writing those slogans on the walls she felt she had personally participated in the Holocaust. 'When Richard Dimbleby went into Belsen,' she said, 'I felt the guilt of the whole of the world on my shoulders. I felt utterly responsible for what happened in those camps in Europe.' But the confession all those years later brought her no relief. As she described it, the guilt had 'dug right into me' and she could find no route back to self-absolution.

Stella, Aunt Pam's sister and the mother of my husband Charlie, lived all her married life with the consequences of a secret. When she got engaged to her boyfriend Philip, she didn't know he was secretly in love with another woman. That woman was expecting his child. The day before the wedding Philip confessed his secret to his fiancée, and admitted he loved the other woman more. He gave Stella the choice of going ahead with the marriage or of calling the whole thing off. The stigma attached to being jilted in the late 1930s felt unsurvivable. So, without telling anyone in her family what had happened, Stella agreed that the marriage should take place. For the rest of Philip's life, Stella never mentioned the other woman. But she tormented her husband in other ways and he tolerated her anger because of his guilt. Their children grew up through the 1940s and 1950s powerless to diffuse the tension that sometimes infected the whole household, with neither parent openly addressing the source of the antagonism.

I envy a dear friend who will not let her mother die without recording her life and their relationship in as full, honest and enquiring a way as they both know how. With the help of a sensitive and professional camera director, Helena and Elena have made a film together. Elena, born in 1934, her vivacity evident within five minutes of meeting her, understands the precious significance of this record-making all too well. Mother and daughter are banking memories about things big and small, confiding in one another and discussing everything that matters before it is too late. Laughter gives way to tears in a conversation that radiates tenderness as they address the inevitability that, one day, Helena will watch the film alone.

No such film would have been possible for me and my mother Philippa, who was born in 1928 – the first year of the era defined in 1951 by the American magazine *Time* as 'The Silent Generation' to describe those born between 1928 and 1945 and who reached adulthood in the 1950s and early 1960s. The parents of these 'Silent' children, arriving in the interval that divided the economic dip of the Great Depression from the end of the Second World War, were still reeling from the decimation of so many young men. The memories of those lost boys were cherished, their special significance transferred to the male children who succeeded them.

Philippa didn't stand a chance. Insignificantly positioned between two brothers, effectively silenced from the word go, she knew her place. As laws rendered married women, however qualified, ineligible from most salaried occupations, education was considered secondary to the housekeeping skills that were necessary for a successful marriage and for motherhood. The only daughter of a businessman and his class-conscious wife, my mother was raised never to object. Countryside life contributed to her isolation. Her brothers were either away at boarding school or up in town. Her parents were often holidaying in their villa in the South of France, satisfying their love of canasta and cocktails, while their daughter remained at home sweeping and dusting the Edwardian house in the New Forest, riding her ponies and avoiding the sharp-edged gorse bushes which pricked up through the surrounding scrub.

Secrecy was my mother's go-to protection. Even if she had attempted any confession while she was alive, I doubt I would have listened. As part of her mother's legacy, her stories were repetitive and showy-off name-drops, full of kings and queens, prime ministers and celebrities that she and her parents, and even her grandparents, had once seen/met/dined with. There were conventions around food – the order in which to eat cheese or pudding, the precise position in which to lay down cutlery on a plate, the use of a fish knife or the temperature of water in a finger bowl, for heaven's sake. As a child I swallowed this guidance whole but as I grew older I felt these codes and affectations belonged to a previous, class-contained generation and I wanted no part in them. I now feel guilty about treating my mother with such impatience. A woman awarded considerable material privilege but whose confidence, both as a child and as a wife, had been undermined by a suffocating patriarchal contempt and whose opinions were neither heard nor sought, simply moulded, did not deserve such harsh judgement from a daughter.

Philippa was fourteen when her school was requisitioned by the army in the middle of the Second World War, bringing her formal education to a sudden end. As this was also the government's cut-off age for mandatory school attendance, no one considered extending my mother's academic instruction, which sons would have merited. When the Second World War ended and the soldiers, sailors and airmen returned home, the freedom that some women had become accustomed to during the conflict stalled. The decade following the Great War of 1914–18 had been quite different. A limited suffrage was won for women over the age of thirty in 1918 at the time of the Armistice, bowling its newly empowered voters through the 1920s when the extent of eligibility was widened to cover the over twenty-one-year-olds in 1928. With their hair cropped, and their bosoms flattened, a modish androgyny symbolised the new equality. In contrast, women who grew up in the aftermath of the 1939–1945 conflict found themselves expected to slip back into a state of acceptance, the 'second sex' returned to its proper place. My mother's educational lack was a source of shame throughout her life, and the fact that it was readily explainable did nothing to ease her sense of inadequacy. Her parents considered her hands-on experience at keeping house for them followed by a stint in the kitchens at the classy Dorchester Hotel in London sufficient to qualify her as good wife material. She knew little of adult relationships growing up. But courted and flattered at a neighbour's drinks party in 1952 by the attention of the local Conservative MP more than a decade her senior, my twenty-four-year-old mother jumped at the chance to escape. The mismatch in my parents' relationship was obvious from the start, her youthful, spontaneous gaiety and innocence clashing with her husband's relentless reminders of the gaps in her education. Sometimes the language in her surviving letters to him indicate how she tried to impress him, using unfamiliar words, experimenting with similes and descriptions with lots of adjectives. I didn't realise why at the time, but her jealousy of the educational opportunities offered to me became a source of unspoken tension between us, only openly erupting in letters exchanged between my parents where my mother argued that I was not the right 'material' to attempt to land a place at university.

Although distressed by her husband's criticism of her intellectual limitations, it was the physical side of her marriage that upset my mother most. Sexually inexperienced right up until her 1953 wedding night, she discovered she had married a man for whom love-making was, at his own later admission, a source of 'repugnancy', his self-reproach manifested in open resentment of my mother's evident longing for demonstrative love. Even if she had overcome her shame and embarrassment, she would not have known where to seek advice. So, she kept her confusion to herself, even from, or *especially* from, her husband. My father was barely more sexually conscious, having been fixed up by a friend just a few years before his marriage with a 'resting' actress who had relieved him of his innocence. The 'event' was as functional for him as passing his driving test, and he probably remained borderline-competent in both 'skills' for the rest of his life.

In 1955, a couple of winters into her marriage, my mother was diagnosed with tuberculosis and admitted for a lengthy stay to St George's Hospital in London before convalescing for a year at her mother's house in the New Forest. Total bed rest and incarceration were considered essential for the cure, and to prevent others from catching a disease thought to be spread through speaking, coughing or singing. This serious illness meant a year's enforced isolation from her still-new husband and her ten-month-old baby. What did she feel about being separated from us during those days she spent back in her old childhood bedroom? I longed for a photographic record to help me find my way back to her again. But the albums which covered those very early years of her marriage and her subsequent motherhood went missing after her death. I could only guess at her loneliness and sadness as marriage and motherhood were put on hold. Since her death many years ago I have made many attempts to understand her. Even though I know 'things' should not matter, I am conscious that I have almost nothing tangible to remind me of her. Just as the Russian wedding ring she was wearing when she died, one of the very few things of hers that I owned, slid off my finger one careless day and fell between the cracks of a pavement, my long-tentative grasp of my mother has slipped over the years to what felt like irretrievable depths.

I would love the chance to begin my relationship with my mother all over again. I have imagined, in an admitted spirit of stagey styling, seeing her walk into my house on a perfect summer morning, a soft breeze blowing rose petals in through the open door. Sitting across from one another at the kitchen table, I would try to persuade her to give herself up to a conversation inhibited in life and truncated by death. Aunt Pam's late willingness to confide suggested to me that my mother might also eventually have agreed to talk. Would my own understanding of secrecy and a hard-won twenty-first-century ease with the baring of the soul, with asking for help, with admitting ignorance and fear, mean anything to her? When memory is the narrative device we use to make sense of our past, would we ever be able to untangle the edits and arrive at something that felt like the truth?

In my make-believe scene, embellished with teapot and cake, we would travel between her youthful past and the days we shared as mother and daughter. If I could bring her back just one more time, maybe we could dismantle the barbed wire muffled in the memory mist, remove the hazards of mistrust and disappointment that existed between us when she was alive. I would ask her to forgive me for judging her so harshly, for abandoning her after her second unhappy marriage. The years when I was away at university, easing myself into adulthood, friendship, love affairs, were the ones when I avoided her most, was quickest to judge her, failed to talk to her, failed to listen to her, failed to show her my love. These were the years when she drank so much that she could not remember if she had eaten either lunch or dinner, years when she sat slumped for hours unconscious in front of the horse-racing channel on television, years when she was covered in bruises from falling down stairs, years when she needed help most. But I was too young, too selfish, too free to realise. If I could talk to her now I would tell her how I wish I had done things differently. This time I would listen to her, give her my whole attention, hope to soften her fear of intimacy, try to love her into courage and honesty. I would tell her how I have learned that the exposing of vulnerabilities and the sharing of uncertainties releases fear and shame. The writer Helena Lee talks about the 'danger in the preservation of silence, in assuming that the experiences of previous generations exist in isolation'. Maybe my mother and I would have found common ground in places we never expected to.

I have discussed this fictional reunion with my own two daughters. 'Would your mother mind you asking her about why her secret life has puzzled and preoccupied you so much?' they wanted to know. 'And then writing about it? Has this whole idea actually come about just because you are still angry with her for being so absent, so elusive?'

The prospect of getting to the truth of my mother's life all these years later was admittedly daunting, and my daughters' questions about my motivation were valid. I had three answers for them. First, quite simply, I would love the chance to hear from someone who grew up almost a century ago about how the need to cling to secrecy trailed her and women like her through-out their lives. Secondly, from the perspective of a daughter's curiosity, I would like to know some of the truths buried within my parents' relationship. And thirdly, if I don't speak up for my mother now, champion her, prevent her from being forever silenced, I will have failed her and those others who also strug-gled at that time to find their voice. Writing about her doesn't feel like an act of betrayal but one of nearly-too-late filial respon-sibility. I am not angry *with* her. I am angry *for* her.

CHAPTER 2

Is That Normal?

At the end of the Second World War, the insularity of island life remained as deep-rooted as ever, deepened by a wartime patriotism that had on occasion encouraged xenophobic thinking and behaving. The Conservative Party manifesto in the 1951 general election, when Winston Churchill was returned as prime minister, emphasised that 'we must guard the British way of life, hallowed by centuries of tradition'. During the Second World War, when men were away defending the nation's liberty, the recognition of women's capability for managing all aspects of life in their absence had indicated progress. In 1945 sexual freedom was at the top of the agenda for those who had hoped the relatively liberal wartime codes of behaviour would last. But patriarchal control had returned, consigning many women to the position of understudy and to live once again in the shadow of their fathers, brothers, husbands, fiancés, uncles and cousins, as the male principals reclaimed their leading roles. The popular series of children's early reading books starring 'Janet and John' symbolised this attitude. Published in 1949, young Janet's weekends were spent helping her mother with the housework, while her brother John was busy cleaning the car with his father. During weekdays the father went to his office leaving the mother at home to do a bit more cleaning until the father returned to sit down to a wholesome supper cooked by his wife.

Janet's mother would have been grateful for the assistance of the new shiny machines that freed up time previously spent on washing clothes and dishes so women could, for example, focus on further enhancing their physical appearance for their husbands' approval. As the practical land-girl army breeches were packed away in attics, the moulding and shaping that went on beneath women's outer garments, corsetry famil-iar to their grandmothers, returned with all its buttoning and zipping and hooking and stretching and breath-holding and, above all, obscuring. The Playtex Cross Your Heart bra that 'lifts and separates' arrived in America in 1954 and soon crossed the Atlantic. The garment flattered as it held you in, kept you firmly in place, while providing a contouring emphasis on small waists, around which apron strings could be tied and finished with a tidy bow. While most women kept their bodies under wraps, there were provocative exceptions. Movie stars like Lana Turner and Jane Russell brought back the conical bra, which had first been popular in the early 1940s. Worn beneath clingy sweaters, the 1950s movie stars demonstrated its appeal and attracted the renewed attention and admiration of the male gaze. Those who desired the ample curves of Marilyn Monroe could invest in the 'Trés Secrete' bra, which concealed pads that could be inflated with a straw until the desired cup size was reached.

Domesticity was the idealised template. Conformity was not only admired but expected in all things, from religion and politics to sexual monogamy and clothing. Risk-taking was discouraged. Rationing restricted the adventurousness of menus. Nobody swore in polite society. Elvis had not yet recorded a single or swung his provocative hips. This was the context in which my virginal mother grew up, wearing her flowered and belted tea dresses, going to the local Church of England service on Sundays, voting Conservative, remaining eager to please, to be approved of, hoping but not expecting to be noticed.

The marriage bar was still in place, except for in the teaching profession and the BBC, which meant that women who had worked prior to marriage were obliged to exchange their jobs for keeping house the minute they made their vows. After marriage they needed spousal permission to open a bank account and were banned from getting a mortgage. Women jurors were disqualified if they were not the formal owner or occupier of a property, if the judge preferred a single-sex jury or if he took objection to an individual juror. With most juries comprised of men, the judgement of one half of the population was statistically considered less valuable than the other. In his 1952 pamphlet *Social Work, A Quarterly Review of Family Casework*, social researcher Professor Richard M. Titmuss profiled a 'normal or average family' in which a husband should not disclose his earnings to his wife but be 'generous' with housekeeping money and not gamble or drink. A wife, as well as being 'clean respectable and tidy', should 'run the house efficiently'.

This wasn't only a British post-war phenomenon. The segregation of duties and entitlement applied just as much across the Atlantic. Elizabeth A. Rogers, an American self-described member of the Silent Generation, described in her blog 'As Time Goes By' how 'being submissive, taking a back seat and not rocking the boat were prized female traits, while laying waste to the potential of a generation of women'. Only in 1960 did she begin to question the status quo 'and rejected much of it entirely by the mid-1970s when I started learning to speak my truth'. The American feminist Gloria Steinem, born in 1934, described recently in a BBC radio programme how, as she was reaching adulthood in the 1950s, she still believed the previous generation's teaching that 'the reality of choice' meant marriage and children, 'supported by a man's income'. The prevalence of 'conservatism in the public imagination' went unchallenged by women like herself, who she regarded as 'a 1950s person'.

By the early 1950s women were expected to tolerate a climate of sexual secrecy, widespread ignorance and a dearth of advice in a culture where contraception, abortion, illegitimacy, sex before marriage and sex across cultural and religious boundaries all risked consequences. But the freedoms of the war had brought a culture of acceptance. Historian Dr Caroline Rusterholz has observed how 'British couples were trying to navigate changing sexual norms while caught between two cultures: rigid emotional restraint versus a new sense of self-awareness and openness . . . so this period created opportunities but also huge pressure and suffering'. Shame and ignorance about anything considered 'unmentionable' held women back from speaking to their mothers, sisters, friends, doctors and especially their boyfriends, fiancées and husbands. As feminist Katharine Whitehorn observed, 'people have this idea that no one had sex in the 1950s because the convention was not to talk about it'. Everything that involved sex, conception and birth demanded an approach that was polite at best but more often embarrassing, surreptitious, ill-informed, illegal, dangerous, fearful and secret. In 1953 the sexologist Alfred Kinsey published his report, *Sexual Behaviour in the Human Female*, which revealed that 69 per cent of men had engaged with a sex worker and 10 per cent of men were gay. Rape of a wife by a husband was legal (and would remain so until a new law was passed in 1991). Loneliness emerged as the most frequent underlying cause for women's suicide.

However, statistics indicated that desire was, as it were, on the rise. While 19 per cent of women who had come of age in the 1920s admitted to pre-marital sex, 43 per cent of my mother's generation confessed they would not wait for a wedding band. Those tempted to 'go all the way' were confronted by two distinct deterrents: the stigma of being thought of by men as 'used goods' and the consequences of an unwanted pregnancy. The shame of unmarried motherhood blazed through all classes of society. But ignorance and unreliable contraception, combined with a new sense of post-war stability and the happy reunion of couples, resulted in a baby boom in the late 1940s and 1950s. Abortion was a procedure undertaken only by the desperate. The 1929 Infant Life Preservation Act had continued to outlaw abortion except when the woman's physical life was at risk. But there was no mention of the risky methods and physical consequences involved in a back-street termination. Jennifer Worth, a London nurse and midwife working in the East End in the 1950s, treated women who had lost their sight from the after-effects of lead poisoning; women suffering from the use of knitting needles, crochet hooks, scissors, paper knives and pickle forks, all of which formed part of the amateur surgeon's arsenal. 'From everything we heard, abortionists were in it for the money: the going rate was between one and two guineas,' Worth wrote, half a century later. Although these 'doctors' were simply responding to a market created by the absence of a humane law, she admitted she had 'never heard of one who was conducting a philanthropic practice', and ignorance, incompetence and avarice continued to characterise the work of the post-war abortionists. In the 1960s laws around abortion were revolutionised, beginning with the passing of the Abortion Act of 1967 when abortion was certified as legal if carried out by a qualified doctor before the twenty-fourth week of pregnancy, if the continuation of the pregnancy would cause physical or mental harm to the woman or if doctors anticipated that the baby would be born with a serious physical or mental handicap.

But in the 1950s, while abortion was the riskiest of undercover solutions to unwanted pregnancy, adoption offered another harrowing and often equally secretive alternative. In 1952 parents were permitted by law to give away unwanted children to anyone they chose, usually a grandparent or an aunt but, if no family member was willing, anyone who might answer a newspaper advertisement. In Britain the government passed a sequence of Acts including the Children Acts of 1948 and 1958 and the Adoption Act of 1958 specifically designed to 'safeguard the interests of the child, natural parents and adopters' and making 'fresh provision for the protection of children living away from their parents'. An estimated 13,000 adoptions were legally processed every year in the 1950s, but it is estimated that a further thousand were arranged without the involvement of local councils. There were reports of babies being left for collection in cardboard boxes in railway stations and telephone kiosks, while some children were sent even further out of sight. During the 1950s and 1960s between 3,000 and 7,000 children were shipped to Australia and a combined total of over 1,000 were sent to New Zealand, Rhodesia and Canada. In America, the Adoption Institute estimated an increase of 80 per cent in the number of babies put up for adoption between 1944 and 1955. Many of those babies would have no access to information about their origins.

For those women who did wait until marriage, the rewards of the wedding night were not always worth the suspense. The 1953 edition of Dr Helena Wright's book *More About the Sex Factor in Marriage* said that 'fifty out of every hundred wives still got through their years of married life without discovering that physical satisfaction can and should be as real and vivid for them as it is for their husbands'. Professional advice was limited. But Joan Malleson, doctor, gynaecological consultant and writer, was an exception. She had followed in the pioneering footsteps of two game-changing medical practitioners who had campaigned for the reproductive rights of women. In America Margaret Sanger had led the way. The sixth of eleven siblings (a further seven died before birth), Sanger had worked as a nurse in New York City before the First World War where the levels of poverty and the dangers of abortion motivated her to lobby inexhaustibly for sexual education and reform. Towards the end of her life, Sanger helped source the funding for research into a contraceptive pill (which she argued would eliminate the need for abortion to which she was militantly opposed), although her controversial views and evidence of a semi-tacit support of eugenics damaged her posthumous reputation. In 1918 Marie Stopes, the thirty-eight-year-old campaigner for women's rights and birth control, known as 'the agony auntie to the Empire', and founder of Britain's first contraceptive clinic, published *Married Love*. This bestselling book defined what she called 'the plain facts of marriage'. She explained to her readers the significance of the word 'pudenda', the collective noun for the female genitalia, derived from the Latin verb 'pudere', meaning 'to be ashamed'. And shame was the prophylactic that Stopes set out to peel away, demystifying the options for birth control for a generation shackled by fear and superstition. During the Second World War contraceptive 'caps' had often been made from the thick red rubber used for hot-water bottles. A baffling range of Edwardian contraceptive options and devices were still available in the 1950s, including jellies designed to inhibit sperm, cocoa butter, the diaphragm, the condom, the douche, the pessary (resembling an upturned bowler hat) and the age-old practices of withdrawal and rhythm. None of these methods were reliable. But these were the ineffective choices that prevailed alongside beliefs that conception took place during open-mouth kissing, that babies were for sale in jars in chemists, born from tummy buttons or delivered to the house by a midwife who brought round the new arrival neatly wrapped up inside her medical case.

By 1956 Dr Joan Malleson, a Victorian born as the century was turning, had been in medical practice for three decades. Educated at the progressive, co-educational school of Bedales, she had a passion for hats, an aversion to blood, a hopeless memory for names and a faultless recollection of the size of a patient's contraceptive diaphragm. She was the second of the three wives of Miles Malleson, an eccentric and libidinous actor with whom she shared an open but tricky marriage. Having graduated from University College and Charing Cross Hospital in 1925, Dr Malleson became a specialist in gynaecology, family planning and sexual difficulties. In 1938, she was involved in a famous trial involving a fourteen-year-old girl who had become pregnant as a result of a gang rape. Dr Aleck Bourne, who performed the termination for the girl, was accused of criminal practice, but his defence and subsequent acquittal, supported by Malleson, resulted in a law change to allow abortion in cases of mental suffering, even though the expense of a psychiatrist's testimony in court put the option out of the way for most. After the war, Malleson continued to campaign for more legal flexibility around a patient's right to choose an abortion, and for their individual circumstances to be taken into account whenever that choice clashed with the law.

Malleson also gave broadcasts about sexual issues for BBC Radio, and contributed to medical journals under the pen name 'Medica'. And yet despite her progressive approach to sexuality, she was also a woman of her time. Her book *Any Wife or Any Husband* (1951) included a chapter covering 'common sexual deviations', including homosexuality, fetishism and sadomasochism, even though these subjects did not amount to 'a topic that the average person particularly likes'. But the book dealt largely with concerns about relationships slipping into trouble. 'If only he didn't treat me as a housekeeper' . . . 'he will never speak at all about sexual matters so I can never explain' . . . 'he expects me to be ready for sexual intercourse without a kind word having been spoken' . . . 'he is so close with money that I can't forgive him', were among the comments Malleson had heard from a variety of women. She found that men also kept complaints to themselves. 'How can I make love to her if she is always too busy?' they asked her. 'I know she tells her mother everything I say' . . . 'she does not think my food and comfort matter at all'. Malleson concluded that 'people seldom express such thoughts to one another and possibly few of their partners would pause and really listen should they try. Yet these trivial inflexibilities may disturb the very heart of marriage.'

But no book could match a face-to-face consultation. While teaching at University College Hospital and the North Kensington Marriage Welfare Centre, Malleson established her own practice in Kent Terrace in London's Regent's Park; she also gave advice at London's University College's contraceptive clinic. She was a pioneer in psychosexual counselling, which was an almost non-existent practice in the family planning clinics of the 1950s. Under the Family Planning Association guidelines, consultants were not supposed to advise unmarried women, so Malleson's patients, as described later by her son Andrew, were mostly but not exclusively married, ranging from 'working-class women many of whom were prostitutes to middle-upper-class, left-wing intellectuals'. Known for her charming manner, the more Malleson listened to her patients, the more she realised they needed something more than practical advice about where to buy lubricant, how to apply it or how to insert a 'dilator'. One woman, rescued from her regular beat on the streets in a state of physical collapse after a botched abortion, became one of Malleson's sons' nannies. Some were directed to Malleson's practice by GPs who not only valued her gynaecological expertise but felt themselves to be less qualified in advising patients about psychological or emotional problems, especially those experienced by women. Patients who were referred to Malleson's consulting rooms ostensibly to ask for advice about contraception and sexual health, gradually realised that Malleson might be able to help them beyond the ostensible problem. Having initially struggled with embarrassment and self-censorship, Joan Malleson's patients would finally admit their suspicion and hope that there could be more to their sex lives, if only they knew what. Malleson, much more than a woman's medical specialist, offered sympathetic and constructive advice, inviting her patients to open up to her in a way they had never dreamed possible, encouraged to tip over the boundaries of a conventional consultation into something that became intimate and often heartbreaking.

As she listened to tales of ignorance, inadequacy and plummeting self-esteem, Malleson was keeping a huge secret of her own. Over the winter of 1955–6, trusting in the discretion of their one-to-one private consultations, these young women had no idea that a hole drilled into the vase of dried flowers beside Malleson's desk concealed a microphone. A large tape machine hidden beneath Malleson's desk was controlled by a discreet switch on top of the desk. In her other consulting rooms at the hospital she had installed a smaller, less cumbersome dictating device that could be moved around and operated by a foot pedal. With the help of Andrew, Malleson had set up a system in which every hesitant word spoken by fourteen of these women was secretly recorded. Explaining later that his mother was aware of the research value that these sessions might hold for her, Andrew described how she would switch on the tape 'when she had an interesting subject for teaching material'. And while it seemed highly unlikely her patients would have agreed to cooperate, Malleson hoped that the results of the deception would offer invaluable insights for young student doctors of the future.

Some seventy years later, I was on my way to listen to the results of her unusual methods of information gathering. Passing University College Hospital on the Euston Road, a building I had not visited since the day my first granddaughter was born there ten years earlier, I thought of the vast changes in approach to pregnancy, childbirth and intimacy that had taken place since Malleson counselled her patients. The glass-faced Wellcome Collection gleamed in the morning light as I took the lift up to the audio and manuscript department of the beautiful high-tech library where the items I'd ordered up from the archive were waiting for me.

As I put on the bulky headphones and prepared to press the play button for the first tape, I hesitated. The action felt intrusive even though I knew that none of the fourteen women had been identified by name or background or even by the date of their appointment. I would be listening to confidences entrusted verbally so long ago, listening to unprecedented admissions by women who had never voiced, identified or shared these secrets and anxieties before, recorded without their permission, their words locked away for many years but now available to a complete stranger. I thought about my mother, about her vulnerability and her shyness. I would be listening to women like her. I pressed the button and entered the consulting space of the 1950s. Perhaps the rooms were overheated during those winter months and the windows slightly open as I thought I could just about hear the London buses rumbling along the road outside and a motorbike roaring away from a busy junction. Bursts of muted laughter floated out – perhaps from adjoining flimsy-curtained cubicles in the outside passageway. Occasionally the double incoming tring-tring of the 1950s telephone on Malleson's desk interrupted the calm questioning. The sound of a pencil tracing across a page was in my ear, the amplification faultless.

As the past collapses into the present, the authoritative voice of Malleson begins. She states briefly the year of birth of each woman and their age, ranging from twenty-two to thirty-eight, presumably recording this information before the arrival of each patient. And then, clear as daylight, each of these innocents begins to speak, feeling her way cautiously, the questions and answers both respectful and hesitant. Gently, Malleson tries to get to the heart of the matter.

A woman for whom childbirth (and therefore copulation) is terrifying describes her phobia.

'I know it is stupid,' she says, 'but I can't bear to see a pregnant woman. When my husband's sister was pregnant I felt physic-ally sick.'

Asked to expand, the patient says she does not know how her husband feels about this. If he knew, she 'wouldn't expect him to stay married to me', his release from the imprisonment of 'wed-*lock*' apparently more acceptable to him than it might be for her.

For another patient, having established that there has been no 'stroking' between her and her husband and that this young woman is therefore 'on very short rations', Malleson analyses the problem.

'You are too tight because you are frightened. Do you cry a lot? Feel very miserable? Wonder if it's all worth it? A sense of hope-lessness?' A note of criticism about other medical professionals creeps in. 'Did your doctor not show you how to relax when fitting the cap?'

Another woman, unusual because she is unmarried, follows each concerned statement with the same question.

'We've only done it three times. Is that normal? I've never cli-maxed. Is that normal?' And then, a little more explicitly, 'Last time it was like hard manual labour. It was hard to start, so to speak.'

'Mmmm. I see,' Malleson replies gently. 'Being unmarried *is* slightly anxious-making. Better circumstances will change things.' She continues at a rattling pace, evidently responding to the silent nods of the woman facing her. 'You do really love him now, do you? Yes? Well, that's a help, isn't it? Do you think he loves you? Well, that's a help. Might this go on to marriage? . . .Yes. Well, that gives you a bit more confidence, doesn't it? 'Cause some people are . . . afraid to love if they feel it won't go on to marriage, 'cause they're afraid of getting hurt, you see?'

Another admits her fear that she is 'undersexed, whatever that may mean'.

'Mmmm. Mmm. It's all different for everyone,' comes the reassuring opinion. 'Like if you laugh easily or not.'

One woman describes with pride that her man 'can last twenty minutes'.

'Oh yes,' says Malleson approvingly, 'that's a very confident man. Exceptional.'

Yet another patient is encouraged to set a precedent and 'take the lead' with a husband whose nervousness is attributed by Malleson to his upbringing. She suggests he may have had a 'weepy mother' which contributed to an 'unconscious guilt' that made him nervous of showing or evoking any feelings and a tendency to behave 'prudishly'.

Joan advises her patient to help him through his impotence by being 'cheerful'. 'Take the lead,' she advises, before enquiring, 'Has he been inside?' I have to concentrate very hard to hear the faint answer through my headphones.

'I don't really know.'

The importance of orgasm is emphasised. 'It's a difficulty of your generation. Because twenty years ago, thirty years ago, hardly any women knew that anyone could get an orgasm. It wasn't talked about. Now it's talked about, everyone thinks it should be a standard measurement and wonders if there's something wrong with them if they're not exactly like someone else they've heard about, you see.' After one patient admits to taking half an hour to apply 'artificial moisture', Malleson responds with undisguised astonishment: 'Why? . . . My dear! It shouldn't take . . .WHAT?!' But such innocence is rarely patronised. Indeed, Malleson herself favours euphemistic words and expressions for body parts, re-enforcing the 1950s taboo of using the anatomical terms for the vulva, vagina and clitoris.

'If you put a little more [lubricant] on just on the outside and outdoors of the passage . . . so that the tension at the doorway is at its very minimum. Do you see?' Suggestions are made for self-arousal and specific positions that might make sex more enjoyable. 'Bend your knees,' she instructs as she encourages her patients to relax.

Occasionally the patient is invited to step behind the screen and undress, at which point the tape falls silent: either it is switched off or the range is not powerful enough to reach the examination bed. One woman, who can't tell if her husband 'is getting in all right', was pronounced, after Malleson's examination, to be still 'intact'. On two or three occasions a male voice speaks through my headphones. Malleson's pencil, noting down his words, is picked up on the tape. The man and his wife have been trying to consummate their marriage for a year without success.

'He doesn't sort of do anything to me,' the wife tells Joan. 'He's forgotten it takes two.' She confesses that all she feels is 'boredom'.

Her husband explains the problem to Malleson. 'You have to stop and do one of these cold things like washing your teeth,' describing putting on a sheath. He would prefer it, he told Joan, if his wife took responsibility for contraception. He is gently reprimanded. 'You're a tiny bit backward in learning it all.' Does he understand about wooing? 'They like to be told how pretty they are over and over again. Women don't have the confidence that men have.' For the sake of her woman patient, she is conspiratorial with him, allowing the husband to believe she is on his side.

Sometimes her questions guide patients into their past as she enquires about half-remembered incidents or some secret event as far back as childhood, too painful to recall and therefore repressed. She suggests that their inhibitions and fears might be decreased, erased even, if past experiences seemingly unrelated to the current relationship were recalled and examined. Given her own marital unhappiness, the challenge of keeping her emotions out of some of these sessions must have been considerable, no matter how professionally she explained the workings of the psyche, as the secret recordings were not the only thing Joan Malleson kept to herself. She did not feel able to tell anyone, even those closest to her, about her husband's promiscuity, that his leaving her for another woman had caused her great distress despite their agreement to an open marriage, or about her experience of post-natal depression.

Andrew explained that his mother 'took great pains to hide her depression from the world. She worked hard for hours on end but then escaped into solitude and exhaustion.' Her ability to conduct her professional role with such empathetic skill, combined with her first-hand knowledge of the complexities of human relationships, gave her a set of unteachable credentials even though, despite many friends, she may have felt as lonely as her patients. But they, at least, had Malleson. In 1957, having left the taped consultations in her office drawer in Regent's

Park, she was en route back to Britain from a holiday in New Zealand when she stopped off in Fiji and went swimming in the South Pacific Ocean. She never returned to dry land. The cause of her death was officially attributed to complications from her 'slipped disc', but Andrew knew the truth. He remembered she had stated that if her private despair grew too much to bear she would 'inject herself with a large dose of insulin and swim out to sea. The cause of her death would remain undiscovered.'

In her meticulous analysis of Malleson's work, Dr Caroline Rusterholz considered various motives for Malleson's secret recordings. Although 'ethical guidelines in the 1950s didn't prohibit recording of this kind', if Malleson had asked permission to record the sessions, Rusterholz suggested the spontaneity of the consultation would have been inhibited, regardless of whether the reply was affirmative or negative. Andrew Malleson believed she mainly intended to use the tapes as an aide-memoire. Any act of breaking the Hippocratic Oath, in which a physician is required to swear to 'respect patients' autonomy and dignity, and uphold their confidentiality', remained safely unchallenged in the drawer, until nearly half a century later, when in 2003 Andrew gave the tapes to the Wellcome Collection.

After I listened to the words exchanged between Joan and her patients, and learned through her son's reminiscences about his mother's own secret suffering, I looked in the files at home for the account of my father's life written in his seventies, a confession which he had stipulated was not to be seen until after his death. As I read his description of his wedding night, I kept my mother in mind. Grateful that he had been spared 'the ordeal' expected of the first night of marriage, because his new wife 'had the curse', he confirmed, as if reviewing a West End play, that when 'the performance' came two nights later, 'it was adequate, but certainly not brilliant'. Almost immediately after their marriage he began to seek the undemanding privacy of the spare room. Fifteen years later he admitted to my mother's divorce lawyer that he 'did not realise that my sexual abstinence was causing her great distress, which accumulated over the years'. With some eventual insight of how his refusal (not even reluctance) to make love to her had affected her, he recognised her 'physical deprivation', as well as what was 'almost an insult, a humiliation' to her as a woman. But he was too late with his understanding. The physical void in their relationship was a source of secret anxiety for her and shame for him, amplifying the tense atmosphere of their marriage and not brought out in the open until the relationship had drifted beyond repair. In 1956, while Joan Malleson's patients were among a tiny minority of newly-weds to be given sexual and emotional guidance that year, others, like my parents, were not so fortunate. Without the know-how, courage or willingness to access marital or medical advice, marriages could become tangled in webs of secrecy and shame that would either end in divorce or sink to a level of unhappiness from which it was difficult to escape with your head and heart held high.

CHAPTER 3

I Was Something Once

Sex, and its perplexing role in romantic and marital relationships, was only one source of isolation felt by the young women of the 1950s. Obvious differences in class, race and wealth added to the insecurities of post-war life when, after a relative period of freedom, attitudes had reverted to their original conservatism. Feelings of shame and fear that developed in anyone who didn't obviously fit in were followed by a desire to disguise the truth. Individual freedoms were inhibited by the various taboos associated with 'outsiders' who threatened the concept of 'Britishness'.

These questions of belonging could become most acute within the context of skin colour. Initially the shortage of a labour force in post-war Britain needed to rebuild not only an economy but also bombed-out cities, to extend roads and to work in the newly established National Health Service had led the government to recruit white Europeans. But the prospect of employment in 'the Mother Country' especially piqued the interest of men and women from the Caribbean. For the generation that became identified with their journey from the Caribbean to Britain in 1948 on *HMT Empire Windrush*, unemployment, uncertainty and oppression at home contributed to the desire for a more secure way of life. But legal discrimination and an entrenched prejudice meant that many new arrivals found themselves living in impoverished neighbourhoods in cities throughout Britain, their isolation feeding the perception of 'differentness'. The government had assumed that their stay would only be temporary, but by 1957 42,000 immigrants who had come to make their home in Britain found their hopes of integration and acceptance disappointed, as toxic sections of society closed ranks against outsiders, claiming the importance of preserving the national identity. While building work and public transport offered opportunities to men and nursing and manufacturing to women, some of these immigrants, including the most highly qualified, were reduced to accepting work in the lowest paid clerical and domestic service positions, often kept out of sight behind machines and in the basement of houses.

Prejudice wasn't confined to the new arrivals. The actress Merle Oberon, albeit privileged by wealth and fame, never stopped trying to escape the obstacles she faced with judgement levelled against her 'darker' complexion. Born in India in 1911, Oberon was one of the silver screen's most famous stars. In a career that had taken off in the 1930s, playing Anne Boleyn in *The Private Life of Henry VIII* and Catherine Earnshaw in *Wuthering Heights*, with an Oscar nomination in 1935 for the film *Dark*

Angel, Oberon made seven more movies up to and during the 1950s, playing opposite the leading actors of the day, including Laurence Olivier, Douglas Fairbanks and David Niven.

Married four times, Oberon's official biography, albeit complex and rumour-fraught, stated that she was born in India, the daughter of Arthur, a Welsh engineer, and Charlotte, his part Sri Lankan, part Māori wife. Charlotte had a daughter, Constance, from a previous relationship. And Oberon was rumoured to be Constance's child, born after Arthur had groomed and raped his twelve-year-old stepdaughter. At the outset of her professional career, in order to land the English-rose parts she coveted, Oberon was desperate to disguise her South Asian appearance, changing her voice and bleaching her skin so she would sound and look like an educated white girl. But the whitening products she used, with names like 'Afghan Snow' and advertised as 'Asia's most famous beauty aid', and the bleach which included poisonous ammoniated mercury to reduce the melanin in the body, played havoc with her skin. Resorting to surgical treatment for failed dermabrasion procedures, she covered the scars with special whitening make-up until in 1957 she finally gave her skin a rest and told the press that the appearance of darkness was due to exposure when holidaying in the Acapulcan sun. Only many decades after her death in 1979 were her origins revealed when her birth certificate was found and identified her mother as Constance.

While those in the public eye had professional reasons for 'managing' their image and the financial resources to pay for it, children were powerless in the face of any adult prejudice against an 'unusual' skin colour. For the 'brown babies' – as the contemporary African-American press in the US called them – who had been conceived in Britain in the 1940s and grew up in the 1950s, questions of belonging and identity were at the core of their existence. Nearly a quarter of a million African-American soldiers were stationed in Britain during the war. The War Office had ruled that white women should not 'walk out, dance or drink' with 'coloured' soldiers, warning that 'such relations would in the end only result in strife'. If an American soldier or sailor married a British woman without his commanding officer's permission, he risked a court martial. The secret romances that developed between African-American GIs and British women, a third of whom were either already married or engaged, resulted in the birth of 2,000 babies who did not know who their fathers were. The double taboo of having a child with an unaccountable skin colour and out of wedlock was very difficult to explain away. The historian Norman Longmate was told of one 'none too bright' husband who had been convinced by his wife of a once popular theory that had otherwise lost all credibility a century earlier. On the birth of her 'dusky baby' the wife explained that she had been 'startled by a Black soldier' who had been walking by her at night when she was pregnant. The colour of the soldier's skin had been 'imprinted' on the baby in the womb. Either way, it was the children, caught in the middle of these broken relationships and society's prejudices, who suffered most.

In 2019 Professor Lucy Bland published her interviews with sixty of these children, conducted when they were mostly in their seventies. Their accounts of their experiences are heartbreaking and enraging. Carole T. said she 'stuck out like a sore thumb'. Mary found that name-calling at school included the N word. 'You didn't exactly know what it meant,' she said. She was ten years old and simply knew the word was a colour. But she also knew she wasn't 'the same as everybody else', keeping this anxiety to herself. 'I kept a lot to myself,' she said. Some children used chalk to whiten up their skin or washed their faces with a bleach-soaked flannel. Jennifer K. was called 'Blackie' and 'little chocolate girl'. At the age of six months, when her skin darkened, Babs was sent away to a Dr Barnardo's home for four years, before being moved on to a foster home. At school the teacher told the other children that Babs had the ability to climb a pole like a monkey, gave her a seat at the back of the classroom and only allowed her simple jigsaw puzzles to do because of her inferior brain. When Babs was ten, news of the abuse she was receiving from her foster father reached Dr Barnardo's and she was brought back to the home for a further four years. She was fourteen when her mother eventually came to claim her. The sight of this strange women with her white skin astonished Babs. She could not imagine how they might be related, gradually realising that her mother had come to collect her not because of any maternal longing but because Babs was now old enough to go out to work and therefore contribute to the family wages.

Although the majority of the GIs had left Britain after the end of the war and returned to the United States and Canada, inter-racial relationships continued with the new wave of immigrants. The breaching of society's boundaries and the fear of discovery remained very real for those couples, for whom love trounced prejudice. Andrew Augustus, a carpenter from Dominica, arrived by ship in Britain – a destination that he considered 'the mother country' – in 1956, and found work in Selfridges department store in London, distributing goods to the various floors from the service lift. When he met Doreen, a sales assistant with glorious 'golden' curly hair who looked after customers in the fur department, Andrew was smitten. The lift became their safe, out-of-sight route in which to travel together up to the roof of the store, where a shared cigarette led to mutual expressions of love. As the relationship blossomed, they would venture out for a picnic in the little park near the store. 'People would see us having a kiss and a cuddle,' Andrew remembered, 'and they'd point and stare and say: "Look, look! They're kissing!" They'd just watch us because you never saw a mixed-race couple together then.' When Doreen and Andrew decided to move in together they embarked on a long search to find a landlady who would rent out a room to a bi-racial couple. Eventually, with the realisation that Doreen was to have a baby, they decided to share the news of their secret love with Doreen's parents. The reaction was explosive. Horrified, they insisted that Doreen should give the child away 'and pretend nothing had happened'. Doreen and Andrew refused point-blank.

However, when Doreen's mother hesitantly went to meet her new grandchild, she couldn't fail to notice the way Augustus cherished her daughter, cooked for her, and cared for their child. She was won round. But Doreen was unable to find a childminder who was prepared to look after a 'brown' baby, so she was forced to give up work, money was tight, and the comments the little family attracted when out in public didn't get any easier to hear. But the couple loved one another, married one another in 1961, had another child together and spent another fifty-three years together, rising far above the suspicious attention their relationship attracted.

A generation after Doreen and Augustus began courting, I saw for myself how love and subterfuge can prevail in the face of prejudice. I was walking down the main street in Las Vegas with my brother when a girl in a flower-patterned sundress came up to us and asked us to do her a favour. Her name was Holly and she was going to marry her boyfriend Gregory later that morning. There would be no guests but by law they needed a couple of witnesses. To decline the invitation was unthinkable, so we made our way past the neon flash of casinos to the incongruously cute Little White Wedding Chapel, with room to seat just ten guests. A brilliantined and quiffed Elvis look-alike, in dazzling-blue rhinestone rig, lip-sync-crooned the bridal couple up the aisle to 'Love Me Tender' accompanied by a crackly recording coming from an unmanned miniature organ. And there, in front of a little altar festooned with red and white plastic roses, Holly and Gregory made their vows. Three minutes later they were pronounced man and wife. As we co-signed the register, the newly-weds told us they had been planning this event for two years. Holly's mother would have tried to forbid the marriage if it had taken place at home in Chicago because Gregory was Black and she wasn't.

Back in a time when Holly's mother would have been a young woman herself, Natalie Meddings's family were caught up in a maze of prejudice, their own awareness of the judgement of society often dictating the way they led their lives. Her two grandmothers, Helen and Minnie, shrank from confronting and exposing the stigmas that hung like a shroud over their backgrounds, feeling powerless to change their circumstances, their accumulated troubles, suspicions and resentment preventing them from travelling through life with contented ease. Only when their granddaughter Natalie was ready to uncoil the family secrets did the weight of decades of insecurity about race, class, money and birth emerge into the light for the first time.

As one of nine children of an Irish Catholic baker, the young, bright-eyed and ambitious Helen left her home in Ireland in the 1930s to look for a new and prosperous life in Egypt. By the mid-1930s Helen was enjoying her new existence, working as a French translator in Cairo, the city which had been architecturally transformed in Victorian times from its medieval origins into 'The Paris of the East'. Helen's work at the British embassy soon became part of her glamorous colonial existence but when the dashing Frenchman to whom she'd lost her heart died suddenly in one of Cairo's frequent cholera epidemics, she met Alfred Abadi, an Arabic Jew, on the rebound. Alfred worked as a 'businessman' trading carpets and as a charming and indefatigable 'procurer of goods', he was ever anxious to fulfil the smallest of requests. At the beginning Helen thought she had fallen on her feet with her new suitor, with whom she would spend her evenings at Groppi's café, the epicentre for Cairo's ethnically diverse and cosmopolitan elite, drinking strong coffee and eating chocolate-covered dates in the thrilling company of the haut monde of Cairo.

When Helen became pregnant with Alfred's baby, they travelled briefly to England to satisfy her Catholic roots and to legitimise their relationship before the arrival of their first son. Maurice was born in 1939 and Helen and Alfred then took up their married life in Cairo where Daniel, their second son and the future father of Natalie, arrived four years later. While Alfred would spend his days wheeling and dealing, consolidating his 'business' contacts, playing backgammon with his friends and smoking his hookah, Helen had the run of a luxurious apartment. As a nanny tucked the babies into their fancy bassinettes, Helen, or 'Queenie' as she later came to be known, might relax by listening to the hugely popular actress and singer Umm Kulthum, known as 'The Voice of Egypt' or 'Egypt's Fourth Pyramid'. Spreading delicately embroidered doilies beneath her porcelain tea cup, a linen napkin held daintily to her lips, Queenie would adjust her pearl necklace, lifting her nose above any distasteful market smells.

Challenged by her new maternal responsibilities, with Alfred out at his 'office', and missing the camaraderie of the translating work she had exchanged for a domestic life, Helen's good humour began to recede. Then when the boys were fifteen and eleven, with the rise of nationalism, King Farouk was deposed. Those Egyptians who had long been a part of the old regime were forced to leave the country and Helen and Alfred and the children became part of the subsequent repatriation of foreigners. Helen's life would never be the same again.

Once they returned to live in Britain, Alfred's status as a man-about-town vanished. Where once his be-ringed and manicured fingers had twirled his elegant cane as he walked Cairo's sunny boulevards in his immaculately pressed cream trousers, he was now at a loss to fit into the grey, damp fog of the Victorian streets of Battersea. Despite the popularity and respect that had been shown him by his own community in Egypt, Alfred had never prioritised social standing, valuing instead the pride he took in providing for his family. But Helen felt severed from her old self. Mourning a lifestyle now confined to her memories along with the membership of an elite society, Helen took her associated fall in status badly. Conscious of the subtleties of judgement now imposed on her by the class-conscious stratification back in Britain, Helen's self-worth plunged. In an attempt to retain her dignity, she lived a duplicitous existence, pretending to society that she was something she no longer was, trying to conceal her distress at the contrast in her circumstances but succeeding only in allowing her discontent to alienate all those who came across her. As she watched her boys swap any residual Egyptian mannerisms for those of cheeky London street-boys, her readjustment hit a further low. Begrudging her diminished husband for remaining resilient and cheerful, Helen treated Alfred as the scapegoat for her disappointment with life, regularly tipping him bodily out of their bed with such force that he would crash to the floor.

When Daniel married a woman he had only known for two weeks, his mother Queenie, who had once held Mrs Bennet-like ambitions for her son's marital prospects, was now mired in thwarted disappointment. 'I was something once, you know,' was the message she signalled to all and everyone night and day. A self-styled 'Grand-mère' she would deliberately speak to her son in French with the fluency acquired from her past and in front of her new daughter-in-law, who could not understand a word she said. An evolving work of concealed rage and blame directed secretly at herself, Helen was eaten up by resentment. No one in the family ever remembers seeing her smile.

Meanwhile the aspirations of Natalie's other granny's family had been punctured by poverty and the obstacles of working-class life. Minnie Finedon had grown up with her seven brothers and sisters in Wandsworth in the 1920s. After their mother's death when Minnie was two, her father Bill worked all hours as a freelance barrow man at Covent Garden, Billingsgate and Smithfield markets. But despite Bill's industry, the family had so little money that the children would pile newspapers and coats onto their beds to keep themselves warm. Poverty as well as having so many mouths to feed meant that Minnie and her siblings went undernourished, causing her to lose all her teeth in girlhood and develop rickets, a common childhood condition at the time that resulted in weak or soft bones.

As soon as she turned thirteen and could look after herself she went into domestic service. But the absence of maternal care left Minnie aghast when she began to bleed inexplicably, learning the meaning of her first period from the resident cook. Minnie's innocence contrasted with the knowing, sexual culture that pervaded pockets of the South London working-class streets where teenage girls would go down the alley with a boy, extinguishing the street lamp by kicking up a ball into the bulb before 'getting it on' in the dark. But Minnie was a 'good' girl. When her first boyfriend offered her a ring in exchange for her favours she told him he could 'sling his hook'. The Finedons occupied a level of society described by Natalie as 'under-class' beneath which, in the perception of the working men and women of Wandsworth, there was only one more indignity to which they could slump. Minnie would do anything in her power, even sacrifice her freedom, to prevent herself from slipping down to that final rung and landing on the socially bankrupt floor with 'gypsies' or the sort of person, Minnie later described to Natalie with horror in her voice, who would have 'been forced to keep livestock in the front garden' as a means of survival.

Minnie was eighteen when she saw John Goldsmith out dancing. He was a good waltzer and his offer of marriage was an opportunity to do better for herself. Even though she knew nothing about John, she seized the chance to haul herself out of poverty onto the safety net of conventional prosperity, little knowing that the consequences of her decision would be as entrapping as those made of Queenie. Three days after the wedding Minnie was alone, cleaning the house, retrieving unwashed handkerchiefs from her new husband's coat pockets, when she found something unexpected. Although Minnie had never used any birth control, she knew what this cylinder of latex tubing was meant for. Marching straight round to the pub and finding John already ensconced at the bar with a fancy-looking woman, Minnie slapped the rubber johnny on the counter, demanding an explanation. With no response offered, Minnie carried the incriminating object over to the local police station. Surely there was something they could do when a marriage contract, only just made in law, had been broken? There must be a punishment? Rejected by their patronising laughter, she returned home to live out her life with a man she did not love. After her discovery of the condom Minnie had only submitted reluctantly to the occasional 'roll on and roll off' encounter. After Natalie's aunt was born in 1938 and Natalie's mother in 1942, 'Minnie understood the terms of engagement and disengaged,' Natalie explained.

When war broke out Minnie escaped the unhappiness at home, working first for a munitions manufacturer before finding employment painting the tops of gasometers black to hide them from German night-time bombing raids. Many years later Minnie was ready to confide.

'I used to stay with my nan every weekend,' Natalie told me, 'and we would watch *Dallas* on TV and have cheese on toast and we would talk.' Minnie loved to remember her years in the factory. 'Talk could be so open back in those days,' Minnie told her granddaughter, describing the sort of uninhibited female confessional that was still a couple of decades away for so many women. 'We would hatch plots to get rid of babies immediately after sex as none of us wanted to be pregnant,' Minnie remembered. 'We would jump off a table or have a really hot bath.' On another day chatter trickled down the assembly line about a famous woman named Marie Stopes who was coming to Wandsworth Town Hall to tell them how not to have babies. And yet Minnie had more than an inkling that physical love *could* be joyous. 'My nan realised,' Natalie explained, 'that women had found something in their bodies that meant they were desired and that there was a way to have sex for that other reason and not just to get children. A woman on the munitions line would say to her, "Oh, it's Friday night. Friday night's our night," and my nan would say, "What do you mean?" and the woman would have such a glint in her eye and would be so excited that Nan would be intrigued.' But years later, as Minnie described the romances her friends had enjoyed with the American GIs while their husbands and fiancés were away at the war, she admitted she had never experienced any romantic yearnings of her own, even though she knew those 'other kind of feelings' which eluded <u>her</u> clearly existed for others.

The gaiety of the community spirit at the factory contrasted with the hidden horrors of life at home. John's employment and daytime activities, apart from a stint as a security guard, remained a mystery to Minnie. Once she had watched John through the letterbox and seen his arms encircling a young man who she did not recognise. But such was the gulf of communication between Minnie and her husband that she did not question him about the incident. And neither of Minnie's daughters ever mentioned that anything was out of the ordinary when they were left alone with their father. However, when Minnie's elder daughter was about ten years old, she confided the truth of the abuse she was enduring secretly at home to her best friend. Before long, the best friend had told her mother and that mother told Minnie. Sitting her up on the kitchen counter, Minnie asked her daughter to tell her everything that had been going on but the poor girl was in such a state that she was unable to lift her chin high enough from off her chest to speak.

Once again, in an act of bravery, Minnie went to the police station, risking the shame that she was bringing on her family and exposing secrets that others would not have dared to reveal. This time Minnie was taken seriously and her accusation brought John to court. But instead of receiving any conviction, John was sent for treatment at the Maudsley Hospital, pleading innocence and arguing successfully that he had problems with his mental health, leaving him free to offend again. Their daughter never recovered from the abuse, fearful and diminished after the violation of a childhood that Natalie defines as 'soul robbery'.

After a two-week courtship, Daniel, Queenie and Alfred's son, and Minnie and John's daughter, chose to marry on a Wednesday early-closing day so Daniel could take time off from his job working in a television shop. The two sides of Natalie's troubled families were captured in the wedding photograph taken in October 1965 in Wandsworth Town Hall, the uneasy bridal couple flanked by an equally wary group of relations radiating distrust. Queenie, widowed since Alfred's death in 1958, is in a black hat, stiff black coat and pearls. The bride, her mother Minnie and her sister, each as unsmiling and nervous as the other, carry outsized white handbags, emblems of purity and defence, as if shielding themselves from the battles that might lie ahead. On the extreme right of the picture, standing apart from the group, is John Goldsmith, his eyes impossible to read through his thick glasses. Natalie has another photograph from those days in which Queenie, her little finger crooked as she enjoys her tea ritual, is sitting at one end of the sofa while John, clutching his glass of brown stout, glowers from the other, chalk and cheese personified.

But Alfred had taught his son well. The security of family must come first and it was up to the husband and father to make that a reality. After a few years of marriage, Daniel – or Danny as he was known by then – left his job in the television shop. He was determined to lift his three children over the financial hurdles, the cultural and class prejudices of his post-Cairo life that had troubled and inhibited his mother. He became a successful electrical engineer and then broadened into 'business dealings' so lucrative that he was able to afford to move the family out of their cramped London flat and into more expansive comfort in the Surrey countryside. No one was quite sure what Danny's lucrative 'business dealings' exactly were. But his connections were profitable enough to enable the purchase of a nice house in Esher with a swimming pool, to send Natalie and her brothers to local private schools and to buy his mother-in-law, Minnie, a rose-embellished bungalow so she would never be bothered by John Goldsmith again. Danny was a devoted father. A passionate Conservative, a committed fan of Margaret Thatcher, he would take his children into town every Sunday in the early 1970s to have breakfast in Dino's café on the King's Road before standing with them in admiration outside 'Mrs T's' house in Chelsea's Flood Street. 'She'll make a marvellous prime minister,' he would tell his kids as they spied on the MP, unaware of her audience as she adjusted her hair rollers in an upper window, getting ready for church.

While Queenie never got over her shame at losing her original status in Cairo society, and never stopped pretending to be someone she no longer was, the generational cover-ups snaked down the two families and began to seep into her granddaughter Natalie's own life. When she was a teenager she stopped bringing friends home after school, fearful that she would find her mother 'acting silly, or swaying while at the oven, or already in bed by 4 p.m.'. Natalie had found the changes in her mother confusing and scary, changes which she felt she certainly couldn't ask about. One day, the unsaid – the 'secret' behind her mother's now erratic behaviour – was revealed. Her father showed her an understairs cupboard full of empty wine bottles. There was no discussion, no exploring the source of her mother's sorrow or why alcohol had become necessary. Natalie's mother, now elderly, still struggles to speak about the terrible things her father did to her sister during their childhood or about what might have happened to her as well during those long days spent alone with John while Minnie was out at work at the factory. The unpredictability of her mother's behaviour, her lengthy bouts of depression, her closed-down-ness, all hinted to her daughter that she was possibly another untreated victim of grooming and of paternal abuse.

Worryingly underweight and burdened with the exhaustion of life, Minnie smoked constantly as she delivered her life story during Natalie's regular visits, speaking without any apparent censorship, self-pity or even emotion except when she talked of the war, when the closeness of the factory camaraderie had brought her unprecedented happiness. Only once did Minnie betray a sense of fear. As Minnie's account reached the moment when she got engaged to John aged nineteen, she spoke to her granddaughter, then also aged nineteen, with a special solemnity of the consequences of marrying for any other reason than love.

Minnie died in 1996 and, three decades later Natalie continues to honour her memory and heed her warnings. A friend she had known for almost twenty years provided her with the longest and most important friendship of her life. Layer upon layer of understanding and trust had been established between them until the romantic connection, obvious to everyone who knew them, finally revealed itself to them both, and the only remaining secret between them was dissolved as they married for love. The process of pattern breaking and healing in a new generation became symbolised in Natalie's work as a doula, through which she offers emotional and physical help to women in the lead-up to and the aftermath of childbirth. The treasured lesson she learned from the behaviour of the women who came before her is, in her own words, simple. 'The darkness will come to get you and bad things will happen if you never tell your secrets to those you love.'

CHAPTER 4

People Would Look at Me and Say, 'What Is It?'

As a new generation of women came of age at the start of the 1960s, the pre-war hierarchy and even those survivors of the more distant Edwardian world remained ever tenacious. Men made the decisions that affected the world's stability while society bent to the laws that governed female subservience and sexual choice. And yet, even before the new decade was under way, a fledgling confidence was growing among women that their collective voice might soon be heard and acted upon both on the international stage and in their private lives.

In the years since America dropped the atom bomb on Hiroshima in 1945, the maintenance of peace had remained at the top of the political world agenda while Russia, with its nuclear capability, represented the greatest threat. From 1950 to 1954 the extreme right-wing American Republican Senator Joseph McCarthy conducted a ruthless campaign to root out the Russian communism that he claimed was infiltrating the heart of the establishment. The climate of scaremongering and suspicion throttled everyday life, including the livelihoods and work of innocent individuals like school teachers, artists and journalists.

In the UK, the nuclear threat produced a different response. The Campaign for Nuclear Disarmament (CND) was attracting women in greater numbers than any political movement since before the war. The Aldermaston March in 1958 was sponsored by prominent individuals, including women in the arts such as the actor Peggy Ashcroft and the artist Barbara Hepworth. Three years later Dagmar Wilson, an American artist and gifted children's book illustrator, enraged by men's ineffectual protest against the atomic weapons and consumed by fear of the effects of radioactive milk on children, embarked on a mission to 'end the arms race not the human race'. In November 1961 Wilson helped galvanise 50,000 women in sixty cities across the United States to join her newly founded Women's March for Peace (WMP) against atmospheric nuclear testing. In Washington, when 1,500 members of the WMP led by Wilson reached the Washington Monument, President John F. Kennedy was watching from a window at the White House. 'You know how men are,' Wilson explained to journalists. 'They talk in abstractions and the technicalities of the bomb, almost as if this were all a game of chess. Well, it isn't. There are times, it seems to me, when the only thing to do is let out a loud scream . . . Just women raising a hue and cry against nuclear weapons for all of them to cut it out.'

In Britain women weren't just concerned with speaking up

about politics. A 1950s survey conducted by the *Manchester Guardian* found that 50 per cent of the housewives they contacted were bored and, in corollary, lonely. In February 1960, the *Guardian*'s 'Mainly for Women' page published a frank, taboo-challenging piece by Betty Jerman. In 'Squeezed Like Sardines in Suburbia', Jerman accused women themselves of being responsible for the dullness of their own lives, and for succumbing to the 'blunting effects' that 'home and child-minding can have on a woman's mind'. Maureen Nicol read the column, thinking of her own neighbours who had clearly surrendered their brains to domesticity. The thirty-year-old Cheshire housewife wrote to the newspaper saying that since she had become a mother, she had found it difficult to find anyone with similar interests and views. Describing her own sense of isolation, and the 'voluntary exile' chosen by new, first-time mothers, she suggested that while they loved their children, that wasn't 'enough', and that 'perhaps housebound wives with liberal interests and a desire to remain individuals could form a national register so that whenever one moves one can contact like-minded friends'.

When her letter was published in the newspaper complete with her home address, Nicol received such a deluge of enthusiastic responses from other women that her letterbox fell off. As a result of the powerful reaction from women keen to seize a chance to air a dissatisfaction they had been keeping secret, she set up the National Housewives' Register in 1960 for a shilling subscription per person. 'We didn't want to know what washing machine somebody used,' remembered Pat Bowers, a 1970s NHR member, talking to the *Guardian* in 2020, 'all talk about home life or cake baking was discouraged.' Instead, they met to discuss literature, politics, the government, 'what was going on in the world, and things women weren't supposed to be interested in'.

Despite this growing openness and engagement with the outside world, discussion around sexual and marital intimacy, especially homosexuality, was still confined to whispers. The American tennis player Billie Jean King described the traumatic effects of keeping her sexuality secret. Four years after her marriage to a man in 1964, she admitted to herself, but not to her family, that she was attracted to women. 'I wanted to tell the truth but my parents were homophobic and I was in the closet. As well as that, I had people tell me that if I talked about what I was going through, it would be the end of the women's tour. I couldn't get a closet deep enough. One of my big goals was always to be honest with my parents and I couldn't be for a long time. I tried to bring up the subject but felt I couldn't. My mother would say, "We're not talking about things like that", and I was pretty easily stopped because I was reluctant anyway. I ended up with an eating disorder that came from trying to numb myself from my feelings.'

Regardless of the recommendations of the Wolfenden Report of 1957, sexual relationships between men were still punishable by law. The decriminalisation of homosexuality would not come until the 1967 Sexual Offences Act, just a year before my grandfather Harold's death and five years after my grandmother Vita had succumbed to cancer. Harold had always known that the revelation of his homosexuality could invite serious legal consequences, possibly even jail. Vita's passionate extra-marital love life with women was an open secret among her family and friends and a source of gossip indulged in by many of them. No law explicitly forbade lesbian love and through conversations and in her letters and diaries Vita had often indicated that she would be willing to be open about her 'secret' existence. But she knew that in her own lifetime society was unlikely to accept the admission of same-sex relationships and she was particularly worried that the public knowledge might ruin her writing career. She tried to conduct her affairs with relative discretion, protecting her professional life rather than retreating from the judgement of friends. Although she died when I was only eight years old, my memories of my grandmother have remained powerful. She was inscrutable, in part terrifying and yet always thrillingly different from all the other grown-ups I knew. Formidably tall and baritone-voiced, she wore breeches, laced-up and knee-high boots and her hair was Turkish tobacco-scented from the roll-ups she smoked from a long tortoiseshell holder. I remember the strength of my awareness of her watching us, sitting at the head of the table at lunch, less of a talker, more of a listener, attentive and amused, especially to the chatter of us children who, under her scrutiny, suddenly felt like beings of unusual and flattering curiosity. Despite the arrival of her two boys, she was never a hands-on mother. And perhaps her own status as an only child had left her wondering about sibling banter. After she died my grandfather gave me the carved wooden angel that had always stood sentinel facing her large bed in the cottage they had shared, but with separate bedrooms. Three foot high and rescued from a deconsecrated church in Venice, the impassive figure, the sole surviving witness to the love Vita had shared with other women, has never divulged its secrets.

As children we had no idea that our grandparents managed their happy marriage by mutually accepting each other's romantic liaisons. Although they rarely discussed their extra-marital love lives face to face, they would sometimes use the letters they sent to each other on a daily basis whenever they were apart to refer to a latest relationship with surprising candour and even mutual advice-seeking. At home a black-out system operated where exchanges of information not deemed suitable for children's ears were often communicated in mysterious encrypted language. But we listened, if only to have confirmed that there were things we would only ever half know. Why, for example, did any mention of Great-Aunt Gwen, my grandfather's married sister, the mother of five children, always prompt such a rapid change of subject? Only with Gwen's death in 1995 did we learn that for many years Vita's sister-in-law had also been one of my grandmother's most devoted lovers.

Within a week of Vita's death in 1962 we had moved into Sissinghurst, the house and garden she had left in her will to my father. She and Harold had designed the garden in the 1930s, with its hedged and walled enclosures forming, as Harold said, 'a series of escapes from the world, giving the impression of cumulative escape'. Inside the house, the whisper of secrecy breathed its way into the walls, curling through the crevices of my childhood landscape. Almost two hundred years earlier, the Elizabethan house and its buildings had served as a government-run prison camp for seamen when Britain was at war with France in the eighteenth century, and hundreds of French sailors were

held captive there over seven years. The beams in the window-
less roof cavity beyond our attic bedrooms still carried the faded
black painted numbers denoting the number of prisoners held
in each claustrophobic space. We knew nothing of the sailors'
lives, but we had evidence that they had been skilled craftsmen
in their civilian existence. Somehow a pair of two-inch-high
French poodles had survived, exquisitely carved from a piece
of stray wood, perhaps dug out from a beam. The dogs' fluffy
coats had been rendered almost strokable, their wooden fur so
tenderly made from memory, each carving small enough to fit
into the palm of a child's hand. Beneath those roofs the dusty,
spider-infested spaces, jammed with musty-smelling trunks
full of forgotten-about documents shoved up there for storage,
surely contained horror stories and a yearning for freedom and
for home that would remain forever unsatisfied, forever secret.

After my father died of leukaemia in 2004, at a time when I
was still coming to terms with the end of my first marriage and
my daughters were away at university, I lived alone for several
years in the Sissinghurst cottage in the garden at my grandparents' home. I felt untethered by the changes in my life. Uncertain
of the future, I did not know how to tell anyone about a 'guilty
secret', a phrase that had become tautologous: alongside the persistent ache of missing my father, I also felt relief at his death,
relief not only for him and his release from illness but for me
at being liberated from the limbo of fear. The event that I had
dreaded for so long was over. Now I slept in Vita's childhood bed,
the perfume from little dishes of her home-made pot-pourri still
retrievable with a gentle crumble of the desiccated leaves. *Her*
ghost – for that is what the unexplained awareness of a benign

presence felt like to me – drifted across the room at night. Yes. She was there somewhere. Fancifully I sensed her blessing that I had returned to this place that she too had loved, a place that offered both continuity and refuge.

One night I woke suddenly, disturbed by a movement on the bedside table. Convinced that ghost and granddaughter were finally to meet, I switched on my light to see a little mouse gazing at me, unblinking, motionless except for a twitch of his whiskers. Throughout the garden, through what Harold also called a 'succession of privacies', a tortoiseshell cat stalked the paths at dusk, slinking in and out of the shadows of the hedges, sometimes to be found curled up asleep in the dark recesses of my grandmother's abandoned potting shed. White doves, descendants of those Vita had once encouraged to roost in the eaves, continued to flutter and settle on the tiled roofs. Robins with an unnerving tameness would hop onto a table just inches from my hand and give me their version of that mouse's steady gaze. These living creatures, a mouse, a cat, a bird, time spent in spidery attics and later in my grandmother's cottage, all convinced me of the viability of an invisible imprinting of a self on a place after death.

Forty years before her death Vita had written an uncensored account of her rapturous love affair with another married woman. The affair had threatened to schism Vita's life, ending marriage and motherhood. She had locked the manuscript away in a leather bag and thrown away the key. My father found the notebook when she died, concluding she had considered the affair to be too private, too damaging, too volcanic for the manuscript to be published during her lifetime.

If queer freedom was still either illegal or taboo in the early 1960s, gender identity was an even more sensitive topic. In November 1961, six months before Vita's death, leading model April Ashley hit the headlines. Born in 1935 in the docklands area of Liverpool, Ashley said that although she was 'born a boy', she believed she had always been a woman with some physically male characteristics. Many years later she spoke to journalist John Preston and told him that she was three years old 'when she first realised that she'd been born into the wrong body. There was no one she could tell about this, of course – not then, or for years afterwards.' Taunted at home, where her mother was aghast and ashamed about her son's unmistakable womanliness, and teased at school for her effeminate appearance, Ashley had twice attempted suicide. She told Preston that she grew used to being referred to as 'it'. 'People would look at me and say, "What is it?"' Aged ten, Ashley was sent out to work processing sides of bacon. At eleven she was raped by a family friend. At fourteen she ran off and joined the Merchant Navy, which was 'one of the things that made you a man'. But Ashley's own efforts to dim the conviction she was a woman occupying a man's body proved futile. Electric shock therapy and psychiatric attempts to brainwash her out of her 'deviancy' and into full-blooded maleness brought her to the edge of suicide. Escaping to London, she joined what she called 'the twilight world' of marginalised individuals, working as a table clearer in Lyons' Corner House in London, where the amnesiac relief offered by drugs helped soften the anxiety of her circumstances. Soon she moved to France, suddenly happy working as a cabaret dancer in a celebrated Parisian nightclub, where Elvis Presley became her greatest fan.

Having read about early examples of successful gender transitional surgery, Ashley saved enough money to undergo the dangerous and rare six-hour medical procedure in Casablanca. The operation liberated her both physically and emotionally. As she changed her name from George to April, she became *Vogue* magazine's most popular underwear model and managed to keep the news of her transition hidden until a friend shopped her to the *Sunday People* newspaper for £5. After the headline that shouted '*HER* Secret is Out' appeared under a photograph of April cocooned in a glamorous fur coat, all her modelling work was cancelled and she became a figure of derision, distrust and suspicion. With remarkable strength of mind, she replied to her critics just six months later with a fully frank memoir that was serialised in the *News of the World* in May 1962. I remember watching April once in a swanky London nightclub in the 1970s, as she reclined on a velvet sofa, leaning against a plump of cushions, surrounded by devoted admirers. Wearing a long satin evening gown, a feather boa thrown round her shoulders, her eyes canopied by huge false lashes, she personified glamour. Her courage never failed her. During the rest of her long life she campaigned for LGBTQ rights, especially transgender equality, and in 2012 her work was recognised with an MBE.

As April had experienced, any deviation from the sexual 'norm' fuelled conservative society's love of speculative gossip. Members of our village and our family were no different. In 1962 we still shared our home with those who had cared for Vita and her garden and who had all attended her funeral in the village church. Vita's secretary, Mrs Staples the cook and Jack Copper, the odd-job man/chauffeur, were part of a flotilla of staff from a grand and swiftly receding era, a community of individuals whose roles soon became unaffordable and inappropriate for our family. But for a while Copper continued to work for us doing odd jobs, including driving my brother and me to the local riding stables on Saturday mornings. Two bored ponies, Sunshine and Patch, never deviating from their prescribed circle, carried their wobbly riders around the loose-earth floor of the riding school while Copper waited in the old Ford Zephyr puffing on a sweet-smelling pipe. Afterwards Copper would drive us home, stopping to buy us sticky penny chews at the village sweet shop.

We loved Copper but the grown-ups were suspicious of him. For years he had kept a home-made cider press in the back of the garage which accounted for the tipsy behaviour of several Sissinghurst inhabitants, including, on occasion, my grand-mother. Vita called him 'my wicked, warm-hearted old Copper', knowing that he had more than an eye for the young women of the village, despite being married to Marjorie, the shy, dark-haired, well-to-do daughter of a family of local Baptists. Margie and Jack's daughter Fay grew up to marry a local boy and have a family of her own. But their son, Gordon, was never any-where to be seen. In our small community his name was only spoken under the breath, just like April Ashley in her own city of Liverpool, because at some point in the 1960s, while living in America's Deep South, Gordon had broken unthinkable boundaries and the shock of it, the scandal of it, was too much for a small village to cope with.

The story began prior to Marjorie's marriage. Her devout family didn't approve of her courtship with Jack Copper, and condemned her subsequent teen pregnancy. Her aunt Elise called Margie's condition 'a disgrace to virginhood'. Margie hid herself away in her bedroom for nine months, the curtains drawn tight against the world. When Gordon was born, the doctor and nurse who delivered the baby were faced with a dilemma. The baby's clitoris and penis were both said to be so small that the medics couldn't define conclusively whether the baby was male or female. In accordance with the law of the time, because the sex was in doubt and there hadn't been an internal examination of the child, the baby was registered as male, all ambiguity conveniently solved with the flourish of a pen on a birth certificate.

But Dawn, as she would become, could not remember a time when she doubted that she was genetically and emotionally female. The terminology of the 1930s for someone assigned a sex at birth that didn't match their gender identity included 'abnormal', 'hermaphrodite' and 'weird', and Dawn spent the first thirty years of her life hiding what she termed her 'deep, dark secret'. Open discussion of gender dysphoria was still far in the future. Had she been alive today, Dawn might have chosen to identify as intersex or as a trans woman, but back then neither Dawn nor medical science had access to any knowledge or supportive resources to offer her.

Dawn was a small and slight child, known by her contemporaries – including my father, who was five years her senior (or possibly ten, or even twenty, depending on which of

several records and memories one consults, according to Dawn's
own adjustments of dates) – by the pejorative nickname 'Dinky',
a reference to her 'effeminate' and delicate physique. My father
remembered 'a suggestion of bisexuality, impishness, a deal of
Ariel, just a streak of Puck'. Margie had also guarded Dawn's
secret even while she delegated much of Dawn's upbringing to
her many female relatives. Seeking a further maternal anchor,
Dawn looked to older women outside her family for guidance
and affection. Fascinated by stories of Pepita, Vita's flamenco-
dancing grandmother from Andalusia, the mother of seven
illegitimate children, and admiring of Vita's literary reputation,
Dawn developed a lifelong respect not only for Vita but also
for her friend and lover Virginia Woolf. Watching her arrive for
lunch with Vita at the beginning of the war, Dawn remembered
how Woolf would be carrying a home-made suet pudding in a
china basin knotted up with a linen cloth. Both women were
kind to this perceptive young person, encouraging Dawn's love
of books and her ambition to be a writer, praising her early
poems, instilling in her the necessity of rigorous research.

But as Dawn grew up she found deception more and more
difficult to live with and on reaching the age of sixteen the
scrutiny of family and village life became intolerable. Having
secretly contacted her Aunty Alice, her father's well-off sister
who lived in Detroit, Dawn used her aunt's life-saving cheque
to buy a boat passage across the Atlantic to Canada. Still identifying publicly as male, Dawn worked at first among the
indigenous Ojibwa people as a missionary school teacher in
Ontario, before persuading a local journal to employ her as a
reporter. Within a couple of years, she had made her way to

New York, hired by a newspaper syndicate to cover 'human interest stories'. Soon Dawn made unlikely friends with a pair of influential and wealthy women – the celebrated English actress Margaret Rutherford and the painter and heiress Isabel Whitney. Both women became her willing and intimate confidantes and patrons, encouraging her writing career. On Isabel's death in 1962, Dawn inherited two million dollars from the Whitney fortune and an elegant 1840 mansion in Charleston, South Carolina, in America's Deep South. Charleston's anglophile grandes dames welcomed Dawn, who was becoming a well-known biographer of women. Continuing to live the existence of a young male heir, Dawn restored the elegant old house on Society Street, the bohemian part of the city, filling it with Chippendale furniture, and mirrors said to have once belonged to George Washington. However, when Dawn began walking down Society Street wearing a pillbox hat and 'a Dippity-Do hairstyle – a dowdy doppelganger of Jackie Kennedy', as one Charlestonian observed, the neighbours' tolerance was tested beyond their limits. And there was more. The news broke that Dawn had fallen passionately in love with a Black twenty-two-year-old garage mechanic called John Paul Simmons.

Dawn was ecstatic to have found such a companion. 'I responded to John Paul's joy of life, his smile, the bunch of wildflowers tucked into his jeans back pocket. He always picked me flowers . . . he had a great compassion for animals and old people. He promised to love and care for me.' Just as John Paul treated Dawn with the unconditional, romantic affection she had craved all her life, so Dawn introduced John Paul to the arts, to history, to an English sense of humour and to a belief in himself. And, because she could afford to, she bought him a red Thunderbird car. They had both found their perfect match. But the relationship appalled Charleston. Not only had this charming, if eccentric, British newcomer, the author of a biography of Britain's Princess Margaret no less, revealed her 'perverted' sexual preferences, but she had crossed the town's uncrossable racial divide. Further shocks followed. In 1968, Dawn made no secret about the news that the Whitney legacy had paid for her to have a ground-breaking operation at Johns Hopkins gender-identity clinic in Baltimore. The procedure made her one of the first to undergo gender transitional surgery in the United States after undergoing 'endless' physical examinations, and a rigorous psychological questioning process. But on 24 September 1968 'Gordon died', as his successor put it, his name and identity becoming a thing of the past the moment that Dawn Pepita left the hospital wearing a blue and white mini-skirted suit. She owed the choice of the first of her two new names to John Paul, who wanted to celebrate a beginning and his girlfriend's emergence into the light. The second was chosen by Dawn herself in homage to my bisexual grandmother who had been so kind to the young Gordon and whose grandmother Pepita had also defied the conventions of her time.

But the same person who had once been so welcomed into Charleston society now found herself shunned. She was targeted with relentless name-calling, her dogs were poisoned, shots were fired at her front door and when Dawn and John Paul disclosed the details of their impending wedding – Charleston's first inter-racial marriage – the local newspaper moved Dawn's paid announcement to the obituary pages. Threats to burn down the local church if the ceremony was conducted within its pretty cream-painted walls meant that Dawn and Jean Paul's marriage in January 1969 took place in Dawn's sitting room, the union solemnised by a brave, defiant priest. As the vinyl containing the anti-white, Civil War's 'Battle Hymn of the Republic' spun on the gramophone's turntable, the bride, who made her vows wearing a white, full-length, satin dress, was attended by her dogs whose collars had been woven with flowers.

Jack Hitt, a ten-year-old schoolboy in Charleston, never forgot the town's treatment of the couple. In an interview in Mark Jones's book *Wicked Charleston*, Hitt describes Charleston's reaction to Dawn. 'When one crosses forbidden lines, inter-racial marriage, announcing one is gay, taking a lover from another religion or class, or even changing one's sex, at least there is a community on the other side waiting for you. But Dawn charged across so many borders at once that she slipped into a country where she was the only inhabitant.' And yet Charleston, the town at the heart of 1960s segregated America, smacked of hypocrisy. Dawn and John Paul threatened Charleston not because they were truly different, but because their differences might reveal the same transgressions in Charleston society. When news of Dawn and John Paul's relationship had originally broken, a trio of residents paid Dawn a visit, bringing water melon for John Paul and apple pie for Dawn and asking her, 'Why can't you be like other white ladies who fall for their Black butlers? *We* marry a proper white man and keep the Black man on the side.' Another visitor advised Dawn that 'sex between Black and white' was 'always behind closed doors'. And Charleston's clandestine gay community, many of them married with children, continued to live in smug duplicity behind their elegant Georgian facades, deflecting attention from their own secret relationships by openly attacking the newly-weds.

News of Dawn and John Paul's marriage hit national and international headlines. The *New York Daily News* came up with 'Troth is stranger than fiction' for their coverage of the event, while *Newsweek* ran a full-page article about the nuptials. Margaret Rutherford told the British press that she gave the relationship her blessing. 'I am delighted that Gordon has become a woman, and I am delighted that Dawn is to marry a man of another race and I am delighted that Dawn is to marry a man of a lower station, but I understand the man is a Baptist!' Margie, Dawn's mother, also offered her support. In a letter to Dawn she reminded her of the old English proverb that 'a man worth lying down with is worth standing up with'.

All the international attention for 'Copper's lad', as Dawn was still referred to in our village, was suddenly focused on Kent when the couple came to England in the winter of 1969, one year after Gordon became Dawn, to have their marriage blessed by the Catholic Church. The *News of the World* went to town on the story and my father hid from the shame of it all, actively blocking the use of our village church for the blessing by having a quiet word with the vicar. Eventually Dawn persuaded a priest in nearby Hastings in the adjoining county to officiate at the ceremony and she came down the aisle of St Clement's Church in November 1969 in her second full-on bridal finery, this time a cream gown, a glittery tiara holding her embroidered veil in place and John Paul handsome in a perfectly cut dinner jacket. As the couple emerged arm-in-arm from the church, a large crowd of Sussex onlookers were agog. Nine months later, after Dawn had spent the bulk of the year in flowing maternity dresses beneath which her swelling shape had been obvious, she was seen in Charleston pushing a pram down Society Street, a proud mother followed by a gaggle of children chanting, 'He-she, he-she.' Holding her head high, Dawn attributed her 'strange new courage' to her reading of Virginia Woolf's novel *Orlando* and the real-life parallels she drew between her story and Woolf's gender-transforming heroine-hero.

If the birth of Natasha had provided Charlestonians with a last straw, when Dawn discovered that her husband had been hiding his own secret her resilience was shaken. Not only was John Paul revealed to be a compulsive drinker of Scotch and a gambling addict, but he was beginning to show signs of schizophrenia.

Having managed to gain access to Dawn's inheritance, John Paul whirled away the Whitney fortune on the roulette tables. Dawn was forced to sell the Charleston mansion and the little family fled north in debt and fear to the town of Hudson in Upstate New York. But John Paul's gambling habit, compounded by new levels of violence, resulted in his admission to a hospital for the mentally unwell. Dawn was left almost penniless, her unfamiliar gender classification preventing the payment of the social housing and child benefits to which she should have been entitled.

My father had always brushed off the Dawn/Dinky story as a source of faintly amusing embarrassment, a long-rumbling saga belonging to the past. He would move from the subject at speed whenever Dawn's name was mentioned. But it was more than that. For the product of an unconventional marriage, he was surprisingly troubled by anything he considered 'out of the norm'. Visiting the house of his oldest friend once, he spotted a new painting hanging in the sitting room. It showed the couple's six children gathered around the piano. But on closer examination the figure of the youngest child in the charming scene was sitting on the floor, half turning away, leaving only the back of his blond head and a barely discernible profile by which to identify him. My father assumed that a decision to conceal the face of the child had been made because the parents were ashamed of having a son with Down's syndrome. But the truth was that Martin, this much-loved two-year-old, adored by his parents and siblings alike, was, as with most two-year-olds, incapable of sitting still for long. The artist had simply drawn what he saw. Any suspicion of shame was felt not by the family but by my father.

Dawn's notoriety and her openness about her gender and her sexuality deeply unsettled him. His discomfort at any public discussion about the physicality of sex, especially same-sex relationships, led him to rely on euphemism. A writer friend could never be thought of 'in the same way' after my father had read his lusty novel and could not bear to imagine the friend 'doing those awful things'. Not wanting to think 'what might be happening on the other side of the wall', he would give separate bedrooms to gay partners who came to stay the night with us. When in 1972 his old friend, the writer James Morris, met him at the male-only Travellers Club in Pall Mall, my father was mortified to discover that after transitional surgery James had become Jan and was therefore not allowed any nearer to the club than the steps leading to the front door.

During a post-Sunday-lunch washing-up session, my father once urged me to have at least three passionate, full-blown, physically satisfying relationships in my life. But he wasn't able to admit to his fourteen-year-old daughter that this conviction came from the shame of his own inability to follow that advice. When he was dying, his face hollowed, his skin stretched tight over his cheekbones, he confided to me that his chief regret was never having known sexual passion. He was a complex man. He took ten years to reach the decision in 1972 to publish his mother's confessional account of her love affair with another woman. But the book, to which he contributed more than half the total text in analytical and contextualising sections, was the book for which he too became best known. His ultimate insistence that he would not shirk a story of lesbian love and would publish that story even in the still shockable and critical 1970s was an act of courage. But although he could be open and honest and validating about the significance of his parents' gender-fluid relationships, that openness deserted him when confronted with Dawn's story. My father's self-loathing around what he saw as his own sexual inadequacy may have contributed to a tendency that therapists call 'projective identification', when an alcoholic might condemn the drunkenness of someone more obviously inebriated than themselves, or a bully might point to the belligerent manner of another, in order to divert attention away from their own similar behaviour. Towards the end of Dawn's life, and also Nigel's own, my father began to recognise the unkindness and intolerance he had shown towards her. Reviewing Dawn's autobiography in 1995

in the *Spectator*, Nigel wrote 'there is not a word of reproach for
me in her book. Like everything else about Dinky, it is gallant,
resilient and unfailingly generous.'

When I lived in America in the 1990s, without knowing
quite what my intention was, other than wishing to demystify
a woman who had been whispered about all my life, I wrote to
Dawn to ask if I could visit her at her home in Upstate New York.
I had an inkling of what I would find. I had seen an interview
she gave there in 1985 to the television journalist Alan Whicker.
The sitting room in which Whicker had spoken to Dawn, her
hair teased into a candyfloss up-do, was still furnished with elegant chairs, the walls still hung with portraits of what looked
like Victorian ancestors, Dawn's pride demonstrably intact.

It was raining as I parked on Dawn's street, on the edge of
the town of Hudson. The terraced house, with its peeling paint,
had, like Dawn herself, known better days. She was waiting for
me, sitting on a high-backed chair, an indeterminate number
of cats dozing in her lap. There was no evidence of the stylish
up-do – her grey hair had been home-dyed orangey-red, a slash
of self-respect still evident in her scarlet-painted lips. Although
I knew she was suffering from osteoporosis, I was taken aback
by its cruel effect on the tall but fragile frame which was folded
in on itself with weakness as she shook off the cats, struggling
to stand. But reaching out her hand in greeting, warmth and
welcome in her eyes, she indicated her determination not to be
beaten, even by age. A neighbour came over, made us all tea and
then vanished. I sat in the only other armchair, its covers fraying,
and we were left alone to talk about life back in England, about

the sadness of her mother Margie's marriage, about books, about her daughter and mine, while ignoring the smell of cats and the sound of rainwater dripping into a bucket in the corner through a crack in the roof. She wanted to tell me about Charleston, responsible for so much emotional and physical damage, but still a town for which her devotion was undimmed. Her loyalty to memories of my treacherous father was hard to listen to. She allowed no hint of resentment or blame to affect our long conversation. There was something not only unworldly but beatific about her. As I stood to leave she handed me a small red-framed faded photograph of my grandmother. 'I would like you to have this,' she told me. 'In memory of the kindness your grandmother showed me.' I walked back to my car, the shame impossible to shake. When I heard that Dawn had chosen to spend her final years in Charleston, I understood why. She died there in 2000 with her daughter Natasha by her side.

Twenty years later, on a trip to South Carolina, I was invited to speak about Dawn in the church in which she had been prevented from celebrating her marriage. Dawn's story had filtered down through generations of families in that beautiful town and the tiny church was packed. When I climbed the stairs to the pulpit, the impact of those events so long ago hit me with a new force. I owed it to Dawn to address decades of cover-up and injustice and to acknowledge our own family's part in that cruelty. When I finished speaking there was an appalled silence. People were in tears. But their presence in the church and their visible shock at hearing about the cruelty directed at Dawn and John Paul by their own 'conservative' town, with all its hypocrisy and double standards, seemed like a sign of awareness, even progress. Several people came up and spoke to me afterwards, remorseful about a story that usually featured as a passing curiosity in guidebooks to the city, but in which the humanity that I had seen in a dilapidated room in Hudson with a hole in the roof was never mentioned.

CHAPTER 5

Something Wasn't Right

The children of secret-keepers learn how to be secret-keepers too. If those children also went to the sort of boarding school where I was a pupil in the 1950s and '60s, secrecy became an additionally stubborn inheritance to overthrow. My own school was filled with teachers who had come through the traumatic instability of at least one world war, experiencing rationing not only of food but of romance. With ages ranging from forty to seventy, the elder staff had grown up in the Victorian age while the younger group were born between the two conflicts. Most were unmarried, some finding companionship and often love with one another. Even to a schoolgirl like me, it was clear that the unworldliness of this particular group of women made them unsuited to a pastoral role – in loco parentis, as the phrase of the day went. Nevertheless, they were charged with guiding three hundred hormone-fizzing girls through the maze of adolescence just as a new psychedelic world was bursting outside the confines of the black school gates.

I had dreaded being banished to one of these locked-away places with their archaic uniforms and code of manners. The incarceration of children in freezing-cold institutions far from home for months on end was a fundamental, complacent and expensive response to education nurtured by a class system built on experiences most parents like mine had gone through, unquestioning, themselves. My own stint in a couple of these establishments gave me a six-year lesson in faltering self-confidence and the habit of keeping feelings under wraps. The skill of secret-keeping was all but written into the curriculum as I learned how to conceal and almost never to reveal anything worrying, puzzling or shameful. There was no requirement from these institutions to show empathy or concern. The teenage hailstorm of inexplicable physical and emotional changes would drive any adolescent to cower in confusion, but such failure of interest by the adults was not considered irresponsible. Nor did it really occur to me that the convenient absence for weeks at a time of me and my younger brother (who had been sent away to board at the same time as me, but at the age of eight) allowed my mother the freedom to travel abroad and to escape any unhappiness at home.

I was sent first to a prep school by the sea where every Sunday we walked a mile in crocodile formation to the huge, freezing Victorian church where the pounding organ couldn't quite hide the sound of homesick children's weeping. In my first summer term a new history teacher arrived. She was called Miss De V. She was small and round, her face partially hidden by a purple felt hat, squashed so far down on her head that it pushed her smeary bifocals off balance. I told my parents about her in my letters. 'The other night Miss De V. was on duty and she took off her shoes and jumped up and down in a most peculiar way. And she doesn't know a thing about history.' A week later I reported that Miss De V. had announced to the class 'Juliet is like Hitler trying to make war and she doesn't believe in the true God of love', unaware that Mss De V. had plans to teach me how to mend my ways. After the end of the next history lesson, she asked me to stay on. Shutting the door behind her and pushing me into a corner, she leaned in. She was very close. She said I must learn the beliefs of Roman Catholicism if I was to be saved from eternal sin. And then, with my back pushed up against the wall, she kissed me fully and open-mouthed on the lips.

I reported every detail of this encounter in my daily letter to my father: I wrote from previous experience. A year earlier my brother and I had been sent to spend the summer holidays on the Norfolk coast with my mother's adult cousin and her family. An artist friend of theirs had borrowed the barn at the back of their house for a few weeks so he could paint. One day I was exploring on my own when the artist spotted me through the open door and invited me to come and have a look at his paintings. A radio was playing 'Do Wah Diddy Diddy' by Manfred Mann, my favourite song of the moment. So, in I went, a pop-music-crazy ten-year-old. I stood there in my summer dress, singing along with Manfred Mann and the painter. The painter remarked what a pretty little girl I was. He held out a hand, beckoning me to come a little closer so I could see the picture on the easel. With an arm curled around my waist, he said he would like to see even more of me. He suggested I take my knickers off and twirl around for him. Without thinking, I complied. And then I burst into tears. And ran. But I did not dare tell my mother's cousin. What if she did not believe me?

I had seen the post-box at the end of the twitten so I wrote, on that occasion, to my mother and asked her to rescue me but she never replied, never came, which is why, this time, when Miss De V. kissed me, I appealed to my father instead. Unknown to me, he got straight in the car as soon as he read my letter, drove the two hours from home to the school, spoke to the headmistress and left without me knowing he had ever been there. That afternoon a figure in a purple hat was seen walking out of the front door with her suitcases before getting into a waiting taxi. That evening the headmistress told us that Miss De V. had to leave because she was 'tired' and 'not feeling well' and would not be returning to school. We were given no further explanation. I wrote to my parents that evening, still oblivious to my father's loving lifeline, saying the reason we'd been given for her leaving was 'a load of cobblers' but that I was going to 'put it all behind me'.

Even before Miss De V.'s attack, the approach of my teen years, the prospect of physical maturity and anything that hinted at sexual activity felt terrifying. When I was about ten years old my mother had visited me on a school exeat in her Rover car, the smell of its leather upholstery making me car sick even before we had left the school gates. Looking in the driver's mirror she spotted me and my best friend on the back seat holding hands like ten-year-old school friends do. But the spectre of same-sex love such as that practised by her in-laws alarmed my mother so much that, determined to do all she could to arrest any hereditary 'invertedness', she stopped the car at once. Opening the door she wrenched our hands apart and I learned that if I ever wanted to hold the hand of a girl it would have to be done in secret.

When I was twelve my mother went to great lengths, and in language that was often hard to understand, to warn me that there were 'womanly matters' ahead of me that must be kept hidden from everyone else, especially men. I had already cringed and blushed my way through the surreptitious handing over of a brown paper bag containing bulky cotton wool pads and a booklet that explained their purpose. Then a minuscule bra arrived, disguised in department-store wrapping, and which would not have offered any support to a doll let alone a blossoming adolescent. A year or so later my mother finally arrived at the crux of the matter, the heterosexual act that was the essential alternative to my grandparents' lusty and unappealing practices. 'What a man must do to a woman to produce a baby sounds disgusting,' she cautioned me, as I sat on the edge of the sofa watching her light a new cigarette from the glowing embers of the last, before inhaling deeply. 'And it is,' she confirmed, exhaling with an emphatic sigh, as the plume of smoke curled upwards, impregnating the folds at the top of the curtains as I too absorbed the grubbiness of this newly imparted knowledge. And yet somehow, despite my innocence, I had an inkling of insight. That self-revealing 'facts of life' evening, as my mother smoked and grimaced in front of me, imprinted itself on my mind in pinpoint detail. Even then I had some understanding of how unhappy she must be as I watched from the margins of her emotional confusion. Only later on, possibly only even now, have I come to realise how a complicated fear of and yet yearning for sexual satisfaction, along with the wish to be fancied, appreciated, taken on her own terms, all contributed to her confused and fragile state of mind. She had been pigeonholed into a female stereotype of subordination that some men of my father's generation had been educated to endorse. But it came with a bitterness and resentment that she was passing on to me, wrapped up in nicotine-impregnated anger.

Within my father's papers I found a photograph of my mother, Philippa, in a bathing suit marked in her own writing – 'P. in 1962' – in pencil on the back. She is standing alone on the deck of a smart-looking boat in the South of France. The picture was taken the summer that my paternal grandmother died, that her own grandmother died, that her beloved Border terrier died and soon after I had been released from a six-week stay in hospital having been treated for osteomyelitis, a dangerous infection of the bone. My mother's frequent absences went unchallenged. We were used to her keeping the details of her life hidden but the opportunities for spying on her were plentiful. When she was away I would tiptoe into her bathroom to look in the cupboards for clues. Once I found a plastic compact that revealed not a mirror, but a three-week supply of tiny white pills marked in a Monday-to-Sunday sequence. Whenever she was at home I was on alert. In order to reach my own room on the attic floor of our house the staircase wound past a large beam, with a small hole at its centre which bored its way through to my mother's bedroom. One ear pinioned to the splintery wood, I would strain to make out what she was murmuring into the telephone receiver. Words that she obviously did not want anyone else to hear were being whispered to an anonymous recipient and remained a frustrating mystery until a couple of years later when the truth of her secret love affair with a much older man was blown into the open.

At the beginning of the spring term in 1969, when I was fourteen years old, my mother drove me back to school and while we were still sitting in the car with the engine switched off, she told me she was leaving my father. She was going to live in a flat in London, the gulf of differences between my parents proving unbridgeable. Although the Divorce Reform Act of 1969 made 'irretrievable breakdown' a legal reason for the annulment, some proof of that collapse was still required; evidence of 'behaviour that the plaintiff could not live with' included adultery or cruelty. Not until after my father's death did I learn that instead of taking the adulterous option, he had chosen to cite his own cruelty in denying my mother a sexually satisfying relationship as the justification for their eventual divorce.

So I had seen the signs that had led up to my mother's news. I had listened to her whisperings through the crack in her bedroom beam, watched my father's increasing indifference to her prolonged absences abroad, accepted her withdrawal from family life as she sat in silence at one end of the dining-room table. But the shock of her announcement in the car was still immense. Reaching for the handle of the car door, my mother said it would be better if I kept the news of the separation to myself. A perfunctory kiss on the cheek was followed by the slamming of the driver's door as she opened the boot and heaved out my trunk. She drove away without looking back.

It is only now that I wonder if tears prevented her from saying anything else, either about her own state or to offer me words of comfort or explanation. Maybe the final admission of something that had been hidden for so long was so painful that she had silenced herself with hearing it spoken aloud to her daughter for the first time.

Being able to write about this moment some sixty years later gives me the chance to think about how much she must have dreaded that car-locked confession. Only now do I understand why she had to save herself from the marriage if she was to survive. But I have not forgotten what it felt like to be me, as I pulled my trunk towards the school door, determined not to watch the car's receding lights as they vanished down the drive, the sense that I too had somehow failed to keep our family whole suddenly overwhelming me.

That night in my dormitory, under the cover of sheeted darkness, I hugged my tap-filled hot-water bottle tightly, but its tepid warmth failed to comfort. Even so, I was unaware then that my mother had not quite given me full disclosure. Recently I came across an entry squashed into my father's little five-year diary, written in the 1960s during the years in which his marriage was falling apart. There it was in just one cramped line of biro. 'If either of us is killed, Philippa is making R. the guardian of the children.' It is the small things, not the murders, or even the infidelities, but the incidental comments that are the secrets which have the power to hurt most. The idea of my mother deciding without any consultation that we would be cared for by my ultra-conservative stepfather, an arrangement that would have wounded not only us but my father, shocked me deeply.

Difficult as the confrontation would be, I would add this dis-covery to the agenda for my planned kitchen-table conversation with my mother.

At school any girl whose background and home life diverted from the mainstream was whispered about. When the story of my parents' separation broke I joined the odd ones out, the targets of the community at large who thought of us as 'dif-ferent'. Our motley group included the girl whose father had died when she was only four, the girl who was adopted, the girl who shaved her lower arms after lights out, and a pair of Jewish sisters who were exempted from the religious rituals observed by the rest of us in a C. of E. school. There was one girl who used the lidded confidential box in the chapel, placed there during our confirmation classes, to send secret notes to the visiting nun to ask how she too could join the holy orders. As the entire class lurched pretty much simultaneously from childhood to the physical and emotional challenges of adolescence, I still felt like an oddity. My nose was too big. My teeth too long. My hair too thin. Despite, or because of, my mother's idiosyncratic spin on her 'facts of life' talk, I existed in a state of self-exclusion, con-fusion and shame. What was happening to my body? Had it happened to anyone else? Even if there had been someone in my dormitory who already knew something about the facts of life, I would never have dared to ask. And teachers were way out of the bounds of consultation. I had learned my lesson with Miss De V.

In the spring term of 1958 eleven-year-old Augusta Hope arrived as a new boarder at West Heath School in Kent. Founded by a vicar in 1865, the school was intended for children of the 'well-to-do' and those of 'like-minded people'. All these years later Gus remains puzzled about why her parents chose such a school for their own child where 'every girl was christened and the parents all voted Tory'. Speaking to me in the sitting room of her cottage by the sea she explained, 'I was meant to go to the more progressive Bedales but as I had failed my Eleven Plus they did not think I would pass the Bedales exam. So, they panicked. What to do with their daughter's education? My father's sister, Aunt Barbara, had been at Cambridge with Phyllis Elliot, an undergraduate of the same age, both of them by then in their early sixties. Phyllis Elliot was now the headmistress at West Heath and as long as the fees were paid, the girls were accepted. So, I went.' Elliot was described by the West Heath Old Girl's Association (WHOGA) as an intellectually formid-able figure whose 'brilliance' at teaching (history and literature) was 'legendary'. She charmed the adults. Tall, 'stolid' and dressed in fitted tweed suits, her hair was permed in a grey frizz. Elliot was admired, according to the WHOGA, for her 'generosity, her teasing, and her passionate desire that everyone should share her love of music and painting'. She drew universal approval from parents and governors alike, overseeing a school which was 'friendly, communicative and inspirational'.

Gus arrived at West Heath holding and maintaining a double secret. 'I immediately knew I was different,' she told me. First there was the question of Church. West Heath was another Church of England school and although Gus had visited churches with her mother as places of cultural interest, she had never been to a church as a worshipper. Also, unlike every other girl, she had not been baptised. The second secret was the political persuasion of both her parents. The newspapers that were dropped through her letterbox at home each morning were *The Times* and *The Daily Worker*, where her mother had worked. Both of Gus's parents were signed-up members of the Communist Party.

On the first night, Gus was let into the big school secret. She was told that at bedtime, just before lights-out, the headmistress, known by all the girls as P, would come round to kiss every one of the hundred or so girls goodnight. And this was confirmed by P's arrival at Gus's bedside later that evening. P shared a house with Miss Anne Brown, who was responsible for the administrative and bookkeeping side of the school. All those years later, Gus jumped up to demonstrate for me the angle at which Miss Brown would approach you, the middle of her body bent in a perfect right angle. As she reached you Miss Brown would open up, unhinging herself until she was upright and looking you in the eye. But there was no sign of Miss Brown when P came nightly and unfailingly to bestow her kisses on the cheeks of the young pupils. 'Within a week,' Gus told me, 'it felt entirely normal. For most girls it was never more than an affectionate kiss, but for a few it grew into something else. I suppose nowadays you would call it grooming.'

No one actually discussed the bedtime ritual much, the routine less of a formal secret than an unspoken contract between headmistress and girls that had existed for many decades unchallenged. No one told their parents. Only one act of rebellion occurred when a particularly beautiful girl suddenly vanished from the school. No explanation was given but Gus had a hunch that it might be connected to P's interest in her.

'Early on, I sensed something wasn't right about P's behaviour, even if I didn't feel it was exactly "wrong".' At the beginning of term each girl was required to have a medical.

'You would take all your clothes off, put on your dressing gown and wait outside the headmistress's study.' Inside, the female doctor would be waiting with the headmistress as the girls were asked to remove their dressing gowns and twirl around naked in front of the two women. 'That's odd, isn't it?' Gus half asked me.

Twelve-year-old Gus received P's kisses with neither encouragement nor protest. And as she grew a little older, she felt herself to be especially chosen, although she could not explain why. Gradually the intimacy increased.

' "Darling, what lovely little breasts you are developing," P would say to me.' Gus paused. 'I think you would call what she did inappropriate. She would be sitting on my bed. And she would run her leg up under my nightie. And she would fondle my breasts. Kiss me full on the lips as I kept my mouth firmly shut.'

When Gus became head girl she would be invited to P's study to share a tiny after-dinner cup of coffee with her. The sophistication of the miniature cup made the experience feel grown-up and exciting for Gus, while P seemed to be part motivated by the adrenalin of risk.

'Do you think you have minimised the lasting effect this had on you?' I asked Gus.

Her reply came slowly and carefully. 'No. I don't. The fact that P shared a house with Miss Brown and that they almost certainly had a love life meant that P didn't have to insist on our compliance. Although my mouth remained closed during kissing, there was no moment in which P forced it open. If the girls had indeed been mass-groomed but, on the whole, did not suffer any long-term effects, then where was the harm in it? P got her satisfaction. The girls were shown that there was no shame in touching, as long as it wasn't spoken about.'

Gus never talked to anyone about the dormitory or sitting-room activity, but not only because she did not know how to or with whom to discuss it. There was another reason for her discretion. Any shame that Gus felt was not because the kissing and stroking had ever taken place. On the contrary. 'It was nice to be favoured. I was the chosen one. The real truth of the matter is that I didn't mind it. That's what's embarrassing.'

Did Gus's home life help to explain the way she reacted to P? Despite the harmony of their political allegiance, she admitted 'my parents' marriage was one of silence. There was not much talking between them. My father was reserved with me too and we didn't speak much. In fact, I never had a private conversation with him. My relationship with my mother was closer. But not that close.'

Had there been there much physical affection at home? I wondered.

'Almost none. Although my mother did kiss me goodnight, we didn't hug.'

And so while Gus admitted to no one, perhaps not even to herself, that she did not want the stroking and kissing to stop, so P remained safe with her secret. The mutual code of silence, the omertà, was intact. In the holidays Gus was able to keep what she and P got up to during term time 'in a box'. At no point did she consider herself a lesbian because in the barn at home she had a 'very nice time' with a boy who lived in the village, 'although we didn't go the whole hog as I must have known, aged about sixteen or seventeen, that the whole hog could lead to a dreadful, dreadful result'.

Gus took her A levels and then left the school, 'left it all behind. I had nothing to do with the school again and never saw P again.' She is confident that she emerged from West Heath unscathed, neither scared nor scarred. 'P certainly abused me. But I don't *feel* that I was abused.'

However, there *were* others on whom P's abuse inflicted life-long damage. When, for the purposes of research for this book, I asked to meet another West Heath old girl from P's years, I received a polite but definitive refusal. I was told that almost seven decades later the old girl still found the memories of what happened at West Heath 'too painful' to contemplate. I wrote to the West Heath Old Girls Association to ask whether they had any photographs or any memories or obituaries of their previous headmistress. A huge trawl through the school records by the helpful archivist did not throw up any photographs of either P or Miss Brown. Her image seemed to have been erased even though she had remained at the school until 1965, aged almost seventy, having completed a tenure of thirty-seven years. P's secret assignations were never detected by the outside world, only defied once (by the girl who vanished in the middle of the term) and never called to account by the girls, their parents or the other staff.

With the lack of proper scrutiny of the teachers responsible for the boarding school residents of the 1950s and early 1960s, assumptions went uncontested about the instinctive nurturing nature of women which allowed female paedophiles like P to hide in full view. Boys' schools, on the other hand, were packed with male paedophiles who got away with abuse of the pupils that inflicted suffering that lasted a lifetime. In his memoir *A Very Private School*, Charles Spencer described how he did not tell anyone about what went on at his prep school in the 1970s. In 2024 I went to St James's Church in Piccadilly to hear Spencer talk about his experiences. The pews were packed as he spoke to the journalist and writer Justine Picardie, sitting together against the beautiful backdrop of the wooden Grinling Gibbons carvings that hang above the altar. The incongruity of discussing such depravity in a place dedicated to the sanctity of morality and goodness was not lost on anyone there as we heard how predatory teachers had preyed on innocence. But the audience responded with the greatest intake of breath when Spencer revealed that one of the teachers who sexually abused him most consistently and dangerously when he was eleven years old was the twenty-year-old female assistant matron. In the hushed church, Spencer described to Picardie how, with a 'calculated deployment of feminine warmth', she groomed the youngest boys to comply with her sexual demands, creeping into their beds and having sex with them, manipulating their own yearning for maternal affection in an institution otherwise devoid of female comfort. Spencer's dependence on this young woman became most acute when she threatened to leave the school, a prospect that drove him to such despair that he cut his body with a knife. 'If I hurt myself enough,' he said, explaining his thinking at the time, 'maybe God would let her stay.'

A decade after Gus left her school, Spencer's sister Diana

became a pupil at West Heath. She had managed to escape P's kisses by a matter of years and, unlike her brother, sexual abuse by a woman. And even though Gus is confident that she emerged unscathed by her experience, at least one pupil has not, her reluctance to speak about her experience intact all these years later. Spencer lived in secret with his trauma for many decades. In both cases the criminals were never brought to justice, the truth of their hideous activities only emerging lifetimes after the damage had been done.

CHAPTER 6

The Letter Was a Love Letter

In Britain the Mental Health Act of 1959 had highlighted the incarceration in specialised asylums of people considered 'lunatic' or 'defective' – terms that had gone unchallenged for centuries. Increasingly, instead of electroconvulsive therapy (ECT) delivered under anaesthetic, which some doctors were beginning to consider inappropriate, patients with mental health problems were being recommended to take courses of talking therapy. The Act removed the category of 'moral imbecile' and said that, instead of being institutionalised, individuals should be offered the chance of community care. The controversial psychiatrist R. D. Laing believed that insanity was often a valid emotional response to world-madness and that therapy was the solution, even in the case of 'conditions' such as schizophrenia. Laing advocated that self-healing was effective enough that the 'insane' could then be released back into the wider world. But these clinical developments didn't filter through immediately. In the early 1960s most forms of mental instability still attracted suspicion and sat uncomfortably with the general public, and most of the healthcare community.

When Rebecca John, born in 1947, and her one-year-younger sister Caroline came to adulthood in the mid-1960s, the shame attached to the taboo of mental illness that had run through their family for two generations had resulted in a sequence of disintegrating relationships. Secrets held by their grandmother and mother affected their young lives until the sisters eventually rejected the whispering and began to question events that had remained mysterious to them for so long. The John sisters' maternal grandmother Margaret was the eldest of the twelve children of Amy Cullen and her husband William Cullen, an Irish confectioner and baker. After leaving her home in North London for Auckland in New Zealand in 1912 in 'search of better prospects', Margaret met and married Stewart Vanderpump, a fellow émigré and a solicitor's clerk who had arrived in the country four years earlier. Stewart had become a passionate follower of the nineteenth-century religious and philosophical practice of theosophy before he suffered a nervous breakdown that landed him in a psychiatric hospital in 1917, a year after his daughter Mary was born. When the New Zealand doctor confirmed to Margaret that 'the patient is in an exceedingly disturbed state of mind', with 'intense headaches', he recommended that Stewart be given 'Mental Hospital treatment'. Margaret left Stewart in Auckland and returned to Britain after the end of the First World War, taking three-year-old Mary with her on the six-week sea voyage home; her actions were considered neither questionable nor cruel. And there it seemed the relationship between Margaret and Stewart Vanderpump ceased, leaving what Caroline describes as 'a blanket of silence, a veil of secrecy that was impossible to penetrate'. Within the family theosophy came to represent something 'unfriendly, unloving, divisive', a belief system which made Stewart culpable for putting oceans and continents between himself and his family, and for enforcing the separation of a father from his daughter, a wife from her husband and eventually grandchildren from their grandfather.

Back in England Margaret became a successful travelling saleswoman, working for a Central London clothing company specialising in elegant hand-made blouses of lace and silk. The financial rewards provided her and her daughter with a comfortable life, although Margaret's work consumed her days and Mary was packed away, first to boarding schools and then to a Belgian convent, the unhappiness of those lonely, fatherless years never forgotten or forgiven. During the Second World War, while working as an ambulance driver, Mary met her husband Caspar John, a distinguished naval officer and the son and nephew respectively of the painters Augustus and Gwen. In Rebecca's words, Mary was 'a tough and spirited girl without airs and graces' but 'with an energy and spontaneity that Caspar found immediately appealing'. Rebelling against her mother's love of smart clothes, regarding them as 'something to which the minimum of attention should be paid', Mary worked on the wartime barges, transporting a cargo of steel north from Limehouse to Birmingham and, on the journey south, bringing coal down from Coventry, a three-week round trip.

By 1960 Caspar had risen to the very top of his profession, becoming First Sea Lord and Admiral of the Fleet, and in 1961 Caspar and Mary travelled together to New Zealand as part of a world tour visiting other countries' navies. For Mary, the prospect of meeting a father she had last seen when she was three years old, almost half a century earlier, was a once-in-a-lifetime opportunity. With a demanding schedule of commitments to meet dignitaries and to appear as guests of honour at lunches and dinners and ceremonies, only one afternoon remained free to make the visit that mattered above all others. In the absence of any firm evidence, Rebecca and Caroline assume that prior to the trip Margaret had probably denied all knowledge of the name of the mental health hospital in which Stewart was spending his days. And when Mary tried to telephone Curley, Margaret's best friend in Auckland, to ask for the address, Curley's number was 'unattainable'. Rebecca and Caroline can only speculate that if Margaret had already failed to give her daughter the address of the 'Mental Hospital', she had also warned her friend to keep Stewart's whereabouts secret. The reunion between father and daughter never took place. When Mary realised what her mother's obfuscation had denied her she 'lost all the love she might have felt for Margaret' overnight.

In her retirement from the clothing business, Margaret lived in a bungalow on the Sussex coast at Shoreham with two of her unmarried sisters.

'She would take us out for treats,' Rebecca remembered. 'We would go to the Strand Palace Carvery, tea and cake at Fullers (one of her favourite places), the ballet, sometimes a film (I remember *Pollyanna* and *Fantasia*). The excitement!!'

But after the abortive trip to New Zealand, the anger Mary had come to feel towards her mother had begun to infect the children too.

'I dreaded going to Margaret's bungalow for half term,' Rebecca said. 'It faced this bleak shingle beach stretching as far as the eye could see where it always seemed to me to be windy, cold, grey and treeless.'

On one of Caroline's visits, Margaret professed herself to be mystified as the conversation turned towards the source of Mary's anger. How could an only child be so unkind to her eighty-seven-year-old mother? she asked her granddaughter. Taking up her mother's defence and challenging her grand-mother's decision to prevent a daughter from meeting her father, Caroline was shaken to see how Margaret, once so independ-ent and strong-willed, appeared to be 'overcome with guilt and unhappiness', her lower lip trembling as Caroline accused her of 'blanking out a life, a person'. Her granddaughters continued to visit her in the care home that she moved to in 1976 at the age of eighty-eight. But Margaret still insisted to the carers that she was puzzled and distressed about the rift with her daughter and over the telephone complained to her son-in-law in London that no one ever wrote to her or called her.

Almost twenty years after Margaret's death in the care home in 1981, this sad and unresolved story took an unexpected turn when Michael Vanderpump, a previously unknown second cousin, Stewart's great-nephew, got in touch with the sisters out of the blue after reading Rebecca's published biography of her father. With Michael's help, Caroline began to trace Stewart's fate, the new information from their cousin prompting her to think of her family in two ways. At times they were 'full of flowers, blue skies, green grass, mossy glades'. But then, as with any landscape, she realised there were also dark places 'hidden, unexplored caves where, when you make a noise, shadows flap out like bats disturbed from their roost, flap and clap noisily, chaotically, frighteningly'. Michael's research revealed that a year before Stewart's death in 1976, Helen Vause, a *New Zealand Sunday Times* journalist writing a piece about mental health patients, had been to the hospital to interview Stewart. The eighty-seven-year-old was amazed to have a visitor.

'I thought I was a forgotten man,' he told Vause, who found him to be 'slight, with fine features and well spoken . . . the epitome of an English gentleman'.

Stewart told Vause about his love of astronomy, showed her his room filled with 'a maze of gadgets and books' and his two telescopes, his most precious possessions. He would spend the evening hours looking up at the stars. His other passion, he told Vause, was cowboy stories. And it was with conviction that he spoke of a contented life, sustained by contemplation, meditation and yoga. Incarcerated for fifty-seven years, he had been quite unaware of the changes that had taken place in the outside world since he had left it aged twenty-nine at the end of the First World War. Vause found this gentle gentleman to be the embodiment of serenity and acceptance.

Gradually, further truths emerged. Margaret and Stewart had been polar opposites. She loved conversation and was a communicator. He craved quietness and even silence, wearing head muffs held in place with clips to shut out the noise of life. She was a doer. He was a thinker. Far from the practical, capable man Margaret had hoped for and with her heart set on making a home in her newly adopted country, she acquired some pristine land, asking Stewart to clear the terrain in preparation for the building works. But as he explained later to the medical superintendent in charge of his case, he had not been physically strong enough to cope with the 'lifting of heavy clay soil up an incline', and Margaret had grown impatient with his weakness. By the time Stewart had started following the doctrine of the Russian-American mystic Madame Blavatsky, there was little hope for the relationship. Theosophy's teaching about the ongoing presence of the spirits of the dead required its followers to spend long solitary periods devoted to study and meditation. The movement had soared in popularity during and after the First World War when the vast scale of death meant that millions of bodies had not been repatriated from the battlefields and a yawning chasm of untethered grief opened up for those denied a final goodbye, a funeral or a grave at which to mourn. For Stewart, lonely and far from home, looking for a support system to nurture his own sense of alienation, the comfort he found in his theosophical practice felt god-sent.

The more she learned about her grandfather, the more Caroline John understood his struggle to assimilate this new-found devotion into his marital circumstances. 'How to make sense of ancient wisdom? How to relate it to everyday life? How to integrate it into the scheme of things – a marriage, a new baby, the need to make money, the building of a house, the clearing of the land?' Increasingly unable to manage his mental and physical challenges in the face of Margaret's lack of sympathy towards both, he had pitched a tent in the garden and moved in, communicating with his wife in whispers and then through written notes. A conventional woman who felt quite at odds with this fanciful, quasi-religious bewitchery, Margaret found herself stuck with a silent, almost absent companion, from whom she felt increasingly excluded. Far from home and fearful of being contaminated in the eyes of others by what she interpreted as the stigma of her husband's mental illness, she took action. Dammed by his beliefs, punished for his silences, Stewart was admitted to a hospital for the treatment of a mental health condition.

There had been an assumption in the family that no contact had existed between Margaret and Stewart after Margaret returned to England, the explanation being that Stewart had suffered 'a nervous breakdown'. But Margaret was keeping a secret of great poignancy. Among the documents that Caroline received from her cousin Michael was a letter from Margaret written in 1922 to the doctor in charge of Stewart's care in the New Zealand hospital. She asked whether there had been any signs of improvement in Stewart's mental health, whether there was any hope he might be discharged because she 'can never for an instant forget he is there' and she is never 'really at peace'. The medical superintendent's report arrived two months later. The patient has 'abused' the unnamed privileges offered him, the unnamed doctor reported, so those privileges had been removed in punishment. As his mind was still 'centred on theosophy', Mrs Vanderpump must accept 'there is little hope of his permanent recovery'. Stewart's fate was sealed. With the collusion of his own wife, by then suffering from her powerlessness to alter her husband's fate, Stewart remained a man isolated for ever from the warmth of family life.

This unhappy saga, that had rippled through two generations, was not the only source of family shame. There was something else that Rebecca wanted to talk to me about. She invited me to lunch. She has lived in the heart of Covent Garden for more than half a century, just a minute's walk from the underground in an area ribboned with the narrow streets and old warehouses that had once formed the nucleus of London's fruit and vegetable market. On her arrival there in 1969, with a privy in the back-yard, Rebecca would take her bath in the Oasis Rooms at the end of the street where, if she wanted more hot water, she would shout out to the lady in the corridor who would turn on a giant brass tap with a spanner and hot water would gush into the bath. The atmosphere of the market had changed little since the time of Edwardian playwright Bernard Shaw, the flower-baskets, glass halls, stalls and barrows identical to those from which his character Eliza Doolittle had sold her violets fifty years earlier. Boxes of fresh produce would arrive from the countryside in the middle of the night before being loaded into hand carts and wheeled into position by the market traders. The pubs stayed open until dawn and the Floral Hall was, Rebecca remembers, 'a scene of constant activity, brightly lit and quivering with flowers and flitting sparrows'. In Rebecca's sunny living room, sitting at the oak table that had once belonged to Augustus, her paternal grandfather, the walls hung with his drawings, Rebecca showed me some of her own exquisite botanical watercolours – here was wild fennel, here a plump pair of lemons, here a snowdrop, here a tangle of lichens. But I was aware that despite her initiative, confiding in a stranger did not come easily to her as, moving on from the sad story of her grandmother's punishment of star-gazing Stewart, we came to the entangled puzzles of the next generation.

Rebecca's parents had married in 1943 and her fiercely etiquette-observant father, so different to her and Caroline's bohemian, exuberant mother, used to joke that they had married each other's opposites.

'My mother was warm, chaotic and spontaneous,' Rebecca told me. 'She loved people. She loved drinking, loved dancing, creating the beating heart of the street in our house in Barnes. People came and went, dropped in all the time. She was most at home with artists – Elisabeth Frink, Frank Bowling, Sandra Blow all came to our parties. And she was a terrific and effortless cook. All my friends loved her. She was very compassionate, especially with women who had experienced hardship, been abandoned, were hard up, had experienced the challenges of substance abuse. She liked taking in people who were in distress. She could shock. She was great fun. And she rebelled against her own mother in every way she could, never getting along with high heels and stockings, dressing in jeans in 1956 to the mortification of us, her children.'

One afternoon in 1964, seventeen-year-old Rebecca arrived home at 13 Woodlands Road having left school early. An envelope addressed to 'Mary Brown, 19 Woodlands Road' was lying on the hall table. Alone in the house, Rebecca opened the envelope. The letter was written to her mother from Ann Chadwick, a Canadian woman Rebecca and her family knew well. As soon as Caroline arrived home from school, Rebecca shared her wholly unexpected discovery.

'The letter was a love letter,' Rebecca told me. 'Our mother "liked" women.'

Ann Chadwick had left Canada after the war to marry the sculptor Lynn Chadwick. Mary first met Ann when she and Chadwick were living in a remote cottage in Gloucestershire without electricity or running water. Some five or six years after Chadwick won the Venice Biennale in 1952, Ann left him for Bingham Wilson, an antique dealer with whom she started a new life in a disused pub in Bletchley, adopting three children before having one of their own.

An arrangement with friends a few doors down at Number 19 Woodlands Road had meant that Ann could send her love letters there before being collected by Mary. After the initial shock, Rebecca grew to like Ann. She presented no threat. She was quick-witted and enjoyed a drink. Best of all she made Mary happy. Following a summer holiday in the Berwyn Mountains in Wales, they each bought a property in the same area – one a derelict cottage, the other an abandoned malthouse – where their love affair continued. Although Caroline was extremely disturbed by the discovery, Rebecca convinced herself that she had accepted the situation, as long as the 'subject' was not discussed either outside or inside the home. But of course she hadn't.

During my first meeting with Rebecca in Covent Garden, the admission of her mother's affair hung between us. Tentatively and with intervals of silence, she began to talk about that long-suppressed turmoil.

'While I knew it was out in the open that *men* did that,' Rebecca continued eventually, 'I did not know about women.

At school we used to say the art teacher was "lezzie" with the English teacher. But we did not really know what that meant. At the time I learned about my mother's affair, I learned the actual word for it. Lesbian. It was taboo. That word. Out of loyalty to my mother, I felt I must never speak the word aloud. To be "it" was something very weird and very dark and . . .' And, as Rebecca reached for a way to describe how she had once interpreted same-sex love, she concluded, '. . . and not nice.'

When Mary and Ann's relationship came to an end after six or seven years and Mary took up with another woman, Rebecca found herself facing what felt like a new and almost intolerable state of affairs. Jean, 'a feisty forthright redhead living in the Welsh hills', had been Rebecca's friend. They had met in Wales and, as they both prepared for the arrival of their first child, they had bonded over conversations about new theories of natural childbirth. And then, to Rebecca's amazement, Jean fell in love with her mother. For the five years that Jean and Mary were together, and although for entirely different reasons, the relationship between Mary and Rebecca came to resemble the stand-off that had existed a generation earlier between Mary and Margaret.

Eventually, Rebecca knew she must break the tension that filled the house in Barnes where no one ever mentioned their mother's situation. 'We were all affected – my brother, sister and I.' Rebecca needed to clear the air. She knew she must say the 'word' to her father.

'We were sitting together alone on a sofa after a party,' Rebecca remembered, when Caspar was the first to speak.

'Surely it can't go on much longer?' he asked Rebecca.

Assuming he was referring to her mother's mood swings brought on by the menopause, Rebecca seized her chance. Despite her 'excruciating embarrassment', she half-whispered to her father, 'Mummy's a lesbian, isn't she?'

Caspar's reaction, little more than a verbal shoulder-shrug, was interpreted by Rebecca to mean, 'More or less – so be it.' Although Caspar was often described to his daughter by others as 'fabulously handsome' and an 'homme fatal', to her 'he was just Dad with a bald head'. But as a true liberal and the son of a man for whom marriage had imposed no boundaries, Caspar never criticised his wife's choice of lifestyle. He himself and two of his brothers had all fathered children outside marriage. It was years before Caspar's son asked to meet his half-sisters and brother, an occasion regarded with bemusement and excitement on both sides.

These secrets buried within this family story have been revealed during a long process of investigation shared only after much careful thought and discussion. As soon as Rebecca and Caroline began to unravel the details of their grandfather's exile, the missing parts of their genealogical legacy begun to appear. Any regret over the fierceness of judgement with which they may have treated their grandmother has been recognised in hindsight as the reaction of those living at a time when mental health was so little understood and when the opportunities for discussion were hampered by confusion and fear. Despite my own grandparents' bisexuality, I also understood so well myself, also a child of the 1960s, the Victorian code of repression that remained attached to any open discussion of mental health and same-sex love, and how shattering such revelations could be within the family. Caroline's empathy for her grandfather shines through her words and when Rebecca found the courage to address the point of shame that had lain unmentioned behind their mother's love affairs, a new generation of women had begun to face the truth.

My own father struggled for many years over whether to talk and write about his mother's complex and taboo-ridden life, wondering if he was betraying her after her death but concluding eventually that he must do so in the belief that her experience would bring some reassurance, identification, clarification and hope to others going through similar struggles. One day, while staying alone in her mother's cottage in Wales, Rebecca spotted a copy of my grandmother's recently published book, *Portrait of a Marriage*, lying on the floor. My grandmother's 'confession' of lesbian love gave Rebecca 'the revelation' that a same-sex relationship could coexist within a heterosexual marriage. For me, the serendipity of meeting another woman who had been comforted by words that my grandmother had written so long ago was a powerful thing. And although Rebecca had confided in a few, close women friends over the years, sharing some of these stories with a stranger has brought her a new sense of freedom.

PART II

My Generation

1970–2000

CHAPTER 7

Mother's Little Helper

I began the 1970s as a naive schoolgirl, still to discover sex, cigarettes and T. S. Eliot. I ended the decade with first-hand knowledge of all three, in addition to a degree, a job and a husband, the decade as transformative for me as it was for other women of my age. The perfectionism, caution and above all deference that had dictated the lives of so many women of the 1950s had begun to dissipate rapidly through the 1960s. Leading activists on both sides of the Atlantic came largely from an educated, white, middle class, whose marginalisation of less privileged women would soon find its critics. But as the women's movement took off in America, members of this new, albeit elitist, social order produced the literature of protest. It came in various forms, from polemical to personal. Mary McCarthy's novel *The Group*, published the same year as Betty Friedan's landmark book *The Feminine Mystique*, was a bestselling sensation with its candid depiction of a community of female graduates and the taboos of sex and contraception. In 1970 Robin Morgan's anthology of women's feminism, *Sisterhood Is Powerful*, also became one of the Second Wave's most enduringly influential publications. Optimism was spreading that the ancient code of submissiveness, the male stranglehold, might be hovering on the brink of defeat. For these women the imposed code of self-discipline was at last giving way to self-expression.

Observer journalist Katharine Whitehorn led the British cavalry of journalists, television and radio presenters, writers and publishers behind the growing momentum of activists. Whitehorn was already known for voicing the unvoiceable. She had written about her grand aunt, a woman from a previous generation when things were supposed to be just so. 'My aunt's problem was remembering to remove a moustache she could no longer see, and trying not to wander around the house with her mouth open.' But it was Whitehorn's 'slut' article, a call to rebel, that had even greater impact. Dedicated to anyone who had 'ever changed their stockings in a taxi, brushed their hair with someone else's nail brush or safety pinned a hem', Whitehorn appealed to those who had discarded the waist-tied apron and retrieved an item from the dirty clothes basket 'because it had become, relatively, the cleaner thing' and it was less of a sweat to be a BIT dirty than to do the whole washing, drying and ironing thing. Women wrote back in huge numbers, including one who, her mind on higher things, had wiped her kitchen table clean with the kitten.

The novelist Margaret Drabble was candid about motherhood

and illegitimacy in her novel *The Millstone*, published in 1965, which arose, she explained, not from literary ambitions but because she was writing 'to exorcise fear, I was writing for luck, I was writing in hope'. Aged twenty-eight, with three children, four novels and a book about Wordsworth to her name, Drabble was asked in a radio interview at the time to explain her decision to combine work and motherhood when 'most married women make a choice between a career of some sort and their home'. She replied that she could not do without either. 'I could not spend my life wheeling pushchairs round the park. I had to do something else as well. So, in a sense I have always felt there was no choice.' But the double existence took its toll. 'My life is a continual and absolutely exhausting compromise. I am always rushing from one to another and never knowing where I ought to be and feeling totally guilty about every part of my life.'

Living in London while studying at a sixth form college for my A levels in the early 1970s, I attempted to address my sketchy sex education. I never heard my parents utter a four-letter word aloud and I wondered if they actually knew the existence let alone the meaning of mysterious terms like buggery and sodomy. Necrophilia lurked in the darkest, unmentionable corners of my curiosity. Oddly I never looked anything up. Less oddly I never asked anyone else if they could explain these mysteries. I read *Lady Chatterley* and found it utterly arousing. I stood on a chair to retrieve the hidden copy of John Updike's *Couples* from the top shelf of my father's room. I listened obsessively to Anna Raeburn on London's Capital Radio, where she was one of a group of agony aunts – wise, sympathetic, unshockable, fearless matriarchs who played a crucial role in a fast-changing society. Anna and her approachable male colleague, 'the Capital Doctor', would broadcast nightly, encouraging confession, weakening the fearfulness wrapped up in taboos, as confused and lonely women (and some men) sought advice. I heard how violence and sexual abuse had ruined lives, and listened to Anna's mix of sympathy and practical advice. With her precise, swift-moving, rat-a-tat, no-nonsense diction, Anna sounded intimidating, indeed terrifying, but also so reassuringly knowledgeable that I considered calling her up myself and asking her what on earth to do about my mother's undiscussable drink problem. I never had the nerve to do so. Anna identified the peculiar advantage of radio as providing 'a remarkable mixture of intimacy and anonymity . . . as far as I am concerned I'm talking to whoever is on the telephone and the caller is not deceived because he or she knows that there's the presenter, the Capital Doctor and me and the rest are eavesdroppers'.

With the advent of hundreds of personal podcasts in the last ten years or so, especially those conducted by the most sympathetic while at the same time forensic of hosts, such as journalist and writer Elizabeth Day in *How to Fail*, *Laid Bare* with Dami Olonisakin, Shakira Scott and Shani Jamilah in the UK, and psychotherapist Esther Perel in the USA with *Where Should We Begin*, the 'listening in' to people's problems and their solutions has become an even bigger part of our auditory landscape. But Anna and the Doc were not the first to offer solutions to personal problems, having joined a long-established tradition of 'Problem Page' counsellors – newspaper, magazine and radio roles traditionally occupied by agony aunts. In the 1950s and 1960s Britain these women became household names. Evelyn Home had dispensed advice from the 1920s to the 1970s in the pages of *Woman* magazine, never failing to observe proprieties, censoring the word 'bottom' from all printed correspondence, including the 'bottom of the garden'. Marjorie Proops had begun her problem-solving career in 1956 with a column called 'Soul Surgery' in the *Daily Mirror*. She amazed her readership when she revealed in her 1993 memoir that she had been conducting a twenty-year-long extra-marital love affair with a colleague at work, and had herself been on the receiving as opposed to the solving end of the agony.

The advice columns of Kailash Puri were a particular source of solace for those with limited fluency in the language of their adopted country. Born in 1925 and brought up first in a village outside Rawalpindi (now in Pakistan) and then in Lahore, Puri was married to a young scientist whose research in plant ecology involved travelling and living all over the world. In 1966 she joined her husband in Liverpool and started *Roopvati*, a magazine intended for a family readership. As her typewriter could not accommodate the Gurmukhi script required for Punjabi, Puri wrote the magazine by hand and sent it to Delhi to be set. The printed versions were then returned to her in Liverpool to distribute. Every weekend during those early years, she would pack her car with *Roopvati* and drive around towns in Yorkshire, to Coventry, to Birmingham and even as far as London, calling in at Sikh temples across the country. She would sit in the congregation as the Punjabi musicians, the dhaddis, beat their small hand drums 'shaped like egg timers', the children running among them, as voices 'pronounced the familiar words of the Gurus while the harmonium waxed and waned'. When the service ended, Puri would move through the congregation selling her magazine. By the 1970s, writing in Punjabi under the pseudonym Humraaz Maasi, translated as 'confidante auntie', Puri was answering questions from Punjabi women of all faiths, including Sikhs, Hindus and Muslims, and reaching not only women in Britain and Punjab but also wherever Punjabi women had settled, from Canada and America to Africa. Struggling with the comparatively sexually liberal etiquette of a different culture, women wrote to Puri under the protection of anonymity with concerns including 'domestic violence, alcoholism, impotence, adultery, gambling, relations between mothers and daughters-in-law, dowry demands, arranged marriage, husbands neglecting their wives and children to spend their money on themselves'. A woman talking openly about romance and love-making wasn't something that Punjabi society could accept easily. While not wishing to censor the subjects that concerned her correspondents most, Puri found her own discreet, euphemistic vocabulary when the Punjabi language did not have the right terminology. *Madan chhatri* (Cupid's umbrella) was her description for the clitoris, and *pashm* (silk) was the word she used to describe pubic hair.

Questions were sent about whether to allow young girls and newly married couples to go out unchaperoned, how to marry for love rather than dynasty, how to interest a new generation in old cultures and how to face the uninvited curiosity provoked by a burqa or a hijab. Threats of suicide were not uncommon. A dowry was sometimes seen as the price paid for an existence only slightly better than slavery. One young bride from California described how her new brother-in-law expected 'more than sisterly love from her'. She told of how he threatened to lie to her husband, his brother, that the child she was carrying was his. If the young woman denied his claims she would not be believed and would be expelled from the house. The brother-in-law would ensure her name was forever shamed within the family. Her daily telephone calls to Puri were full of talk of suicidal intentions. Puri's advice was consistent. 'Resist the advances. Stay steady.' Puri acknowledged 'this was no easy case' but eventually the young woman's resistance worked and she persuaded her husband that they should live separately from the brother-in-law.

Living in a foreign country, far from family and friends, made any escape from a life of domestic persecution especially challenging. 'In such cases a woman has to be strong, educated and confident of her ability to live on her own,' Puri observed. Breaking cultural traditions was often impossible. 'However much their husbands drink and beat them up,' she wrote in her memoir, 'Asian women here, especially those brought up in the East, continue to suffer behind closed doors rather than to leave and claim their legal rights.' Unlike Britain's home-grown radio and magazine agony columnists, Puri also encouraged visitors to come to her Victorian house for consultation, where, according to her daughter, 'she listened. She counselled. She intervened.' Those people who could not come to her house, and who found it difficult to make an undetected telephone call, would take their chances only to be caught and be forced to hang up. After her death Puri was praised by her country as a breaker of taboos.

Puri was 'the confidante who would answer the questions they could ask no one. Absolutely no one.' Her daughter said that 'everywhere, her message was the same – equality and recognition for women, elimination of patriarchal tyranny, and grasping the new age with confidence'.

Anna Raeburn and Kailash Puri guaranteed their correspondents' anonymity, but as the 1970s progressed, women in the public eye increasingly used songs and books as outlets for personal catharsis and to draw public attention to some of the forms of abuse women might experience, while suffering in silence. After university, my first job was as an assistant in the publicity department of a London publisher. There, I met two American women who wrote and sang openly about secret behaviours in ways I had never come across before. In 1977 the American singer Dory Previn flew over to London, partly for the promotion of her new book, *Midnight Baby*, but primarily for her first ever British concert tour. While the book told the story of her early years, Dory revealed her adult self more fully in the lyrics of her songs. Smiling beneath an exuberant halo of curly hair and through her huge tinted glasses, she embodied not only star quality but an unmistakable fragility. Married to the conductor André Previn, she had been friends with a young, little-known actress named Mia Farrow who would come to visit Dory at the family home. At some point during those visits, Mia found a way to seduce her friend's husband. When André revealed that he and Mia were expecting twins, Dory's lyrics reflected this betrayal. She had no intention of vanishing because of the shame of a husband leaving her for a younger woman. Instead she sang about it. She sang about the problems of communication and the hurdles of being misunderstood. She sang songs about love and sex, despair and hope, and about mental fragility. Packed audiences came to listen to her at London's Royal Albert Hall and watched her on an extended live television session for the BBC's prestigious *Old Grey Whistle Test*. She travelled to sell-out concert halls in Brighton, Leeds, Oxford, Southampton, Edinburgh and Glasgow. Every song had something to say that felt shockingly and valuably honest to the twenty-two-year-old me. But it was the agonising 'Beware Young Girls' that taught me most about the pain of betrayal. With a chorus refrain that she was her friend, her friend, her friend, Dory sang of the subtly pernicious treachery that destroys friendships, marriages and lives.

Previn's public voice gave her a way to express private pain. Where she used her music as a therapeutic tool, another woman, Barbara Gordon, used the written word. In 1980, I went out to Heathrow airport to meet an author whose book I had found so harrowing that I was apprehensive about accompanying her to her hotel. *I'm Dancing as Fast as I Can* was a double confession involving a secret addiction to prescription drugs and an inability to escape an abusive relationship for which Gordon had taken the blame. But when the poised woman in a smart knee-length coat came smiling through the arrivals gate and announced herself, I was taken aback. Given the emotional turmoil she had described in such naked detail, I had been expecting someone less composed. But here she was, beautifully dressed, coiffed, ear-ringed, with a charisma that explained why people had opened up to her in the television documentaries for which she was famous.

Her book told the story of how, as a forty-year-old leading television producer in New York, Gordon had been nominated for Emmy Awards and regarded with the utmost admiration by her industry. But even at the height of her career, she had kept her nine-year-long use of the tranquillising drug Valium secret from everyone but her doctor. Her dependency was so entrapping that she could no longer go the shops or catch a bus, let alone go to work, without taking the pills. She became 'afraid of fear', of the panic attacks that could swamp her even when walking down a familiar street in Manhattan. The psychiatrist who prescribed the drugs had assured her they were 'non-addictive', and dismissed her questions about their long-term side effects. But eventually, even though she had become 'a slave to these pills', they were no longer helping to alleviate her ever-persistent anxiety. Only able to shuttle between the twin sanctuaries of work and home, making elaborate excuses about her reticence to go out in public, she consulted her doctor. She wished to quit the pills cold turkey. He reassured her she would be fine and said she should go straight ahead, insisting there was no need to taper the dosage. She did not think of questioning him. He was the voice of authority. And then the nightmare began. Unable to sleep with 'a fire raging through my head', her body felt 'like a piece of glass'. She stopped going to work at all. She stopped getting dressed. A woman once proud of her appearance, she now took no care of herself, no longer bothering with make-up or washing or brushing her hair. As the physical symptoms of withdrawal increased, her perfect love affair with Eric, a lawyer and her live-in boyfriend, was upended. He began to tell her she was a 'bitch'. That she was a 'bad woman', that she had 'ruined people's lives', that people 'hate' her and that she must be punished. He tampered with the lock on the door to their apartment so that she could not escape even if she had wished to. Subjected to what is now recognised as coercive control, Gordon became the target of not only verbal but physical abuse. She was defenceless. She thought she was going mad.

Reading the book, from which no detail of her appalling physical and mental suffering was omitted, I understood how a sense of shame had prevented Gordon from telling a soul about what was happening. Eric fielded all telephone calls from her friends, saying that Barbara was recovering from the stress of work, that she was resting, that she was tired, that she was 'taking it easy'. One day she overheard him informing her boss that she was a 'schizophrenic'. Another day she allowed herself to glance in the bathroom mirror. 'My neck was black and blue, my arms were covered with huge purple spots.' And then she realised that the insanity was not hers but Eric's. A crazed attempt to escape resulted in a fight in which Eric's glasses were shattered and Barbara was bound and tied up with the cord from Eric's bathrobe.

Eventually her two best friends, desperately worried by her silence and absence, staged a rescue. Arriving at the apartment, the friends pretended to go along with Eric's blustering assurances first that there was nothing wrong with Barbara and then that she *was* mad, in order to get his permission to take Barbara away from him and to safety. Two years of treatment in psychiatric hospitals were followed by a search not only to recover her health but to retrieve her sanity. In every interview for her book in the USA and the UK, Barbara Gordon used her personal experience to urge women to stop being 'docile patients', 'not to ignore your own doubts' and to become part of the 'consciousness raising' that was fundamental to addressing the inequities of dependency and relationship coercion. I held her in the highest regard. I still do.

At about the same time as Gordon's book was published, prescription drugs were also secretly attacking the mental health of America's first lady. Betty Ford, the wife of Gerald Ford, the 38th US president, already nationally admired for publicly acknowledging her breast cancer in 1974, had become a role model and proud advocate of women's rights when she publicly supported women's choice to have an abortion. In an interview with TV anchor Morley Safer on NBC's *60 Minutes*, she said, 'I feel very strongly that it was the best thing when the Supreme Court voted to legalise abortion, bringing it out of the back woods and into the hospitals where it belongs.' This open communication was in contrast to the previous presidency, when the secrecy that characterised Nixon and the Watergate scandal had done such damage to the presidential image. Betty Ford was voted a Woman of the Year by *Time* magazine and her popularity ratings soared above those of the president himself. But the political backlash against such outspokenness worried her husband's campaign managers who were already working on the president's re-election. For a while Betty Ford was quietly sidelined, discouraged, even prevented, from speaking to the cameras, but her influence proved irrepressible and the swell of support for her so powerful that the new badges for the presidential campaign declared 'I'm betting on Betty's husband'.

Not long afterwards, rumours that the president's wife might be drinking to excess began circulating in Washington. A television interview with the formidable Barbara Walters, in which Ford gave an inarticulate tour of the private family rooms in the White House, made denial of Ford's inebriation all the more difficult. When grilled publicly about whether her use of tranquillisers affected the speed of her speech, Ford replied that she had never learned to be a rapid-fire speaker. The White House staff spoke to Ford's doctor about the number of pills they had seen the first lady consume, only to be rebuffed and told not to interfere in his patient's private matters. On an official visit to Russia, public suspicions were raised further when Ford was televised slurring her words during a public reading of *The Nutcracker* and a newspaper report openly stated that she was 'sloe-eyed and sleepy-tongued'. When she and her husband left the White House in January 1977, life became emptier and the drinking increased. Her husband later admitted he was in denial about her condition but the time came when Ford's family could no longer ignore what was evident to everyone else. Just as Barbara Gordon stopped dressing, seeing friends or participating in any social life, so Betty Ford admitted later that she had 'had no urge to live, I wanted life to pass me by'. Ford's daughter, her youngest child Susan, said, 'It was like watching a robot in slow motion.' Finally, on 1 April 1978, Susan, her father and her brothers staged a family intervention. Dressed in a pink, satin, quilted robe, Ford was faced by her family as each one in turn told her how her addiction was destroying not only her life but theirs. At first Ford was furious, rejecting the accusations, calling her family 'a bunch of monsters'. Two days later, in order to deflect the amplifying rumours, she called a press conference to say that she had been 'overmedicating' herself with pills, including the anxiety-busting Valium, also known as 'mother's little helper'. The painkillers were originally prescribed for a pinched nerve in the 1960s, and she had been taking them for ten years, becoming drawn into an unkickable addiction, legitimatised as they had been prescribed by a proper doctor. Immediately after the conference she checked secretly into the Long Beach Naval Hospital. Few places offered rehabilitation from chemical addiction and at Long Beach Ford shared a room with four strangers, wore a name tag and was deprived of privileges just like the other inpatients. The public were not told that she was there for the treatment not only of pill addiction but detoxification from alcohol.

When this further development was made public two weeks later, a shockwave ran through the country. The exposure felt all the more unexpected because of the usual outspokenness of the former first lady, a proud feminist who had always emphasised the importance of being honest. But soon the candour about a subject associated with so much shame and made by this popular role model came to be seen as both remarkable and ground-breaking. 'I had a gourmet collection of drugs,' Ford explained. 'I did a little self-prescribing; if one pill is good, two must be better – and when I added vodka to the mix, I moved into a wonderful fuzzy place where everything was fine, I could cope.'

Her admission resulted in huge postbags from Americans thanking her and identifying with her. Embracing sobriety, she admitted how for her the word 'alcoholism' had always prompted images of a 'dishevelled drunk', and that this taboo had stifled her, preventing her from outing herself as an addict. 'My make-up wasn't smeared, I wasn't dishevelled, I behaved politely, and I never finished off a bottle, so how could I be an alcoholic?' she asked. By emphasising that women were equally susceptible to addiction as men, she encouraged women to confide their secret habits. In 1982 she founded the Betty Ford Center in California, with the aim of 'serving patients and saving families'. Attaching her name so publicly to such a place lanced the shame of addiction and gave the centre credibility and dignity. Patients, many of whom were women, including the actress Elizabeth Taylor, were granted anonymity in order to help them come to terms with such exposure. Betty Ford had made it clear that no one was immune from addiction whether they were TV executives, movie stars, first ladies or housewives like my mother.

CHAPTER 8

What Did You Do to Provoke Him?

At the very beginning of the 1970s, the collective energy of feminism started to operate more formally under the umbrella of the Women's Liberation Movement (WLM). With the milestones behind them of the setting up of the National Housewives' Register in 1960, the revolutionary, choice-affording contraceptive pill in 1961, the publication of Betty Friedan's book *The Feminine Mystique* in 1963 and the new practical freedom offered by Mary Quant's short skirts, British women's visibility in public life had begun to move to the centre of the political stage as well. There was a growing recognition of women who had been previously under-represented, or ignored by the Women's Liberation Movement, excluded by those with an educational and material advantage. Voices were encouraged and heard from sections of society that had up to now been passed over not only by the men in charge but by women wielding their feminist authority.

An increasing focus on legal injustices, including abortion laws and unequal pay, followed the Dagenham car factory protests in 1968, when women machinists who sewed car seat covers at the Ford factory went on strike. They had discovered that their pay packets were 15 per cent less than men's, even though their jobs were equally demanding. By May 1970, Barbara Castle, Minister for Employment and the first woman ever to hold a seat in the Cabinet, had negotiated the Equal Pay Act prohibiting all wage discrimination for 'equal work'.

Later that year a high-profile, annual event accelerated women's refusal to tolerate sexually objectifying behaviour in all forms. The Miss World competition, the premier annual beauty parade, was held that November in the Royal Albert Hall. For some the competition was the apogee of international female glamour and aspiration. For others the swimsuit-and-heels event represented the nadir of debasement in which women were judged exclusively by their looks and bodies. The compere that year was the sixty-seven-year-old American entertainer Bob Hope, who welcomed the audience to 'the cattle market'. Greeting them with an extended 'mooo', breathed low and deep into the microphone, he described how he had already been enjoying himself backstage with the girls by 'checking the calves'. Hope was well under way, playing to what he assumed was a keenly receptive hall, when he was momentarily halted by the sound of football rattles coming from the audience. A puzzled smile playing on his lips, he tried to continue with his routine. But the rattling became louder and suddenly what appeared to be a hailstorm of white thimble-sized bullets whizzed past his dinner-jacketed shoulder and splattered onto the stage. As hundreds of flour pellets, stink bombs and tomatoes were hurled in his direction, Hope moved away from the microphone, the cameras following his expression of bewilderment. The live television broadcast erupted in chaos as a chorus of 'We're not beautiful, we're not ugly, we're angry' resonated around the auditorium. The choir was formed of women activists who had smuggled their ammunition into the hall to protest against the competition and against Hope, the suave, bow-tied figurehead of the event, described by his biographer Arthur Marx as 'one of show business's most incorrigible philanderers'. Returning briefly to the front of the stage, Hope judged the demonstration to have been 'a nice conditioning course for Vietnam' and complimented the speechless previous year's winner on her 'cute little turned-up nose', before vanishing backstage in a dandruffy cloud of flour. The following day *The Times* leader column condemned the demonstration, describing the Miss World contest as 'an activity traditionally regarded as quite harmless by most people'.

In 1970 thirty-one-year-old Erin Pizzey was living in Chiswick in London. Her husband Jack, a BBC journalist, was out at work all day, leaving her at home to care for their two small children. Articles in the *Guardian* by her friend Jill Tweedie and Betty Friedan's book brought her comfort in finding 'that the angry isolated housewife rampaging in my head was not alone'. *The Feminine Mystique* had exposed for Pizzey, as it had for so many others, a problem that 'lay buried, unspoken, for many years in the minds of American women'. By inviting them to ask 'Is this all?' Friedan was issuing a call to action. Nothing would change unless the 'dissatisfaction' that Friedan had identified was addressed openly by all women, including those of my mother's generation too afraid or too conditioned to listen to, let alone answer, Friedan's question. The National Housewives' Register (originally the Housebound Wives' Register and nowadays known as the National Women's Register), set up by Maureen Nicol in 1960 after she read that *Guardian* article about women being complicit in the dullness of their own lives, had moved beyond local get-togethers over coffee, expeditions and talks. By 1970 the organisation had recruited 15,000 women, largely educated and liberal. In an effort to relieve her housewifely isolation Pizzey had been attracted by similar, informal women's meetings held in neighbours' houses while their husbands were out at work. Her chief hope was to become a committed supporter of the WLM by joining the mission to change society's imbalance. As the women confided in one another about subjects many had never discussed before, Pizzey welcomed the unity derived from common experience. Here were women who had never had an orgasm, had never even known what an orgasm was, did not think their husband was a good lover, did not know what a good lover was. A large number had gone through illegal and agonising abortions, an undertaking they had found too shameful to admit to anyone. At first the meetings which encouraged the spirit of shared confession radiated safety.

But over time Pizzey began to feel uncomfortable with the militant tone she detected in the feminist hardcore, their presence changing the original compassionate tone of the gatherings into something that felt more bellicose.

'The promise was we would work together, we wouldn't compete against each other and that we would be powerful in our working. I assumed we would be working in our local communities where I could see things that needed changing. But it was nothing of the sort. My parents had been captured by the communists so I wasn't fooled when I saw the Mao poster on the walls of some of the women's houses. It was fashionable to declare yourself a left-wing communist.'

Hoping that the aggressive attitude would soften, and without a particular political agenda of her own, Pizzey pledged to herself that she would 'stand alone', whenever she came up against any kind of injustice. She became used to raising her voice, especially when she was told not to 'worry your pretty little head about it', as happened when she challenged a supermarket manager about price fixing.

When Margaret Thatcher, the strong-willed MP for Finchley, was made the Conservative Minister for Education after the summer election of 1970, she cancelled the free daily milk allowance for school children over the age of seven in a cost-cutting exercise. There was uproar. The Shadow Education Secretary, Edward Short, called Thatcher's move 'the meanest and most unworthy thing' imaginable. Aware that many families in her neighbourhood depended on this allowance 'as the main source of nutrition', Pizzey campaigned for its restoration. With her slogan 'Thatcher, Thatcher, milk snatcher', Pizzey led a protest march through the streets, accompanied by a real-life Jersey cow. The milk ban was not reversed but the publicity resulting from

Pizzey's determination to speak up for the disadvantaged had made its mark.

On 6 March 1971 Pizzey joined the first Women's Liberation march. Nothing like it had taken place since the Suffragettes' protests sixty years earlier. The elegant green, purple and white sashed dresses and jaunty boaters of the Edwardian age were replaced by floats with giant birdcages in which scantily dressed women had been 'trapped'. Pizzey felt such gimmicks would distract from the serious purpose of addressing women's equality and that the banners carried by Maoists, Leninists and Trotskyists might sabotage the focus on the central cause.

'I feared that to the average woman in the country the march looked like a freak show,' Pizzey explained.

I watched the archive footage of the march and the faces of hundreds of exhilarated women do not share Pizzey's concern. I zoomed in on the laughter pealing from the mouths of children carried on the shoulders of men, and on the police-woman who, with her smiling expression of approval, seems to be saying, 'Let me get out of this uniform and join you.' I saw a joyous crowd of 4,000 women and children, singing and dancing in London's rain and then the snow, to the ironic soundtrack of the jaunty and blatantly sexist 1930s song 'Keep Young and Beautiful' blaring from a tape machine wedged into a child's pram. Taking their children by the hand, skipping together from Hyde Park through Trafalgar Square, here was a group bringing previously hidden lives and concerns out of the shadows and into the daylight. Here were women march-ing for equal pay, equal job opportunities, for abortion on demand, for free contraception, for me and my daughters and granddaughters, footage impossible to watch without being moved to tears.

Pizzey was still attending the neighbourhood meetings when she heard through the network that BIBA, the 'glamorous and liberating' fashion boutique in Kensington, was being earmarked for attack, as the shop represented 'capitalist deco-decadence' to the activists. There were plans for the store to be to be bombed. Instantly Pizzey decided to blow the cover of the secret mission and went to the police. But she was too late to prevent the assault on May Day which damaged the basement of the store and wounded the caretaker. With the WLM supporting from the sidelines, the Angry Brigade, a far-left terrorist group responsible for a series of bomb attacks in England between 1970 and 1972, issued a statement claiming the bombing was intended as a blow against capitalism: 'The only thing you can do with modern slave-houses – called boutiques – is wreck them.'

When Pizzey was discovered to be the mole, she was banned from the hard-line women's collective meetings, her reputation destroyed instantly and irreparably. And yet however isolated she herself had become, she saw and heard the signs of loneliness, poverty and anxiety in the streets and shops that surrounded her. Despite what she recognised as her 'relative affluence', and the proximity of the smarter end of Chiswick, Pizzey was living in a neighbourhood where unmarried mothers, widows, wives of men in prison and women of every diverse racial and religious background maintained an existence that, like the surroundings, was 'worn and battered'. It was for them that, in 1971, Pizzey started her own offshoot gatherings where people could come to share their concerns. While waiting to find a permanent venue, on one occasion she rented Chiswick Town Hall. Abortion and contraception were the two topics highest on the agenda for the fifty women who turned up and who Pizzey saw were 'from all areas, classes and races' and were 'crying out for help'. Unconvinced by the efficacy of marches, cages, placards, flying tomatoes and literature – and even these temporary gatherings in halls – Pizzey persuaded the local council to give her the keys to a tiny derelict semi-detached house on Belmont Terrace and the bank to give her a loan.

From here Erin Pizzey launched Chiswick Women's Aid. Soon the reality of what was happening behind closed doors just yards from Belmont Terrace became all too apparent. Among those who came to her fledgling centre were teachers, secretaries, dinner ladies; the wives of welders, lorry drivers, labourers, mechanics and policemen, as well as the wives of 'so-called gentleman', including 'civil servants, judges, solicitors and councillors'. Here were women whose lives may have started well, but against whom circumstances had turned. Not only were they struggling to pay for rent and food, but some were alcoholic, others anorexic and most were terrified of the violence to which their partners would subject them at a time when the rape of a wife remained a husband's legal right.

The narrative of domestic violence revealed to Pizzey in the 1970s contains an alarmingly familiar ring half a century later, with concerns about abuse of women still so acute. But the fact that this issue is so high on the current reforming agenda, rather than hidden in plain sight as it was when Pizzey started her work, is an indication of change in itself. And Pizzey's role in bringing about that change was pivotal. Now, as then, the abuser was tyrannical, felonious, anarchic. Knives, whips, broken glass and fists did near-fatal and fatal damage. Stories included the fate of a seven-months-pregnant woman who had been electrocuted when her husband threw an electric fire into her bath; another woman had an asthma attack while her husband held a pillow over her face; another was near-blinded by a punch to the eyes; the baby of a fourteen-year-old raped by her father was born with severe birth defects. And yet the women had kept these horrifying states of affairs secret because society would not have helped them. Welfare wasn't available to women who were still married even if they had managed to escape their abusive partners. The law didn't support abused women unless they could demonstrate severe injury by their husbands and even then the police and the hospitals were not always convinced by the evidence. Sometimes the effort required to fight the institution felt greater than accepting the violence itself. Judges had already taken sides when they asked women, 'What did you do to provoke him?' Clergy told women to pray harder, to try harder. Social workers highlighted the masochistic tendencies of women and recommended marriage counselling for relationship problems. GPs and nurses looked the other way and did not ask women how they got their injuries. Pizzey heard that friends and family members would tell women, 'Work it out. Figure out what pleases him and stick with it. After all, children need their fathers.'

The tiny two-up, two-down house in Chiswick was soon filled beyond capacity with thirty-four women and children, bunkbeds jammed into every available space. Any woman who wished to come there – for safety, for peace, for conversation, for help, for food, to use the second-hand washing machine, to feel less lonely – was given a key. This was Pizzey's unprecedented gift to her growing community.

The visible evidence of the treatment these women had suffered was impossible to miss. Skin was marked with cigarette burns, huge bruises, bite marks and glaring bald patches from where hair had been wrenched out. Many women said that the unpredictability of their abuser was worse than the violence itself. On their arrival at the refuge, Pizzey would sit each woman down, take her hand and encourage her to start from the beginning, giving each woman her full attention, stopping whenever the recollection of these suppressed stories became too much. The refuge depended on a process of persuading, encouraging and, above all, waiting for the women to be ready to divulge their stories. Pizzey knew that describing their experiences aloud was essential if they were to stand a chance of staying away from their abusers. And the waiting took time. As Dr Hannah Dawson has said, 'Feminism is often associated with speaking up and speaking out but it is as much about learning to hear.' Pizzey listened not only to what a woman said but 'to what she omitted'. She remembered that 'sometimes it was not the words but the silences between them that was significant. They were telling me things they felt unable to tell anyone else. They spoke about deep, dark secrets of terrible sexual abuse – and sometimes made confessions of their own deviant behaviour.' Their experiences included 'sexual perversion, masochism, incest and bestiality'. Sometimes a pregnant woman would tell Pizzey that the baby was not moving and Pizzey would suggest the baby might be 'frozen with fear'. Gradually and miraculously, with the sharing of the mother's story, the unborn child would sense its mother begin to relax and start to move. Sometimes, when the time spent hearing these accounts felt unbearable, Pizzey's efforts not to cry failed her. She would return home in the evening, 'run a very hot bath and scrub myself clean. I used to have to pray afterwards. But it was the person pouring out her secrets who really needed to cry.'

Gill Margaret Hague, Professor Emerita of Violence Against Women Studies at the University of Bristol, spoke to women who *had* eventually found the refuge after years of suffering. In 1994 'Edna' told Hague, 'You couldn't leave your husband. It wasn't done. I would have been horribly ashamed if anyone had found out . . . And there was never anywhere to go to . . . I didn't have the money for a rented flat – I didn't have any money at all of my own.' By the time she reached her eighties in the 1990s Edna believed her life had been destroyed by violence and the inability to escape. 'I lost my one life.'

Narnia was ten years old when she came to the refuge with her mother, and told Hague how the refuge meant 'safety and escape' and the end to 'walking on eggshells, no more shouting, screaming, banging, bruises, lies'. Another woman described how when she arrived at the house, 'they gave me tea, and I started to cry and there was someone to put their arms around you'. As the women responded to what Erin called 'intensive care', she watched the change in them. 'It was like watching plants grow.'

Pizzey's book, *Scream Quietly or the Neighbours Will Hear*, was written to 'give the women voices' about relationship abuse, because she could find no other book that explained the reality of wife-battering. She included many letters she had received from women admitting they were frightened to ask for help, writing in language that was often childlike, as muted as the act itself was violent. 'He gave me a really good hiding,' one woman admitted, 'and that was followed by a right pasting.' One disabled woman telephoned in anonymity to say she had been left alone by her alcoholic, gambling husband for several days, the wheels of her chair padlocked to prevent them or her from moving. Despite her confession, she refused to identify herself. 'Some keep silent out of loyalty and the wish to keep up appearances. They are ashamed.'

Some women who came to the refuge were not only victims of extreme violence from which they needed to escape if they were to survive, but also the perpetrators of violence themselves through learned behaviour. Pizzey had no reservations in calling them out, just as she had the male abusers. But she was risking trouble. Pizzey was amazed that 'nobody seemed to genuinely want to find out why violent people of *both* sexes treat each other the way they do'. Violent women, who were of course victims too, needed 'therapeutic intervention' and time to unlearn the habits they had acquired over a lifetime. 'The thing is that we don't teach awareness, of how we deal with stress, which requires acknowledgement, or articulating where the problem lies,' she said, developing her concept of 'transcending' to convince these women to get well. 'These are your strategies for survival,' she would tell them. 'You can come from the most abject violent background. But if you don't do the work to *transcend* you will repeat the pattern. If you wish to make a choice for a peaceful life then you must change your strategy for survival.'

Convinced that unless the residents learned to interact with men their chances of a confident return to the outside world would be limited, Pizzey welcomed 'good' and 'gentle' men into the house. Film footage on her website 'Honest Ribbon' includes scenes of men singing 'The Wheels on the Bus' with children sitting happily on their laps, the beginning of an understanding that not all men are violent or to be mistrusted. However, about ten years after opening her first refuge Pizzey was cancelled by her own organisation, alienated when she reaffirmed that experience had shown her that women are equally capable of physical violence as men. She challenged the assumption that the weight and bulk of men means their power over a woman's relatively fragile frame is complete. There are other kinds of violence, she argued. A knife does not require much strength to wield and, as one woman told her, 'knives are a great leveller against the greater physical strength of men'. Another dangerous and more covert kind of violence was psychological abuse, 'with which women are so dexterous. Physical wounds can heal. But words are a different matter.'

Despite the feminist outrage at what was perceived as the disloyal targeting of some women, Pizzey's name became inseparable from the idea of providing a safe place for women who would otherwise have continued to suffer in silence. As the refuge attracted national and international publicity, so Pizzey received letters offering solidarity from Denmark, Switzerland, Canada and Germany, as well as every part of the United Kingdom. Within a few years Pizzey's single place of safety had become the blueprint for such sanctuaries all over the country. By 1974 forty refuges had opened to women whose neighbours had ignored their cries and, as Pizzey learned, had traditionally 'turned up the television to drown out the noise of violence next door'. But Pizzey's work was having a domino effect, encompassing a much wider demographic across the city and nationwide.

In 1973 the Brixton Black Women's Group (BBWG) established their own centre. Founded by women members of the Black Panther Group, increasingly discontented with being sidelined in all areas of society, the BBWG welcomed abused women of African and Asian backgrounds and concentrated on many of the same issues of abuse to which Pizzey had drawn attention. The group also made financial concerns a central issue and worked to right the unfair distribution of wealth. Other groups of women started to set up their own safe places as well: refuges for Jewish, Chinese and Middle Eastern women, and for other groups including lesbians and women with disabilities were also opened. In 1974 the National Women's Aid Federation based in Bristol brought all these refuge services under one umbrella organisation. In 1976 the Domestic Violence and Matrimonial Proceedings Act was passed, and women's requests to place a restraining order on their partners were heard and taken seriously. In 1978, in recognition of the way violence affects every member of a family, including the men, the name of Pizzey's organisation was changed from Women's Aid to Family Rescue. In 1979, a year after the 'Milk Snatcher' had been made Britain's first woman prime minister, Pizzey wrote to her from Chiswick in a spirit of hope. She asked the new PM what plans she had for helping victims of domestic violence. 'A minion replied on her behalf,' Pizzey remembers, 'to let me know Mrs Thatcher was "not interested in women's issues".'

One early spring morning in 2024 I walked through a small front garden with a lone bluebell waving in the breeze. I pressed the buzzer. 'Come on up, love,' Pizzey called through the intercom in the voice that had reassured all those women and children who had made their way to her door over the years. 'Oh yes, they still come,' she assured me as she indicated I should sit on the leather sofa beside her with the sun flooding in from the window behind us and gilding the room. 'They know where to find me, if they need me.'

Well over fifty years after she was first given the keys to Belmont Road, Erin Pizzey's passion for change remained undimmed. Living on her own in the bright top-floor flat of an Edwardian villa in London's leafy Richmond, she seemed contented with life. She has easy access to family love. Her twin sister, her daughter, one granddaughter and some of her seven great-grandchildren all live close by, a visit to her son in America was planned for later in the year. She considered her circumstances 'marvellous'. Nothing matters to her more than family and she lamented the breakdown of multi-generational family life. Reminiscing about the family support that existed, especially in cities and towns, up until the Second World War, she believed its decline led in part to the sort of isolation that can exacerbate violence. The self-policing and protection afforded by uncles, aunts, grandparents and cousins all living close by disappeared, particularly with the arrival of high-rise blocks of flats where no one knew each other, or had any chance of getting to know each other, behind those closed doors. An old man who had been rehoused in the 1970s once told her that the loneliness began when 'they put our streets up in the sky'.

As I switched on the recorder on my phone she settled back into her chair, her black-and-white-patterned dress reaching to the floor, her gaze intent. Secrecy riddles Erin's own story. Her childhood was peripatetic. Born in China in 1939, her father, Cyril Carney, had passed the civil service exam with the highest score of his year, an achievement considered remarkable for a grammar school boy at a time when the Foreign Service was almost exclusively run by Oxbridge graduates. With Cyril in the diplomatic corps, the Carney family moved from country to country as he was re-posted every two years. When her father's right-wing sympathies led to his capture in Tientsin in China by the communists, the family was held under house arrest for three years. Young Erin and her twin sister Kate were sent back to England to a boarding school in a big manor house in Devon, where Erin spent the happiest of days in the care of their teacher, the adored six-foot-seven, twenty-five-stone Miss Williams.

The school was a refuge from home life. Pizzey's parents were 'ill-matched'. Her father was the youngest of seventeen children, seven of whom had died young. There had not been much time in that Irish-Catholic family for being listened to. Brought up in Hackney, London, Mr Carney Senior had run several pubs around Hounslow; owned and managed race horses, ridden by his jockey son Jack; drank a quart of whisky a day and could hold five men against a wall with one arm. Erin's Canadian mother Ruth (known as Pat) had sailed from her home to China on a boat with her best friend on a joint mission to find themselves husbands, knowing there was a dearth of single women in Peking. 'My mother had no romantic interest in my father, who dropped his aitches. But she married him because she could see that he was going to do well in the future. My mother was cold-blooded. She was ambitious. And in those days you married or you were a spinster and faded out of sight.'

Her mother, who had 'very thick, auburn hair right down to her bottom, but which she wore rolled up, was covered in vivid freckles. She was very pretty. She had incredible eyes.' But nothing she said was true; she was a fantasist. She told her daughter she had grown up in a huge house in Toronto but after her death photographs emerged of a simple log cabin. 'I remember realising that my mother didn't love me and that I didn't like her. I didn't like the way she smelled. She used Yardley and she smelled cloy-ey. Not anything like I'd like to smell. And she was an exhibitionist too. Like any good narcissist. "Ta-da!" she would go', the mimicking of her mother's theatricality making Pizzey flinch.

Her father was addicted to her mother, 'an addiction as powerful as morphine'. At six foot four tall and 'the same across', Cyril was explosive. He never hit anybody but 'he was a mess of a human being. He would scream and row and have terrible tantrums. And my mother would sob and cry and carry on and we were just torn to shreds between them.' After her mother's death, Pizzey learned to feel 'tremendous pity and compassion' for this woman who had 'sold herself for a mess of pottage'. Pizzey never spoke about the rowing to her sister. 'You didn't in those days. Children didn't question anything.' She believes that is where silence is learned, in those early days of childhood, and it has to be unlearned if the adult is to have any chance of thriving. For Pizzey, the process of unlearning this early distrust of adults, of keeping quiet and of accepting the absence of affection and care, was the silver lining that made the adult woman. This is when she learned to 'stand alone', never compromising her conviction. She acknowledges the ironic gift of her upbringing. 'I bless the parents I had because I couldn't have done the work I did without experiencing the way they treated me.'

I had gone to talk to her about how and why women especially cling to secrecy and how shame wrapped itself around the women she cared for, and she emphasised how long it could take for enough trust to build between her and these lost women before the full truth emerged. The women's experiences retain the power to shock profoundly half a century later. 'Natural orgasm becomes impossible if you have been forced or even trained to orgasm in pain,' Pizzey said. 'Incest was commonplace.' She remembered a male nurse who used slim glass medical pipettes to abuse his own daughter. The description was so horrifying that I found myself physically recoiling on the black sofa. Eventually it was Pizzey who filled the silence, clearly taken aback by the naivety of my reaction.

'Yes. That's what we are talking about. The rest is vanilla. But nobody else talks about this.' Families who arrived from Dublin, where the refuges were too small, brought some of the most harrowing confessions of incest. 'I remember looking at a child of six,' Pizzey told me, 'and she had had more sex than I had. And when you look into those eyes you see where the most damage has been done. Because the innocence has gone, shattered. And where is she going to go from here? Unlike adults, children can only thrive on NOT knowing. Innocence is the saviour of children.'

After her ostracisation from the women's movement because of her controversial views, and her albeit-long-ago clash with Margaret Thatcher, no one was more surprised to learn that Erin Pizzey was to be awarded a CBE in the New Year Honours List of 2024 than Pizzey herself. Perhaps the Queen was behind the decision. In 2016 the then Duchess of Cornwall had met the mother of a woman who had been bludgeoned to death by her husband with fourteen blows of a claw hammer. The story was so horrifying, alongside many others, that the Duchess immediately made domestic abuse her own cause without disguising her awareness that men too could be the target of abuse from women.

In a speech delivered that year at the WOW Festival (Women of the World), the Duchess said that domestic abuse 'is characterised by silence – silence from those that suffer, silence from those around them, and silence from those who perpetrate abuse. This silence is corrosive; it leaves women, children and men carrying the burden of shame.' She promised the mother of the abused girl that she would do everything to unsilence current crisis levels of abuse and make it a cause of national gravity and urgency.

Pizzey has not abandoned her conservative or Conservative values, and remains not only a fan of the monarchy but wholly unapologetic for the Empire, an enduring legacy of her childhood. Her calm doggedness around not adjusting her beliefs to fit changing viewpoints means that she remains an acquired taste for some. The only point of irritation came when she mentioned the house in Chiswick, the building which became the epicentre of safety and recovery for so many thousands.

'Even though everyone has always known its precise location for the reason that it has always needed to be easily and quickly found by those seeking it in the still terror of the night, the address is now "massively secret",' Erin told me. 'The organisers believe men will come and disrupt it. But they never have done.' I googled one of the refuges that specifically looks after African women. The street address given on the website is 'Unnamed Road'.

If she claims to be baffled by the way feminists continue to 'airbrush' her and condemn her empathy for men, victimhood could never be Pizzey's default position. But as we talked long into the afternoon and the strength of the sun in the window became less fierce, I detected a vulnerability in the self-sufficiency and resilience that has sustained her for so long. The roots of her compassion began with the animals that she looked after as a child. In Tehran, on one of her father's diplomatic postings, she was given a small deer with a broken leg which she and her mother bandaged and nursed back to health, and in another posting in Dakar she was given a pet marmoset.

'Apart from my sister, the animals were all I had to love and be loved by. But it was only when I had young children that the reparation began.' Celebrated and awarded for her work for women, her true motivation comes from deep within her own childhood. In emphasising to boys and girls the importance of talking, she hopes to save them from some of the pain that she herself suffered as a child.

As I turned to leave, I thought once again of the number of

anonymous women who have continued to walk up Pizzey's path, press the buzzer and climb the stairs. Sitting on her black sofa, they have told her their secrets and their fears, before being offered the sort of hope that so many before them have sought – an emotional if not a literal refuge. I wondered about her personal safety. People know where she lives. 'You are brave,' I told her. 'Do you feel brave?'

'I have a cross that I clutch,' she said, smiling again, but she was serious. 'It's God's work.' She leaned forward to emphasise her point. 'I think we have to be taught. At various times in my life God has sent me an angel.' The countless women and men who have been the beneficiaries of Pizzey's own teaching might consider that they too have been rescued by some sort of blessed being, albeit in very human form.

CHAPTER 9

Going in the Same Direction

While Erin Pizzey was addressing the abuse hidden behind closed doors by running a bricks-and-mortar community house, another group of women was establishing a supportive sisterhood through the published word.

In December 1971, a year after Bob Hope had wiped the flour from his eyes, Rosie Boycott and Marsha Rowe, working at the underground magazines *Frendz* and *Oz* respectively, were among fifty journalists who had arranged to meet at the Kensington house which the editor of *Oz*, Richard Neville, shared with his girlfriend Louise Ferrier. These like-minded women were no longer prepared to accept the status quo at work, so they met to discuss what was to be done about it. 'I expected to be encouraged to write and to edit,' one of them complained. 'Instead, all I do is type.' Another agreed. 'I do research, some of the background writing, but do I ever get a by-line?' And yet another admitted how she hated being called 'a chick'. 'I've tried to get the word stopped in the paper but I'm laughed at.'

The British feminist Sheila Rowbotham wrote at the time, 'It is only when women start to organise in large numbers that we become a political force, and begin to move towards the possibility of a truly democratic society in which every human being can be brave, responsible, thinking and diligent in the struggle to live at once freely and unselfishly.' At the Kensington meeting, 'no one was ego-tripping or telling anyone to shut up', Rowe remembered. Before long, personal issues began to take over work grievances and the room seemed to 'swirl with emotion so long suppressed'. It became apparent to Rowe that 'so much of our lives had been concealed from each other it was as if we had been strangers'. They began to see that the confidence afforded by solidarity was the first step in finding the courage to speak out. It was a moment of enlightenment: the fear of expressing what felt like the unsayable began to dissipate and find its voice in a collective power. This collision of feeling and action felt electrifying.

Boycott remembers how 'that early period in the 1970s was tremendously unafraid because of the very straightforward conviction that you were right. And that the world was on our side. We were in the right place, the right river, going in the same direction. The sense of community overcame any amount of panic.' By the time of the group's third meeting it was clear there was 'a huge gap between what their lives were about and the cushioned world of the women's weeklies', and Rowe suggested that they start a new magazine. 'The support in the meeting was unanimous', and when Boycott and Rowe were proposed as the most suitable editors, the two women were 'filled with giddy enthusiasm'. In order to get the magazine off the ground they raised funds by inviting all the wealthy movers and shakers of London to parties where guests couldn't leave until they had paid a departure levy of £20. Discussing the name for their new publication over dinner in a Chinese restaurant, Claud Cockburn, the journalist father of Marsha Rowe's boy-friend, 'picked up a spare rib', and the title was right there in Cockburn's hand.

Spare Rib was born with this sense of optimism and good humour. More than half a century later, Boycott, now a cross-bench peer in the House of Lords, reels at the optimism they felt about changing the world, that 'halcyon-brief time of sub-lime freedom, existing without a secret, able to say "these are my ambitions" and "this is who I am"'. Drinking tea from mono-grammed cups in the gilded grandeur of the guests' bar of the House of Lords, a room upholstered by male power and privil-ege, Boycott and I raised our voices to hear one another above the clink of china and the din of men's chatter.

'No man truly thought any of this would make any difference to their lives. Nobody gave a shit,' Boycott said. 'As a result, people indulged us. They were nice to us. Women's magazines wrote about us. Trendy men thought we were fabulous and wanted to take us out.' She added, 'AND we *were* both terrifically good-looking and sexy.' The fun of the venture was undeni-able. 'There was a joyousness about it,' Boycott remembered. 'We were going towards the sunlit uplands and they were jolly sunny. There wasn't a downside to it. Nothing felt complicated.' Even the male satirists approached the venture with patronising good humour. *Private Eye* spoofed the magazine with a cartoon announcing that 'Two Little Girls in Nursery Land start a new version of *Nursery Times*', while referring to Boycott and Rowe as 'Miss Bums and Miss Tits'.

When the first issue of *Spare Rib* appeared in June 1972, the latest issue of *The Lady* magazine, first published in 1885 as 'a journal for gentlewomen' and described by the *Daily Mail* as 'a bastion of good manners and proper behaviour', featured a double-page spread about storage units for sheets and towels. There was also a piece on the royal family's latest ribbon-cutting activities and an article on the flattering appeal of crimplene slacks. Dozens of situations vacant filled *The Lady*'s back pages, confirming one segment of society's need for another to serve them as cooks, nannies, nursery nurses and maids of all work.

Woman and *Woman's Own*, the two leading women's weeklies, sold about six million copies per issue. These magazines failed either to admit or to recognise their endorsement of the male status quo. The pages were packed with romantic stories which, according to Rosie Boycott, 'always ended with a walk to the altar: the lie was massive'. The watertight message was that marriage was written into a woman's life contract, presented through the pages not only as the goal but as the natural course of things. Boycott and Rowe knew that 'for people to start challenging that message of false hope was a very big deal. The corollary was of course that if you didn't reach that altar you had failed.' As Gill Hague, the activist and academic, observed in the 1970s, 'the male-headed nuclear family could be viewed as the heart and bedrock of how personal, family and sexual relations were organised in society'. But the agreement that with marriage women would promise in front of witnesses and under a rule of law, to 'obey' was no longer credible. While *Spare Rib* aimed to reset the agenda, their manifesto also rejected the caricature of feminists as hairy-legged, men-hating bra-burners.

> The concept of Women's Liberation is widely misunderstood, feared and ridiculed. Many women remain isolated and unhappy. We want to publish *Spare Rib* to try to change this. We believe that women's liberation is of vital importance to women now and, intrinsically, to the future of our society. *Spare Rib* will reach out to all women, cutting across material, economic and class barriers, to approach them as individuals in their own right.

With this editorial intention in mind, the magazine combined personal and political issues covering every taboo subject imaginable, including vaginal orgasm, female genital mutilation, anorexia and 'kitchen-sink racism'. When some newsagents refused to stock the magazine, *Spare Rib* set up a 'floating library' exchange system and continued to publish undaunted. One issue covered Erin Pizzey's refuge and domestic abuse, but just as Pizzey had alienated the 'true' feminists so Boycott and Rowe's magazine also caused divisions. Boycott remembers how 'the gay rights people were shouting that we weren't supporting them, the radical feminists were shouting that we weren't radical enough, not feminist enough. You're always going to displease someone.'

Spare Rib had not forgotten how the French existentialist and thinker Simone de Beauvoir in her 1949 book *The Second Sex* had emphasised that women's liberation should also bring lib-eration for men. She argued that the aim was not the removal of men's power but 'destroying that notion of power'. Equality, as embodied by the democratic principle in all things, was the goal. With this principle in mind, at their first editorial meeting Boycott and Rowe had discussed the extreme feminists' white-washing of the notion that men were also caught in a gender trap, stuck in a job from 9 a.m. to 5 p.m., the sole breadwin-ner with two weeks holiday a year. If male voices were ignored there would be consequences. And so, the first issue of *Spare Rib* not only included a feature on romantic novels and a piece by Patricia Hewitt on women's pensions, but also a men's page fea-turing an interview with the footballer George Best, and another by Boycott's boyfriend about writing for a porn magazine.

'We also wrote an editorial saying liberation was as important for men as it was for women,' Boycott remembers. 'We were adamant that feminism was going to be brilliant for both sexes. Inevitably, that fell away. I wish we'd been able to explore it more.'

'Are we more confused now than we were back in the seven-ties?' I asked her.

'Definitely,' Boycott replied. 'If you go back to the late 1960s or early 1970s it seemed so blindingly obvious that all you needed to do was move into the world and the space occupied by men: an incredible level of naivety. The barriers were clear: you thought, we thought, I thought that you could change laws, change society, by manipulating it at a legal and financial level and that women would then somehow float from one place into another. Later the situation got much more muddied. It was evident to me that women had had a shit time for millions of years and that everyone could see that as injustice. But no one thought through the issues of gender ego or balance. Women wanted the good things in men's life and all we were offering them was the nappies. The father who is in the playground is still perceived as something of a loser. The inbuilt error which held back the women's movement as a whole was the failure to redefine masculinity.' From the clubby, red-leather banquettes in the House of Lords bar, Boycott expanded on how that fundamental error settled into the code of feminist behaviour. It was as if the feminists had been holding tight a huge and misjudged secret: that men would be excluded from their game plan.

'When you slipped off to these women's meetings,' she said, 'you didn't tend to tell your husband or your boyfriend where you were going. That was a secret. If we had confided, we would have emasculated them.' Boycott would return home after an exhilarating consensus of minds and spare her partner's ego by lying to him, pretending that she had spent yet another 'lousy' day at the office. Admitting where she had been would have been tantamount to admitting membership of a witches' coven. Hearing all this, I couldn't help but think about the marginalisation of men now, half a century later, and the development of the manosphere, the cyber space that addresses male pain and encourages, even promotes, misogyny and toxic masculinity.

I asked Boycott where her evangelism came from. She looked at me surprised. 'Evangelical?' she repeated. 'I don't know any other way to be.' And yet Boycott's sensitivity made her wary of men's ego-fragility, as well as hesitant to own the freedoms for which she campaigned. Her background had been as convention-observant as mine. 'I came from a world in which you just didn't say things,' she says. 'My mother was very unhappy. She was keeping herself secret. She sat around as a housewife. She was extremely clever, very beautiful and rather vivacious. But she ended up living in the middle of the country, dressed in shabby clothes. She pigeon-holed herself in how she thought she had to be.'

When Sue, a documentary maker with beautiful hands and 'long thick hair twisted into ringlets' appeared in the *Spare Rib* office with a piece about bisexuality, Boycott took her out for a drink to discuss editorial changes. Drinks led to dinner and dinner led to seduction, an experience Boycott found 'friendly rather than passionate', concluding that although she was 'mildly aroused', she was aware that she 'didn't naturally incline that way'. But at the time she kept the encounter to herself even when honesty about everything was the context in which she operated. 'It was a bridge too far.' She feared Marsha's disapproval. 'Marsha was older and more sensible than I was. And Sue was perhaps a bit hippy even for me.' The conventions, the hesitations, the secrets existed then and, as Boycott admits, 'they still do'.

Two years before the first issue of *Spare Rib* appeared, Betty Friedan had mobilised the Women's Strike for Equality march in America. In August 1970, 50,000 women of every age and background linked arms to stride down New York's Fifth Avenue, holding placards saying 'Don't Iron while the Strike is Hot' and 'Don't Cook Dinner – Starve a Rat Today', the disruption timed perfectly to coincide with rush hour. The sight of those who usually cooked and cleaned, unpaid and unseen, but who were now visibly refusing to do so, illustrated 'the problem that has no name', the elusive but chronic sense of dissatisfaction felt by white, middle-class, post-war women that Friedan had identified in 1963 in *The Feminine Mystique*, which had by then sold over three million copies.

However influential she was, Friedan was elitist, failing to acknowledge the specific discrimination experienced by others, including African-American and working-class women. The Black social activist bell hooks wrote of Friedan, 'she did not speak of the needs of women without men, without children, without homes. She ignored the existence of all non-white women and poor white women. She did not tell readers whether it was more fulfilling to be a maid, a babysitter, a factory worker, a clerk, or a sex worker than to be a leisure-class housewife. She assumed her plight and the plight of white women like herself ran parallel with a condition affecting all American women.' bell hooks was especially critical of the failure to recognise the effects of intersectionality on discrimination. In her book *Feminism Is for Everybody*, published in 2000, hooks wrote about the limitations of the early 1970s women's activism, arguing an 'academy' had replaced the informality and inclusiveness of the first, spontaneous women's group meetings.

'Whereas women from various backgrounds, those who worked solely as housewives or in service jobs, and big-time professional women, could be found in diverse consciousness-raising groups, the academy was and remains a site of class privilege. Privileged white middle-class women who were a numeric majority though not necessarily the radical leaders of contemporary feminist movement often gained prominence because they were the group mass media focused on as representatives of the struggle.'

Among the white women who raised their voices the loudest were the Australian writer Germaine Greer, with her book *The Female Eunuch*, and American Kate Millett, with *Sexual Politics*, both books published in 1970. Greer celebrated women's sexuality not as something to be exploited – as it had been for millennia – but as a subversive weapon against the patriarchy, one which she called 'cunt power'. Her vibrancy, exhibitionism and unashamed sexiness were off-putting to some factions of the movement who chose to de-feminise themselves in drab, non-provocative clothing. Kate Millett took a different tack, arguing that male dominance had come about through society's political, cultural and structural myths rather than any physical differences between the sexes. In France, Simone de Beauvoir was campaigning for women to have autonomy over their own bodies. Although the 1967 Abortion Act had brought greater choice to British women, the procedure was only permitted in France under very specific circumstances. In April 1971 de Beauvoir published her Manifesto 343 in the magazine *Nouvel Observateur* in which the exact number of women stated in the title, including writers, actors and thinkers, joined Beauvoir in signing a document stating 'one million women have abortions each year in France. I declare that I am one of them. I declare that I've had an abortion. We demand open access to contraceptives; we demand open abortion.'

Gloria Steinem was already a well-established journalist and feminist, famous – even infamous – for her May 1963 undercover story in *Show* magazine about working as a Playboy Club Bunny. The club remained open despite Steinem's revelations that Black colleagues were known as 'chocolate bunnies' and all Bunnies were required to undergo internal medical examinations before serving drinks. Like Rosie Boycott and Marsha Hunt, Steinem saw American women's magazines as essentially 'catalogues' of advertisements that normalised the 'working at home' message. They gave no space to the reality of women's concerns or the diversity of the population, no voice to the disenfranchised or the dispossessed. But in New York, in the basements of church halls, women like herself were gathering for 'speak-outs' in which they talked about their most hidden experiences, especially those concerning abortion. Steinem questioned openly why these conversations must be held in secret. In an echo of the journalists' meetings in London, these women also came to the conclusion that collective and pooled wisdom could make change happen. A magazine that would embody this consciousness was the next step.

In January 1972, six months before the publication of *Spare Rib*, Gloria Steinem launched *Ms* magazine in the US with an all-women editorial team, including Patricia Carbine, Joanne Edgar, Nina Finkelstein, Mary Peacock, and Letty Cottin Pogrebin.

The cover of the preview issue carried an image of the pregnant Hindu goddess Kali using eight arms to hold a clock, skillet, typewriter, rake, mirror, telephone, steering wheel and an iron. The founders ordered a print run of 300,000 copies, expecting it to last on newsstands for eight weeks, and to largely do well in urban areas or on college campuses. Instead, the magazine sold out all over the US in eight days. Reflecting de Beauvoir's campaign in France, Steinem and her team's first issue included a letter signed by fifty women, including Steinem, the writer Anaïs Nin and the tennis superstar Billie Jean King, declaring they had all had abortions. There was also an article by Steinem on 'Sisterhood' and one by Letty Pogrebin about 'raising kids without sex roles'.

I first heard Pogrebin on a podcast in which she described the Jewish concept of 'shanda'. Pronounced with a long A, the Yiddish word not only means shame but disgrace, scandal and humiliation. Her manner on the recording was so vital, so current, that I got in touch with her. Born to Jewish parents in Queens, New York, three months before the outbreak of war in1939, Letty has always defined herself as a feminist and a Jew – a group that constitutes roughly 0.2% of a 15.7 billion global population. She has often written about how the Jewish people, like all minority groups, struggle to make their voices heard. For Letty Cottin Pogrebin it is as if 'the weight of secrecy seems to permeate our Jewish identity'.

Although the suppression of truths, especially by women in her own family, helped make Letty such a champion of feminism and a stalwart member of the same activist peer group as Steinem, only at the age of eighty-two did she feel able to address publicly the concept of shame which had characterised her upbringing and forced her family secrets to remain hidden. Her story, she says, is about 'three generations of complicated, intense twentieth-century Jews for whom the desire to fit in and the fear of public humiliation either drove their aspirations or crushed their spirit'. Secrecy masked their anxiety about being shown up, of being shamed, or feeling shameful, leaving Letty 'obsessed' with keeping secrets because of the pressure 'to be a credit to one's family, faith and people'. Growing up unaware that her parents, each of them from a family of seven, had both been married before, she had also never been told that each parent had a child with a different partner. The conspiracy to keep Letty from the truth involved the collaboration of all her aunts and uncles, until the facts were blurted out by mistake one day by a cousin when Letty was twelve. 'Once you know your parents are liars,' Letty said, 'you are unmoored.'

In 1958, when Letty was a nineteen-year-old college student, she became pregnant when abortion was illegal in America. Her mother had died three years earlier but Letty summoned the courage to ask her father, 'a proudly pragmatic but emotionally unavailable lawyer', to lend her $300 (about $3,500 in today's money) for an abortion. Without hesitation or recrimination, he arranged the procedure and accompanied Letty to the doctor, bringing her stepmother along in case she needed a woman's presence. Although Letty worked to pay back every cent of her father's loan, the shameful 'episode' was never mentioned again for the remaining twenty-five years of his life.

But that was not the end of the story. Six months after her abortion Letty found herself pregnant once again. Having seriously contemplated suicide either by jumping off a bridge or by throwing herself beneath a subway train, she finally confided in her room-mate who persuaded her to contact an underground abortion referral network and go to a reputable doctor who terminated the pregnancy. But the effect on Letty was life-long. When she finally discovered another secret truth that her sister, mother *and* grandmother (who was born in the 1880s) had all had abortions, the revelation taught her 'that when it comes to abortion (or any issue important to women) shame and secrecy are self-defeating. They silence us, they separate us, they keep us from confiding in one another and becoming allies in the fight for bodily autonomy and reproductive freedom.'

Writing in her memoir about how 'secrets flitter through the chambers of the heart like ghosts who won't give up the haunt', she attributes this eerie tenacity to a lesson learned from the early death of her mother. Shortly after arriving at university, she quickly discovered that displaying grief in words or tears 'was an impediment to friendship. No one had lost a parent so I was very freakish. No one knew what to say to me or they censored what they said about their own mothers for fear of hurting my feelings.' Writing a book about shame 'got the shit out of her wagon' so by the time her adored husband Bert died in 2024 after sixty years together, she was able to grieve for him without inhibition.

Back in London, in 1973 Carmen Callil founded Virago, Britain's first feminist publishing house. Callil, an Australian-Lebanese dynamo, had arrived in Britain in 1960. After working first in mainstream publishing, Callil had joined *Ink*, a weekly newspaper intended to bridge the underground and national press. 'Whatever we women did for *Ink* – and there were many of us – in my memory the lovely men of the left and of hippiedom treated us like fluttering Tinkerbells,' Callil remembered, 'good for making tea and providing sex.' After *Ink* folded Callil became indispensable during the start-up of *Spare Rib* because she understood the crucial role of publicity. Rosie Boycott is in no doubt that *Spare Rib* flourished in large part due to Callil's commercial instincts, her building of contacts with every woman's newspaper and magazine editor in Britain, and her refusal to be deterred by the high-minded, intellectual individuals who regarded money-making as grubby.

Having read deeply and widely all her life, Callil raged against the diminishing visibility of so many women writers. Those out of print included Adrienne Rich, Maya Angelou, Willa Cather and the novelist Elizabeth Taylor. Women were the biggest readers and buyers of books, but literary agents and publishers' editors were mainly men. Callil's new company was to be run by women and the books they published would be for women. 'How often I remember sitting at dinner tables in the 1960s, the men talking to each other about serious matters, the women sitting quietly like decorated lumps of sugar. I remember one such occasion when I raised my fist, banged the table and shouted: "I have views on Bangladesh too!" '

Virago's first office was in 'an apartment filled with exuberant houseplants, three Persian cats and a large red fireplace', above a Chelsea synagogue. Callil remembered how on Saturdays 'the chant from below mixed with the noise of Carly Simon's "You're So Vain" bellowing from the shops in the road, as I strode up and down the street exuding style and commitment: not just to women and what women did, but to everything that might change the world.' With the founding of Virago Modern Classics, Callil wanted 'to bring women's literature to a mass audience' and 'to break a silence, to make women's voices heard, to tell women's stories, my story and theirs'.

Mary Chamberlain, author of *Fenwomen: A Portrait of Women in an English Village*, was Callil's first new writer to be published under the imprint. Women from Chamberlain's village had told her 'they had little confidence in their skill at story-telling' and that 'they had nothing to say. It was their husbands who were the guardians of the stories.' But, encouraged by Chamberlain's eagerness to hear them, these 'ordinary' women began to speak from their kitchens, from gardens, and from the pub about school, work, religion, politics, recreation, marriage, parenthood and old age. Truths tumbled out, accounts that had once been buried as either insignificant or shameful were shared. Confessions included one from a daughter whose father, popular and demonstrative outside the home, never 'let me know he loved and cared for me'.

Mixed in with the nostalgic shimmer of decorating Easter eggs, wearing ribbons in pigtails, skating on the frozen river, skipping and marble-playing was a description from one woman of the cruelty of another village that had treated her as 'a right slut' when she got pregnant out of wedlock. Women disclosed the strain of working all day, sometimes in a local factory, and returning home to serve a husband dinner. They talked to Chamberlain about feeling that outsiders were viewed with 'suspicion and fear'; they admitted the difficulties of saving for a funeral. And there was beauty in these conversations that none of the women had ever expected to have. A district nurse told of her professional composure crumpling on witnessing the arrival of a healthy new baby. 'It's the most wonderful thing, a birth. Wonderful.' Chamberlain's 'cheapest cassette recorder' captured authentic voices which had been 'disenfranchised from the historical record by class'. From the youngest to the oldest, with memories spanning 150 years, an unseen portrait of a rural community emerged into the light. The accounts are timeless, which is why Callil's pride in Virago's first original publication never dimmed. Chamberlain was not alone in believing that 'Virago transformed the landscape for women as they saw themselves reflected in the culture that surrounded them, in its literature and in its history'.

I experienced Callil's formidable creative energy first-hand during the two years she was my boss at Chatto & Windus publishers in the early 1980s, when she was simultaneously managing Virago. I am not sure she ever slept. With an office filled with fresh flowers, sofas instead of the usual functional chairs and a full decanter of whisky sitting ever ready on a table draped with an embroidered cloth from India, she made male employees wilt under her vitality. When I arrived to work for her I was already the mother of a nine-month-old baby and, terrified that the revelation would compromise Callil's respect for me, I kept my daughter Clemmie's existence a secret until one evening I was forced to blurt out that I was late for the babysitter. Callil was so surprised (or was she appalled?) that she upended her tumbler of whisky over me. Years later she protested that the drenching had not come from horror but shocked admiration at my hidden, multi-tasking ability. But it was Carmen's brainchild Virago that benefited from her own multi-tasking, multi-thinking, multi-passionate, multi-creative ability, the publishing company unlike any other, as it moved women's voices further along this arc of recognition and importance. In the words of the writer and Callil's great friend Rachel Cooke, Virago 'changed the way people thought, for ever'.

CHAPTER 10

The Jungle

After the political intensity of the women's movement during the 1970s, the activists of the following decade consolidated the gains already achieved. In America the voices of women from different races and sexual identities took a newly prominent position in the ongoing campaign for equality, among them bell hooks, Audre Lorde, Toni Morrison and Alice Walker. Concerns about sexual harassment were matched by the establishment's failure to recognise the monetary value of women who ran life at home, both concerns becoming pressing issues on the feminist agenda. The decision about whether to work inside or outside the home should carry equal rewards. Having been married in my early twenties in 1977, I too was consolidating my position as the decade turned.

The news delivered in a telephone call by my doctor in early 1981 that I was to have a child became the most perfect secret I had ever kept, shared solely with my husband. For three months we told no one. Despite my wedding band, and the privileged security afforded me by employment and a home of my own, pregnancy also brought a sense of fragility that persuaded me to keep the secret to ourselves for as long as possible. Also, as the daughter of body-shamed, relationship-dysfunctional parents, I was not only self-conscious about my changing shape but also terrified of losing my much-valued publishing job, not quite believing in the enforcement or effectiveness of the Employment Protection Act of 1975 (passed in the same year as the Sex Discrimination Act), which said pregnant women could no longer be fired for their expectant state. No other woman I knew had experience of remaining in an office while pregnant, expecting to return after the birth. I engulfed myself in voluminous baggy coats and bump-distracting smocks, cloaked in disguise, hiding behind my desk as much as possible, the secret exhilaration tempered by my obligation to function without my altered state being detected.

However, at the weekly birth preparation classes there was no room for deception or embarrassment. Betty Parsons was a splendid sixty-year-old guru with an accent more exquisitely pre-war than the Queen's. Born in Rawalpindi (now in Pakistan) in 1915, she not only promoted the presence of future fathers in the delivery room, but also brought a precious spiritual understanding to my life at a time when I – and perhaps all of the 20,000 women she is said to have helped over her long career – needed insight as well as straight talk. Inspired by eastern philosophy after the death of her own baby son, she explained the importance of the three elements of existence: mind, body and emotion. 'I see these like a three-point plug,' she told us. 'If all three are properly aligned, as they are when we relax, then the divine light will come on.' She moved with the grace and theatricality of a dancer. But when she sat on the floor in front of our class of twelve, dressed in a pair of black tights and a T-shirt, opened her legs as wide as they would go and, through her tights, indicated the birth process by *touching* her vagina, a quiet frisson of enlightened admiration ran through the group. Betty's philosophy was not to disguise but to be truthful about what might happen and, in doing so, remove not the pain, but the fear. It was my first lesson of many (to be frequently forgotten in the coming years) that by admitting vulnerability I could gain strength.

At the same time as I was watching Betty Parsons sitting legs akimbo on the floor, my pregnant stomach covered with a free-flowing Laura Ashley frock, Fiona Gem was in Glasgow, also approaching the birth of her first child. She was sixteen. Fiona's parents, Mary and Bob, had followed convention. They married in 1958 and in their wedding photograph, taken on the steps of Glasgow's 1930s Carntyne Church, the couple radiate their love for one another. They had lived a careful life. Bob smoked the occasional Sobranie cigarette and once in a while had a flutter on the horses. Mary had never set foot in a pub in all her born days and, in the expression of the time, was always 'front door ready'. Her life was 'flowers, fags, tea and books', with a particular passion for the novels of Virginia Woolf. Bob worked for the Cleansing Department of the local council, because his ambition to be a world-class footballer had ended after an accident on the pitch which also left him unable to have children. Mary set her heart on spending any spare money that had once been reserved for a baby, on a new car. But Bob had always longed to be a parent and his wish came true in October 1964, when six-day-old Fiona was delivered into their care.

Born in Edinburgh to Helen, who wanted to keep the baby but could not afford to do so, Fiona was adopted by Mary and Bob and came to live in their Glasgow flat on the edge of Castlemilk, one of the largest estates in Europe. Castlemilk covered a vast area comprised of dozens of grey sky-scraping blocks which rose up from an unredeeming landscape, rubbish-strewn with the clutter of broken bottles and life's detritus. With one pub, no sports facilities, no shops or playgrounds or any other community amenities beyond a church at one end and a school at the other, an environment built on distrust, notorious for nurturing danger and despair, it had little to offer to a vital and curious young girl.

At first Fiona 'was wrapped in cotton wool' and blessed with what she now sees was a 'wonderful' life with the 'best' clothes and the 'best' bike and the 'best' holidays. She was brought up as a member of the Church of Scotland but from her bedroom window she would watch girls her age arriving at the Catholic church for their first communion wearing the white frocks that Fiona secretly desired above anything else. When she grew up she wanted to be a hairdresser. But outside the flat life was tough. Fiona's classmates considered her 'posh' and she was treated as an outsider. She was teased. Her bike was kicked about. And at school, in common with others responsible for the mildest of infringements, she was beaten with a black belt split at the end like a whip and stored in a fridge to make the leather less forgiving. Just a street or two away from Fiona's flat, the Arden Craig area on the southernmost edge of Castlemilk, known as the Jungle, was the most notorious and deprived district in Glasgow. Dozens of homes were semi-derelict and many had been torched. Drugs, crime, unemployment and poor health characterised the community. Tricia, a contemporary of Fiona's who grew up in Castlemilk, remembered life there in the late 1970s. 'The landings became dirtier as no one cleaned them, and the isolation peaked as the turnover in renters increased. Lifts were often broken, meaning elderly people couldn't get out, and the flats themselves were not being maintained the same. The "good tenants" were leaving in droves and for my parents, the end came when their house was burglarised. Due to increasing break-ins, my dad had been increasing security on the door and they had three different locks, as well as a sheet of metal on the back of the door, so that like other neighbours, the lock couldn't be sawn out.' No taxi driver would go anywhere near the Jungle. Rival gangs had turned the estate into a war zone. Drugs blunted the pain of extreme destitution and were the currency which bought each gang its position in the hier-archy. Transactions were conducted from ice-cream vans, baskets of household goods providing a flimsy disguise for the lucrative dealings that went on behind the boxes of chocolate flakes and everyday groceries.

Fiona's father Bob, who was responsible for emptying the dust-bins on all the estates, knew what the Jungle was like and warned Fiona to stay away. But the temptations of the unsupervised lifestyle enjoyed by the young occupants of Arden Craig Road beckoned to her. After the comfortable dullness of her own confined environment, and resenting her parents for not providing her with any siblings with whom to have fun, this new world of wine, cigarettes and boys was irresistible. Desperate to fit in, she waited until she was fifteen before making her move, unaware that in emancipating herself from the loving security of her parents' flat, she was relinquishing her freedom.

Whiling away her days in Arden Craig, she caught the attention of Gordon, a local lad, a Patrick Swayze lookalike. Gordon was a wonderful artist but he was a bad boy. He had acquired a criminal record for robbery aged seven and grew up feeling 'crime is all right'. And he refused to take Fiona's no for an answer. After some persuasion, the estate doctor prescribed her the pill, which she hid in her bedroom cupboard, but on returning home one day she found her mother throwing the contraceptives down the rubbish chute in fury. The consequences were inevitable. The spectre of the unmarried mother retained its taboo status, especially for the older generation. When Fiona told her mother about her pregnancy, her mother's reaction was definitive. 'You've made your bed and now you must lie in it.' Fiona was on her own. Soon she was experiencing the poverty and deprivation such as that described in *Shuggie Bain*. In Douglas Stuart's shattering novel published in 2020 but inspired by Glasgow's working-class districts of the 1970s and 1980s, he revealed 'the truth of living under a patriarchy, even when it's bringing the men to their knees financially, is that women and children suffer'. Stuart's mother had abandoned much of her own life including her education and her hobbies and had instead, he told *Discover* magazine in 2022, 'thrown in with a man who turned out to be a villain, and able to have all the mobility that men seem to have – able to abandon wives and children'.

These women could expect little support from the elected authorities. Margaret Thatcher's Conservative government had promoted the idea of the traditional family, in part to deter single mothers from jumping the housing ladder and claiming benefits. As Thatcher's privatisation of public services led to lower pay, longer hours and deteriorating working conditions, particularly for women, the French President Mitterrand described Britain's first woman prime minister as having 'the mouth of Marilyn Monroe but the eyes of Caligula'. She was not the champion women had expected or hoped for. 'The battle for women's rights has largely been won,' Thatcher said. 'The days when they were demanded and discussed in strident tones should be gone for ever.' As Erin Pizzey had discovered several years earlier, Mrs Thatcher seemed to be in favour of a greater silencing of the concerns of her own sex. In the eighties, the lack of connection between a female role model – the 'lionising' of Margaret Thatcher, the aspirational symbol for woman's progress – sat in sharp contrast to the reality of most women's lives, especially those of the working class. 'Because working-class voices are often marginalised and regional stories are often overlooked, I don't think in history we look at those enough,' Stuart feels. 'It's okay to be a decisive, forthright, powerful person, but you have to look at what the consequences of those decisions were, and we never seem to focus on that.' Thatcher's message of power and ambition could not help the women who felt out of sight of the Conservative government, existing in an environment of fear and brutality in the so-called 'sink estates' of Glasgow in the 1970s and '80s. The irony that Britain's first female prime minister was not interested in women was not lost on journalist Beatrix Campbell, who wrote in her 1987 book *The Iron Ladies* that 'femininity is what she wears, masculinity is what she admires', and called her the first woman prime minister who 'offered feminine endorsement to patriarchal power and principles'.

Many hundreds of miles from the Wimbledon hospital where I was waiting for the arrival of my daughter Clemmie in the autumn of 1981, Fiona gave birth to her own daughter. When Crystal was not even six months old, Gordon attacked Fiona with such force that she spent the following nine months in hospital, her skull fractured, her arm and nose broken, her jaw cracked. Her survival was miraculous: Gordon had also attempted to saw off her legs. Crystal had been taken to stay with Gordon's mother and on Fiona's eventual release from hospital she had no option other than to join her baby, as Gordon circled his way through prison's revolving door, unable to stay away from the violence and theft that characterised the only way of life he knew. Overwhelmed by the shame she had brought on her parents Mary and Bob, too proud to ask them for help, Fiona minded only about the wellbeing of Crystal. With no money for a cot, the baby slept in her pram at night and by day Fiona pushed the pram through the long, characterless roads that ran between the flats, sometimes watching the approach of her mother, who, on spotting her daughter, would cross to the other side of the street.

In 1987, unable to defend herself against his sexual persistence, Fiona was raped by Gordon, and she found herself pregnant. This time, for the sake of Crystal and the unborn child, she felt she had no choice but to marry Gordon. Early on the morning of the wedding Gordon, who had been missing all night, appeared at their flat covered in blood. He had been in a fight and Fiona realised from what he said that he had murder on his hands. Grabbing a milk bottle from the doorstep as soon as the police arrived to arrest him, Gordon smashed the glass and held the jagged end to Fiona's head, threatening to slash her throat if the police came anywhere near him. Gordon was given a life sentence for the murder. His second daughter was born a week after the prison gates closed on him for ever.

Despite Gordon's absence, his family had not finished with Fiona. Using the new baby as a bargaining chip and threatening to ban Fiona from seeing her if she did not do as she was told, Gordon's mother went on the attack. She punched her son's girlfriend, ripping out her hair, breaking her nose and on one occasion smashing an ashtray into her face. Fiona had found a job as an office junior in a film company, and would arrive at work swollen from the beatings and covered in bruises. Trying desperately to hold on to her dwindling dignity, she would reject all enquiries from her colleagues, all gestures of compassion, and insist that all was well. The brutality of Fiona's home life and the shame that consumed her at work engulfed her in an insufferable, secret loneliness. The love of her two children was all that sustained her, the abuse as tyrannical, criminal and violent as it had been for the women who eventually found Erin Pizzey's refuges.

In the spirit of Pizzey's initiative, Scottish Women's Aid had been setting up centres across the country since the mid-1970s to help victims of domestic violence. But the centres were scarce. And even if an abused woman had heard of these refuges, the fear of breaking the family code of subjugation often wiped out the courage needed to seek them out. The Domestic Violence and Matrimonial Proceedings Act, passed in 1976, had aimed to dislodge centuries of female persecution. But in 1983, writing in the *Sociological Review*, leading academic in law and social science Susan Maidment concluded that its legal promises 'do not appear to have been fulfilled in practice'. Although the law may have had 'an important symbolic and educative role' in contributing to change, parliamentary legislation could not, Maidment believed, 'change deep-seated public attitudes'. Douglas Stuart recognised the unyielding physical and emotional disintegration of the lives of women like his own mother, like Fiona. 'It was the poor wives and mothers who had to pick everything up and bear the scorn of a community, deal with the poverty and figure out how to make it work.'

Ensnared by Gordon's violent and coercive family, lonely and fearful, Fiona finally went to visit Gordon in prison, taking her second daughter with her. The baby was just one year old and to celebrate the cutting of her first tooth, Fiona had saved enough from her wages to buy the baby a gold chain. When Gordon wrenched the chain from the baby's neck to pay for his prison drug debts, Fiona knew that she could take no more. Buried deep within this wounded woman was an inner, indestructible resourcefulness. She went to see Wilf, a scaffolder on the oil rigs who came from a rival Castlemilk family with a long-term vendetta against the inhabitants of Arden Craig, especially Gordon's family. Wilf had long held a candle for Fiona and agreed at once to protect her from Gordon's lawless relations. He was as good as his word, caring for her and her two daughters, inviting them all into his own home. Grateful for the safety net, but shattered by the years of relentless violence, Fiona tried but failed to reciprocate Wilf's affectionate feelings. She resigned herself to a life without romance, until one day she ran into Jake. A friend from her teenage years, he persuaded Fiona to go south with him. She had only been to London once before and the prospect of moving there was daunting. But she had fallen in love for the first time and she took the risk, taking her daughters with her.

Never in a million years would anyone guess that this vibrant woman with her turquoise eyes, who sat opposite me, had been through such hardship. She is the mother of four daughters now, each one born in successive decades. She is also a grandmother and a great-grandmother, the life and soul of any gathering, still happily married to Jake, a furniture dealer. She lives a long way from Glasgow in a small village in Suffolk. She has never spoken to anyone outside her family about these events before.

'Deep down I didn't want people to know,' she told me. 'I knew I had made a big mistake but did not want to admit it.'

She described how the guilt of letting her adoptive parents down, concealed for so long, continues to reverberate, her affection for them undimmed, especially for her father. Both

Mary and Bob died long ago but recently a cheerful robin has become a friendly companion as Fiona goes out and about her day. She initially thought the robin embodied her mother Mary's spirit. But now she believes it is Bob who returns to her, the parent she truly loved and who loved her in return. I looked into those turquoise eyes that occasionally clouded with tears for what her children went through, but never with the self-pity of a victim. She told me how when she was about four she was taken on a special outing to Edinburgh Castle, wearing a new pair of red Mary Jane shoes with white socks and her best dress. On an impulse she let go of Mary and Bob's guiding hands and skipped all the way up to the entrance of the castle, the freedom and spiritedness of that memory shining in her eyes as she recounted it. In 2013, Fiona started investigating her adoption papers and found out she has a half-sister, Gaye. The pair speak every day on the telephone. They go on holiday together. And once Fiona took Gaye to visit Edinburgh Castle and they skipped hand in hand all the way to the entrance gate.

A year after our meeting, I spoke to Fiona again. I had been worried that our conversation had been more painful than healing. She had been a sleepwalker for many years and she told me about a recurring dream involving running up and down different staircases. As the sound of the breath of her pursuer came ever nearer, ever louder, the still-sleeping Fiona would stand up in her bed in terror and jump. Once on holiday with Jake, she was still asleep when he reached her just in time to stop her tumbling off their bedroom balcony into the sea below. But since revealing her secrets to me, Fiona has never walked in her sleep again, nor has she dreamed her terrifying dream. The uncoiling of memories, of events embedded for so long, had lifted the burden and banished the ghosts, the toxicity released at last. The healing had been in the courage to tell.

CHAPTER 11

Three of Us in this Marriage

A world away from the grim high-rise blocks of Arden Craig, slick skyscrapers soared above London's South Bank, housing the studios where Michael Parkinson's television show was recorded through the 1970s and into the '80s. A very different kind of deception and concealment was operating here. Parkinson's programme provided, or pretended to provide, a platform for the 'stars of stage and screen' to talk to the public with more openness than ever before. As the unmasked luminaries were ushered into the nation's sitting rooms, the viewing public believed they were being let in on the private lives of the famous that previously could only have been guessed at. Persuaded onto the 'box' by the congenial host, 'Parky', A-list celebrities were invited to plug their new movies, plays, songs and books, the promotion wrapped up in witty, carefully curated and occasionally unintentionally revealing conversations. Audiences were unaware that a 'casual' disclosure from a private life was more often a deliberately rehearsed ploy by the powerful public relations teams working for the famous guest. The hope was that a voracious tabloid media and their consumers would be satisfied with the odd 'insightful' snippet, and distracted from investigating more dramatic rumours. In an industry filled with individuals who feared the publication of a red top in which their marital, sexual and criminal backgrounds might be crimsoned across the front page, this forestalling arrangement was regarded as a solution.

On television screens in America, the formidable Barbara Walters was in a class of her own. Since 1979 she had been a co-host on ABC's programme *20/20* and her serious dialogues with senators and prominent movers and shakers could change a politician's future for good or bad. Her show and Parkinson's programme were anchored on the side of respect, tame in comparison with America's new genre of 'confessional' shows. Speaking in front of a live and curious television audience, Phil Donahue had been a pioneer since the late 1960s in his choice of subject matter. Addressing civil rights, women's rights, consumer rights and gay rights, he offered the predominantly female, day-time viewer a chance to live-grill guests on taboo subjects such as abortion, abuse and same-sex love. 'The average housewife is bright and inquisitive,' said Donahue, 'TV had treated her like some mental midget.' Writer and film-maker Nora Ephron thought that 'if Sigmund Freud had watched Phil Donahue, he would never have wondered what women want'. However, these controlled televised conversations would soon stand in sharp contrast to the anarchy unleashed by an even newer genre of chat show.

From the mid-1980s and then through all of the 1990s the two most-watched 'people' programmes in America were hosted first by Oprah Winfrey and later by Jerry Springer. Members of the public came willingly to their TV studios to confide their deepest and most shocking secrets to huge audiences. Tabloid talk shows, otherwise known as 'trash TV', became, as writer and critic Philip Norman told me, 'the gateway drug to the most manipulative and voyeuristic excess of the media world, providing material that reflected the darkest recesses of our culture'. But Sherryl Wilson, senior lecturer in Media and Cultural Studies at the University of the West of England, described how the formula's success depended on the 'resolution of emotional conflict, coinciding with the closure of the show, but with the anticipation that a new trauma, following the same conventions, will be delivered tomorrow or the next week'. Wilson explained how the shows reflected 'the fragmentation and dislocation characteristic of contemporary culture, but which also holds the attractive potential for a positive and meaningful existence'.

At its most popular, Oprah's show drew an estimated fifteen to twenty million viewers a day, was watched by one in ten Americans and syndicated to 120 countries, leading *Vanity Fair* to claim in 1994 that 'Oprah Winfrey arguably has more influence on the culture than any university president, politician, or religious leader, except perhaps the Pope'. Her choices for her televised book club could guarantee instant bestseller status. But it was her campaigning against racial and sexual prejudice that gained her such respect as a social commentator. She stood up for women who had no voice. She understood abuse. She had been a victim herself. By not withholding her vulnerability from viewers, she <u>represented</u> a voice they had never dared use themselves. Bullied and shamed for her gender, race and weight, she spoke on air in 1995 to a group of female addicts, identifying with their drug addiction. 'In my twenties, I have done this drug cocaine. I know exactly what you're talking about. It is my life's great big secret. It is such a secret because I realise that the public person that I have become, if the story were ever revealed, the tabloids would exploit it and what a big issue it would be.' She chose to retain her authority by revealing the facts herself.

Oprah's programmes had been attracting audiences in their millions for eight years by the time Jerry Springer launched his competing format in 1994. Born in London in 1944 to German-Jewish refugees, Springer moved with his family to America when he was five years old. A one-time mayor of Cincinnati, he had failed to land the Democratic nomination as Governor of Ohio in 1982 and decided to put his political career on hold in favour of conquering television. *The Jerry Springer Show* began as a political discussion forum in 1991. But in 1994 a new producer arrived and the tempo changed. While Oprah insisted she was concerned with dignity and restraint, and white middle-aged women made up her core audience, a younger demographic found Springer's extreme content, bleeped-out profanity and carnival atmosphere more appealing. During nearly 4,000 episodes, over a total of twenty-seven years, chaotic scenes would explode on the rickety, village-hall-type stage, where studio guests perched on uncomfortable, officey chairs, prepared to leap into action when called. For all Jerry Springer's claims that his show offered ordinary people a chance to speak for themselves, the power of secrets began to feel devalued within the showbiz nature of a programme where 'over-sharing' was essential for its success. The Jerry Springer shows were predicated on 'promiscuous honesty', a condition described by the psychotherapist Julia Samuel as arising when an 'indiscriminate outpouring is not rewarded with the empathy hoped for and required'. Tenderness or forgiveness rarely softened the proceedings, tears remained unshed, remorse unexpressed as betrayal, anger and revenge characterised most of the episodes. Female 'guests' yanked hair-pieces and even chunks of real hair from rivals' heads, shirts were tugged hard enough for buttons to fly, and as comedian David Sedaris summed it up, 'curse, fight, disentangle' became the rhythm of each programme. A phalanx of muscle-rippling bouncers stood ever ready to be summoned onto the stage to make pretend gestures to break up the regular fist fights and hurling of insults, when actually their role was to ignore or even encourage the mayhem.

Springer, who always insisted he knew nothing in advance of the content of his shows, would position himself among the gladiatorial audience, who screamed abuse or encouragement depending on which side of the spectacle they were on. Standing in the middle of the aisles, Jerry held his cue cards, a look of innocent bafflement on his professorially spectacled face as each new revelation was made. No potential confrontation was off-limits. The Ku Klux Klan appeared in an incendiary segment with the Jewish Defense League. Confessions that seemed preposterous early on in the series became mainstream. A woman who was 'jealous of her mom's weight loss' was revealed to be a member of a sub-culture of women who were all jealous of their mothers' weight loss. The results of a disputed paternity test were announced live on television to a man's fourteen-year-old girlfriend. A segment on 'interspecies relationships' included a man who had married a Shetland pony called Pixel and who kissed his four-legged spouse on air, insisting the relationship was consensual. 'If she didn't like it, she could always leave,' he explained, with what sounded like credible logic.

Each show competed with its predecessor for shockability, yet Springer always ended with the words 'take care of yourself and each other', somehow managing to make the sentiment sound sincere. The programme aired in forty countries and Springer was voted one of the hundred most influential people of the twentieth century by *Time* magazine in 1998, but it was Oprah herself who eventually condemned his show as 'a vulgarity circus'. Speaking to the London *Sunday Times* in 1999, she commented, 'Unless you are going to kill people on the air and not just hit them on the head with chairs, and unless you are going to have sexual intercourse – and not just, as I saw the other day, a guy pulling down his pants and pulling out his penis – then there comes a point when you have over-saturated yourself.' Her note of extreme caution came close to reality in 2000 when one of the Springer participants, a former wife, was murdered by another, a vengeful husband. The judge in the trial rounded on Springer and his producers, holding them responsible for this dreadful outcome, and in a rhetorical challenge, invited them to answer if 'ratings are more important than the dignity of human life'.

In the 1980s and '90s, the use of television as a lens through which matters of private importance could be seen began to cross all boundaries of culture and class. When the British royal family used the airwaves to expose the minutiae of their personal problems, shattering the golden rule that the monarchy's appeal depended on not letting 'daylight in upon the magic', the medium of TV became the ultimate therapy room.

The romance between Prince Charles, the heir to the throne, and Diana Spencer, his beautiful young girlfriend, eighteen years old at the time of their engagement, had enchanted the public. At their wedding in St Paul's Cathedral in 1981, the BBC had attracted a global audience of 750 million in seventy-four countries. The entire world, almost without exaggeration, was then stunned to discover with the publication of a book in 1992, for which Diana herself had been the main source, that the fairy-tale romance was on the rocks. What is more, during the marriage Diana had been bulimic, anorexic and suicidal. The spilling of these secrets would have been sensational enough from any well-known figure, but coming from a family whose private lives were guarded with utmost vigilance, the shock was unprecedented. In June 1994, after Prince Charles admitted to BBC TV's Jonathan Dimbleby the truth of his adultery with Camilla Parker Bowles, he was followed onto the nation's television sets almost eighteen months later by his wife. The 'People's Princess' declared herself to have been silenced by the institution into which she had married, and spoke openly and at length to a BBC television audience of twenty-three million about how there were 'three of us in this marriage', about the truth of her own extra-marital affairs as well as her struggles with eating disorders. A month later plans were announced for the couple to divorce. The rarefied, gilded world of the royal family had shown itself to be as human as our own. And what was more, they had not chosen to reveal their problems through a carefully worded statement, nailed with a golden hammer to the gates of Buckingham Palace, but through books and the screen that occupied most sitting rooms in Britain.

Diana's decision to dismantle the scaffolding of secrecy around her and demonstrate her own independent spirit helped empower her working life after the end of her marriage. Campaigning for the abolition of landmines and continuing to support charities representing leprosy and HIV/Aids, she was gaining a new authority and public respect right up until 1997 when the end came too soon in the darkness of a Parisian tunnel.

One of Diana's final causes was homelessness, raising awareness of the young and lost people living visible but unseen, on the streets, and who have no one to speak up for them, her individual empathy proving to be as powerful as that of an entire group of activists. At the same time, a young British filmmaker called Pamela Gordon was demonstrating how, by the right person directing a very different kind of camera lens onto people's hidden lives, valuable and constructive lessons can be learned not only by the viewer but by the participant. *Forbidden Britain*, Gordon's 1990s series of BBC television documentaries, examined the lives of 2,500 people born between the end of the Victorian age and the 1940s. Members of society 'stigmatised as delinquents, rioters, mistresses, tramps and the long-term unemployed' were filmed speaking direct to camera. The programmes showed how the problems of crime, extra-marital relationships, child abuse, addiction and homelessness were not new. In discussing their experiences of poverty, injustice and victimisation, as well as the patterns of behaviour inherited from examples set down before them, people of all ages warmed to Pamela, confided in her because she listened and often understood where they came from. With what she admits is 'an almost painful ability to empathise', rather than focusing on a specific issue, Gordon always asked questions about the individual.

'One memory can throw light on an entire issue,' she told me, emphasising that the 'beauty in facing the negative, and talking can make sense of the inexplicable. Just as a Samaritan is constructively listening, so I am constructively filming.'

Accustomed as she is to being on the other side of the camera, over a directing career of more than thirty years, and conscious of her own 'sharp eye for injustice', I detected caution in those eyes, accentuated by winged eyeliner and framed by thick eyelashes, as Pamela Gordon acknowledged the discomfort of speaking about her own background. Growing up on the outskirts of Chester, the daughter of a cleaner and a railway worker, she defied her family by going to university when they wanted her to work in a building society. But she had a sense of her own separateness and a desperate need to get far away. She escaped to Goldsmiths College in London, and felt 'physically sick' trying to fit in with her middle-class contemporaries. While they had spent gap years 'in places like Guatemala doing worthy unpaid things in orphanages', Gordon had worked in a local chemist desperately trying to work out how to escape.

Coming from a family who loved but did not understand her, she began to feel the scope of outsiderishness, an empathy for what it is to be isolated. After making the *Forbidden Britain* series her concern for those living on the very edge of the margins did not ebb. Shifting her focus to the generation of the 1990s (the Millennials), she named her new series *Wasted* (Channel 4), implying not just those wasted by drugs but those whose potential is wasted. One of the 'stars' of the series was Stacey, an addict turned prostitute in her early twenties.

'Rescue was not on Stacey's radar,' Pamela told me. 'She was always trying to make sense of how her life had become this.' For a girl who described heroin as feeling like 'hot fudge running through my body', Pamela saw strongly the waste of Stacey's life and potential. It was an obvious tragedy. A complex but special relationship, unprecedented for them both, began to develop that went far beyond the lens of the camera. Stacey had probably never known anyone who wanted to spend time with her, an extended period of time, since she was a child. 'There was an unspoken contract between us,' Pamela said, 'a contract of trust, that she understood I cared about her and I knew she valued me being around. I was looking at life through someone else's eyes and she felt the benefit of that. We had such a great laugh. Whenever she got thrown out of a squat or wherever she was staying she'd stuff all her hundreds of clothes into black bin liners. We would drive up and down the Romford Road in my little blue Clio car packed full of these bin liners looking for someone she knew who might put her up and listening to her favourite tape at the time.'

In the television programme the camera zooms in on in Stacey's ever-changing squats, where postcards are always pasted carefully on disintegrating walls. The postcards made the most desperate of shelters into a home. Pamela and Stacey would sometimes go to York Baths together and have a few almost normal hours. They spent Christmas together in the infamous Tower House squat. And two years after they had met Pamela was there at the very end, when Stacey's varied group of friends from so many parts of her chaotic life came together in a church to mourn her.

We had been speaking for an hour when Gordon placed a Filofax on the kitchen table between us. The notebook was crammed with handwritten cards and letters, decorated all over with hearts, an archive from participants in her programmes who had found in Pamela an unprecedented willingness to hear out their hidden, unheard stories. Many of the letters had been sent from prison, telling her about the smallest detail of their daily lives, asking her questions, sometimes angry at their circumstances, occasionally remorseful, always grateful and trusting of Pamela for simply being that rare person in their lives who was there to listen to them, whether accompanied by a camera or not.

CHAPTER 12

Don't Die of Ignorance

For all the candour *The Oprah Winfrey Show* encouraged during the 1980s, the host herself recognised that progress is not always linear. 'Communication is like a dance. One person takes a step forward, the other takes one back. Even one misstep can land both on the floor in a tangle of confusion.' In the winter of 1984, I had taken a ship across the Atlantic Ocean with my husband and three-year-old daughter to live and work in New York. This new beginning was an especially magical prospect: in a few months I was to become the mother of Flora, my second daughter, who would grow up in this extraordinary city, absorbing a new culture, a new perspective. But as we arrived in a shiny, liberal-minded, all-inclusive, non-judgemental New World, we were grateful that George Orwell's dystopian land-scape set in the same year only existed in the pages of a novel. We were unaware that an optimistically inclusive city was about to take that step back and of the apocalypse that was unfolding in the adjacent gay communities, even as we docked.

In New York in June 1969 a police raid on the Stonewall Inn in Greenwich Village had been met with fierce resistance by the gay men and women inside their favourite bar. Since then tolerance of sexual choice had been growing. The following year the first meeting of the Gay Liberation Front took place in London, extending a hand across the sea not only to gay men and women but to all of those oppressed, whether because of their sexuality, race, religion or gender. While the decriminalisation of homosexuality had only reached New York in 1980, thirteen years after the law had changed in Britain, areas of New York already felt emancipated. In 1976, on my first ever visit to the city, I had seen male couples walk proudly hand in hand, along the sidewalk in Christopher Street in Greenwich Village.

Progress for gay women was much slower. While lesbianism wasn't even acknowledged by law, queer women still felt the power of prejudice, their sexual choice carrying the risk of job losses, punitive treatment from landlords and ostracisation from their families and society at large. The British writer Maureen Duffy remembered that when she first came out in the early 1960s into a 'completely buttoned-up society', the instinct for gay men and women was 'to hide their terrible or humiliating secret which set us apart from normal society'. Her 1966 novel *The Microcosm*, set in the real-life Gateways Club in London's Chelsea, described this rare safe place where queer women had hung out since 1931. Duffy's book was banned by the Vatican, the Irish government and South Africa's apartheid regime. Ironically the censorship drew more attention to the book and

Duffy received sacks full of thank-yous from women relieved to have their experiences acknowledged.

Throughout the 1970s and '80s in New York, lesbians became more confident at openly expressing their sexuality. The new and prominent gay rights group, the Gay Liberation Front (GLF), organised the first annual Gay Pride March in the city in 1970, the year after Stonewall. Women formed as significant a part of the march as men, the 'Dykes on Bikes' revving up their motor-cycles with celebratory gusto. A photograph of a woman at that first march carrying a placard saying 'I am a lesbian and I am beautiful' became the GLF poster image of that year, while in 1971 another sign advised 'You don't have to be out to be a les-bian but it helps'. Lesbian relationships featured in the many underground publications that flourished at that time. Some only lasted for one issue, although *Conditions*, a 1976 feminist magazine exclusively showcasing gay women writers, including Audre Lorde, stayed in print for many years.

But sections of society remained resistant. In 1981 Marilyn Barnett, the former lover of the married tennis player Billie Jean King, revealed their long, secret relationship to the press. In response King called her own press conference to confirm the affair, knocking for six not only the sports world but any woman romantically involved with another woman, or anyone who either openly condoned or condemned lesbian love. All King's professional work and sponsorship deals were cancelled over-night. Younger tennis players were asked by journalists whether they 'feared' lesbians who might be hiding, unsuspected, within their profession. The *New York Post* claimed that parents were worried about their daughters sharing locker rooms with such individuals, while other sections of the media offered rewards to anyone with information about players 'in the closet'. A few months after Billie Jean King's press conference, another player, Martina Navratilova, aged twenty-four, was outed by the *New York Daily News*. Having just been granted American citizenship after escaping communist Czechoslovakia, Navratilova now faced a different kind of witch hunt – the penalties of living as a gay woman instead of those imposed by the political regime governing her country of birth.

However, when we arrived on our ship in 1984 there was a hope that new laws had brought an unprecedented and lasting sense of freedom for gay men and women who lived and worked and loved in the offices, streets, houses and clubs of mid- and downtown Manhattan. The explosion of celebratory exhibitionism and unfettered same-sex desire in the nightclubs of Studio 54 and Xenon made for an environment reminiscent of the nightclubs of Berlin in the 1930s, when life outside the clubs balanced on the edge of a precipice. One night we watched the actor Liza Minnelli as she writhed and jived on the dance floor with uninhibited exuberance. All around us men kissed men, women kissed women, men dressed as women, women as men. In one trans club where the door to the women's loos opened onto a bank of urinals, Vietnam veterans hung out with the beautiful clientele, smoking joints, hugging tumblers of memory-cancelling whiskey and rye and staring a thousand yards into the middle distance. Bath houses throughout Lower Manhattan, with their swimming pools and cafés, provided safe community centres for gay men to socialise as well as offering rent-by-the-hour cubicles where all levels of promiscuity were unofficially licensed. All observation of secrecy went unheeded.

But Manhattan's liberal embrace was about to be handcuffed by an incurable virus. At the same time as an acceptance of same-sex relationships was moving forward, a secret killer was advancing through America, a disease for which there was no cure and which would push these new sexual freedoms back underground. In May 1982, a *New York Times* headline had announced a 'New Homosexual Disorder Worries Health Officials', and included the phrase 'Gay-Related Immune Deficiency', or GRID, con-firming that the highly infectious virus was exclusively affecting gay men. While intravenous drug users, immigrants and racial minorities were also at risk, the implication by omission was that women were immune. However, the *fear* of catching Acquired Immuno-Deficiency Syndrome, or 'AIDS', was itself infectious. Tables in New York's celebrity restaurants where actors, writers, painters, musicians gathered on a nightly basis, were suddenly filled with apprehensive customers talking in hushed voices about the giveaway, accentuated-cheekbone, haunted 'look' of the sufferer.

When Rock Hudson, a pin-up movie star with a largely female fan base, revealed in July 1985 that he was living with HIV/ AIDS, international panic set in. As a result of the false rumour that you could catch the virus simply by sitting down, lavatory seats in fancy restaurants were covered in disposable protectors. Warnings were everywhere you looked. Billboards carried block-lettered posters warning 'Don't Go Without Your Rubbers', 'Don't Die of Embarrassment' and 'If You Think You Can't Get it You're Dead Wrong'. One arresting television advertisement filmed at a crumbling cliff face featured the actor John Hurt's ghostly voice rising above an apocalyptic scene and culminating in the crashing to the ground of a giant tombstone onto which one word, AIDS, was engraved as Hurt spoke his final words of caution: 'Don't die of ignorance.'

In May 1986 I spent a weekend in Las Vegas with my brother. One evening we went to the restaurant belonging to the legendary entertainer and pianist Liberace. In 1959 Liberace had successfully defended himself against the UK's *Daily Mirror*, which had described him as 'a deadly, winking, sniggering, snuggling, chromium-plated, scent-impregnated, luminous, quivering, giggling, fruit-flavoured, mincing, ice-covered heap of mother love'. The inference was clear, especially the reference to fruit, a codename for homosexuality. Liberace was awarded today's equivalent of half a million pounds and would continue to publicly deny his sexuality, stating in a 1973 press conference that he was 'against the practice of homosexuality because it offends convention and society'.

Dining on surf 'n' turf, the lobster and steak competing for space on generous, black-and-white keyboard-patterned plates, Adam and I had just arrived at the pudding course when the owner of the restaurant glittered into the room wearing a tracksuit scattered with silver spangles, his wig at full bouffant. Settling himself at the piano he caught my eye and beckoned me over to share the piano stool as he ran his fingers up and down the ivories and the liquid melodic sound of Gershwin's 'Rhapsody in Blue' washed over every mesmerised diner in the place. Three months later Liberace was told he was HIV positive. Six months after that, in February 1987, he died from the

AIDS virus. He had been preceded by Rock Hudson, who had died of the illness in October 1986, leaving quarter of a million dollars in his will for AIDS research.

Hiding even further out of the public glare was a single statistic: in 1983 the Center for Disease Control (CDC) reported that a woman had been diagnosed with the virus. By the end of the 1980s one in twelve of those living with the illness were women. Black women in New York under the age of forty-five were more likely to die of AIDS than any other illness. By 1991, about 40 per cent of HIV-positive individuals and 12 per cent of AIDS patients were women. Unprotected sex with a man who had already contracted the virus was one source of infection, the other chief hazard was infected blood. Elizabeth Glaser, married to actor Paul Michael Glaser, AKA Starsky in the *Starsky and Hutch* TV detective series, became HIV positive in 1981 through a contaminated blood transfusion given her after the birth of her daughter Ariel. Not until 1986 did Glaser realise that she had passed HIV on to Ariel through her breast milk and then to her son Jake in utero three years later. With no medication available, or even any research for helping children who were HIV positive, Ariel died of AIDS in 1988. Throwing herself into fundraising campaigns which provided millions of dollars for research for children with paediatric HIV, Glaser herself died in 1994 aged forty-seven. But the full extent of the scandal of untested, contaminated blood would remain unadmitted and lethally dangerous for many years.

At my office, the conspiracy of fear and silence was something with which we were all familiar. The publishing industry was being rocked by the AIDS epidemic and speculation about who might be infected was rife. I was also struggling with my own private anxiety about my mother back in England. Reports of her increasing dependence on alcohol were alarming. Soon after the birth of my younger daughter, my mother managed a period of abstinence and visited us in New York. As we toasted the arrival of her new grandchild, marvelled at a second miracle and refilled the orange juice in her glass and in our own, wine was never mentioned. But the absence of the smell of alcohol on meeting her – a smell which would invariably accompany an embrace on greeting, a sweetness however faint and however half-disguised by a generous spritzing of her favourite French scent – was a difficult new state of affairs to trust. Soon after her return to London she began to drink again and was admitted to hospital. When my father visited her there he caught sight of a bottle of vodka stuffed beneath the spare pillow in the cupboard. A few months later, her funeral took place in London the day after her death. Attended by her three children and her ex-husband, most of her friends had not been given any notice of where or when the service was to be held, the speed, insisted on by her second husband, bound up in the shame of the cause of her death.

My stepfather did not make the journey from his house in Mayfair to the North London crematorium. But afterwards he gave a lunch, where we three, our mother's children, sat in near silence, pushing slices of cooling roast chicken (always roast chicken!) around our plates, the sticky bread sauce congealing, hunger the last thing on our minds. Our stepfather's instruction that our mother's name was not to be spoken during this grim gathering resulted in a stifling silence, punctuated occasionally with stilted, inconsequential talk of the weather. His insistence on verbal censorship was a matter of respect, he said. I am not sure why we were so biddable. Why did none of us object to his ruling? We were certainly terrified of him, or at least I was. But even so, we had just watched our mother's coffin slide into the flames. Desperately trying not to mention her, I hid my food under my knife and fork during that gagging lunch and tried not to think of the pink dressing gown which I had spotted hanging unused on a hook before I had closed my mother's hospital door for the final time.

I returned to New York to experience the silencing of censorship in action. At the office, early copies of Bret Easton Ellis's novel *American Psycho* were circulating. Ellis's descriptions of depravity, of the torture, rape, murder and dismemberment of women, children and animals by the yuppie hero Patrick Bateman had caused some early industry readers to recoil.

The book had already been submitted to our company for consideration when Ann Godoff, the no-nonsense, senior editor at Atlantic Monthly Press, came to my office with the manuscript. 'Have you read any of this book?' she asked. I had.

'Three men we work with are advocating that we go ahead with it. I cannot support the publication,' she said. 'I am asking the other women who work here if they will join me in a protest. I will quit if publication goes ahead. Will you join me?'

Godoff was always a persuasive figure, her leadership a source of inspiration to her women colleagues, and our agreement to support her was unanimous. But although our company declined the book, the campaign to ban the book continued elsewhere. When Vintage Books announced their intention to go ahead and publish, Tammy Bruce, president of the Los Angeles branch of the National Organization for Women (NOW), described *American Psycho* as 'a how-to novel on the torture and dismemberment of women', declaring that Ellis was 'a confused, sick young man with a deep hatred of women who will do anything for a fast buck'. Bruce's plan to mobilise all feminist bookshops in a nationwide boycott of *all* books (except for those by feminist authors) published by Vintage and Knopf, its associated imprint, was supported by nine women writers, including Gloria Steinem and Kate Millett who wrote to Vintage to express their outrage. Speaking to the *New York Times*, Bruce said, 'We are not telling Vintage not to publish', but simply asking the shops to exercise their right of free expression by refusing to stock the novel so the publisher 'will learn violence against women in any form is no longer socially acceptable'. When Bruce's office received calls from three members of the Vintage staff 'talking in whispers' about their fear of losing their jobs if they protested against the book's publication, Bruce informed the press.

'There is an unspoken gag order,' she announced to the *New York Times*, but Vintage proceeded undeterred. As the publication date approached, Bret Easton Ellis received thirteen death threats and was asked by Vintage to sign a declaration saying he had read them all so that if he was murdered, his parents couldn't sue Vintage. Ellis survived, *American Psycho* went straight to the top of the bestseller lists, and when the movie adaptation came out in 2000 Bret Easton Ellis told the *New York Times*, 'You do not write a novel for praise, or thinking of your audience. You write for yourself; you work out between you and your pen the things that intrigue you.'

The writer Kathryn Harrison would follow a similar philosophy. But her book was not invented: it was her own life that intrigued her, troubled her, and which had pushed her to a level of secret-keeping with which she was no longer comfortable. It was a life that provided her with the material for one of the decade's most taboo-exploding publications.

CHAPTER 13

A Transforming Sting

By 1991 the soul-bearing, writing-as-therapy that had encouraged Barbara Gordon into print in the 1980s showed no sign of abating. A *Time* magazine feature highlighted a recent spate of books that took the level of confession even higher. Household names who had recently revealed their own experiences included Oprah Winfrey, former Miss America Marilyn Van Derbur and the comedian Roseanne Arnold who had been sexually abused by both parents. 'It's the secret that's been killing me my whole life,' she said. *Time* magazine reported that 'between 200,000 and 360,000 cases of child sexual abuse occur each year in the U.S. Perhaps 80% of these involve incest'. Surveys in California and Massachusetts in the 1980s found that 'as many as one in five girls and one in seven boys under the age of eighteen had been sexually abused by a relative – anyone from a father to a mother or an in-law'. Increasing awareness of the abuse had triggered the research. And recovery depended 'on the act of breaking the silence', said Laura Davis, co-author of *The Courage to Heal*, the 1988 bestseller and an authoritative text recommended to incest survivors. Davis counselled, 'It's very important for the survivor to tell at least one other person . . . they don't have to tell the whole world if they don't want to.' *Time* described how by speaking out even a little, 'survivors hope they can break the cycle of shame and prevent the next generation from suffering'. The research focused on recovery from childhood abuse. Adult consensual sex between two close relations was another matter.

In 1992 Anaïs Nin, the American writer, published *Incest*, an extract from her 1930s diary in which she describes her brief incestuous affair with her father, the pianist Joaquin Nin, while on holiday together during the summer of 1933. The 'affair' happened after she had not seen him for twenty years. And rather than finding the experience traumatic, she had been ambivalent, fluctuating between a 'deeper, inner holding back' and, after he left, of feeling 'ensorcelled' by him and having a 'great craving' for him. In retrospect, she said, 'It was in my flights with my father that I had found joy.' The critical response to the diary was also equivocal. The influential book trade journal *Kirkus* condemned the book's 'boundless narcissism, preciousness, and grandiosity'. The *World Literature Today* journal, in spring 1993, said that '*Incest* is highly recommended as a literary, psychological, and human work', while the *New York Times* headed their review 'The Sins of the Nins'.

By the mid-1990s the telling of deep secrets for financial gain carried with it the risk of being accused of commercialising trauma. In 1996 Kathryn Harrison, a respected literary novelist, decided, but only after much deliberation, to write about the experience that had obsessed her for years. When she was only a few months old her father left her eighteen-year-old mother and crossed the continent to become a priest. Her mother neither wished to be a mother nor was suited to the role, and handed Kathryn's care over to her grandparents. Apart from a couple of brief meetings with him when she was a child, Kathryn did not meet her father again for many years. He had remarried, become the father of three more children, and risen within the Methodist Church to be a respected figure in the religious community. One day in 1981, when Kathryn was a twenty-year-old student, her father, by then aged thirty-eight, paid a visit to his ex-wife. Kathryn came home from college to meet him. Here at last was the distant and enigmatic figure who had long held for Kathryn the mystery and authority of a god-like icon. Handsome, charming and flirtatious he 'surged into her life like a biblical plague'.

At the end of his week-long stay, Kathryn drove him to the airport. He hugged her goodbye in the departure terminal. He promised they would see each other soon. The flight was called. The father moved his daughter's face closer to his own. And then 'he pushes his tongue deep into my mouth' before picking up his bag, smiling and turning to leave for the plane. The kiss had been 'wet, insistent, exploring'. Kathryn knew at once that this urgent intrusion was wrong and that the wrongness 'let me know too that it is a secret'. The secret changed her life.

'In years to come,' she wrote, 'I'll think of the kiss as a kind of transforming sting, like that of a scorpion: a narcotic that spreads from my mouth to my brain', as, in a reversal of the fairy-tale arousing that wakes the Sleeping Beauty, Harrison's father's kiss was 'the point at which I begin, slowly, inexorably, to fall asleep, to surrender volition, to become paralyzed. It's the drug my father administers in order that he might consume me. That I might desire to be consumed.'

Seventeen years later, when she published her account of what led up to that moment in the airport and the four-year consensual affair that followed, the reaction was tumultuous. Not only was incest illegal in the United States in the 1990s, but any discussion of such a relationship was taboo. However liberal society had become since the buttoned-up puritanism of the 1950s, it seems that a secret story involving a daughter and a father was a love story too far.

I wrote to Kathryn Harrison to ask if we could meet. I had found her book courageous, moving, shocking and unfailingly beautifully written. I wanted to talk to her about regret and risk and about forgiveness. I wanted to know how the release of her secret and the public judgement of that revelation had affected her since publication. Yes, she said, she was more than willing to talk.

I had misjudged the heat of the New York weather as I took the Q Train from Manhattan that autumn day, crossing the bridge to Brooklyn, bundled up in black from point of chin to tip of boot. When the tunnel gave way to the open air for half a minute, I glimpsed the outstretched arm of Lady Liberty, a flash of freedom and defiance in a distant silver sea before the darkness of the tunnel took the silhouette from me.

As I waited at the top of the steps leading up to the brick townhouse, I hoped I would not be asking too much of Harrison. In advance of our meeting she had told me that she had broken her leg, shattered it, falling down some steps on a recent holiday on the Hawaiian island of Kauai and, on her return, the New York hospital had persuaded her that it would heal better if it wasn't put in plaster. When the door opened, she was standing there, wearing a red sundress, her tanned arms leaning on crutches, swinging herself and the crutch deftly to one side to let me in, undeniably elegant despite the naked broken leg. I squeezed past her in my unseasonably dark overcoat, feeling bulky and intrusive in this silent dark interior.

'You aren't allergic to cats, are you?' she asked as I spotted a sharp-eyed creature on the staircase.

'Of course not,' I replied, flunking the truth, before learning that this was one of several strays to have been given a home here. With her injured leg stretched out in front of her, a cushioned stool bearing its weight, I sat in a sturdy chair facing her. I was under no illusion who was in charge as she asked if she might speak first and my questions could follow. She explained how her writing career had begun with an autobiographical first novel, followed by another novel, and she had then embarked on writing a third which hadn't been going well. She had used her father as material for each book but he remained disguised within her fiction and that felt dishonest.

'It rankled.' She longed for 'a sort of pie graph which would help me understand what percentage of the mess was mine, my accountability'. An awareness of the cost of keeping a secret was intensifying. The burden was exhausting her. 'I would be at a cocktail party, a writery do, and while I was talking I was thinking, "You have no idea what I am or what I am capable of." It became an interruption in my life. It goaded me. And I didn't like how that felt.'

So while the memoir itself did not happen 'on purpose', she explained that nevertheless she 'had a compulsive need to confess. This is what I am. Constantly seeking expiation, forgiveness. I needed a jury of strangers, in addition to those people who already loved me anyway. I needed to go out there and be naked in this particular way. It wasn't possible just to be secretive around this one thing and cordon it off and shove it aside.'

Shifting her bare leg a little on the cushion, she told me of the circumstances that triggered the final decision to tell. 'One day my six-year-old daughter Sarah said, "I am supposed to interview somebody about a secret they have. How about I interview you?" She asked me in that way that only a six-year-old can – seeing through your soul.'

At a subsequent meeting with her long-term editor at Random House to discuss how to fix the novel Kathryn was working on, the exchange with her daughter was almost certainly in Kathryn's mind, even if subconsciously. But both Kathryn and her editor were equally 'gobsmacked' when Kathryn made the decision that she didn't want to work on the novel. Instead, she wanted to 'throw it away and write a non-fiction account of what happened between me and my father'. She asked that the

THE BOOK OF REVELATIONS

book be kept a secret from everyone else in the publishing company. She remembered thinking, 'I don't know what this book will cost me. I only know the cost of keeping a secret and I am not willing to do that any more. I am done keeping this secret. The secret was mine but it wasn't really mine. The whole thing depended on secrecy from the beginning. The secrecy allowed it. It was a product of secrecy. The way to finally put it to rest was to expose it.'

Later, having confided her intention to write the book to her husband, her shrink and her best friend, she decided to tell the truth about her relationship with her father to the five women she had been closest to in college. 'There I was, one girl drowning in front of the five of them. When they heard the truth of what had happened they sobbed.'

As we sat together in the shadows of the room, watched by the cat on the stairs, we talked about Harrison's mother. 'My relationship with her was tortuous,' Harrison said. 'She always regarded me as the thing that ruined her life, this thing that had happened to her. She could never disguise her feeling that I was an original sin and she never forgave me. And I spent many, many decades working to undo that feeling.' As Kathryn looked away, the steadiness of my gaze perhaps feeling suddenly too probing, she explained how originally she and her mother had 'entered into our shared project in which I would be made over into a ballerina or something. We both wanted to make me into something she could love.'

Turning back to face me, Kathryn continued. 'I used to excuse my mother because of her youth but the pain sharpened with the arrival of my own children. I knew I would step in front of a train for them. When I was a child I thought maybe if I was cut open I would find a black heart which would explain why she couldn't love me. I wasn't afraid of exposing myself that way because I wanted to know the answer. And then along came a father, a parent to love me. When he said, "God gave you to me," that was an incredibly powerfully manipulative statement. I was suddenly the answer and not the problem. Here was someone saying "be mine" and so I said yes, "take me".'

But Kathryn did not believe her father's agenda was simply to 'seduce' his own child. By ensuring his daughter's loyalty through skilful emotional and physical manipulation, he was also fulfilling an act of vindictiveness against his former wife who had never recovered from his abandonment of her all those years ago. By bewitching their daughter and making her his sexual partner, his exclusion of his former wife was complete. Kathryn thinks her mother probably knew what was happening between father and daughter, 'or knew in that awful knowing, unknowing way. That's the sort of effect psychologically that taboo has . . . so that the person who perceives it thinks, "This is going on," and then thinks, "Well it can't be so what's the matter with me for having come to that conclusion?" It's insidious.'

As Harrison sat facing me, her leg outstretched, she appeared on occasion to be lost in thought, oblivious to the complete stranger and the cat who made up her audience of two. We had been talking about what constitutes the essence of charisma when, for the first time, she stumbled. 'You see . . . my husband,' she began.

Immediately she stopped herself. 'I cannot believe I did that. Can you believe I am still doing that?' she asked me. Taken aback by her 'slip-up', she corrected herself at once. 'I meant to say "my father",' she apologised, smiling, as I watched her, listened to her, beautiful in her red dress, the damaged leg resting on the cushion in front of me.

The affair lasted for four years. Father and daughter would meet in motels, travelling all over the country in order not to be caught. 'We meet in cities where we've never been before,' she wrote in the book. 'We meet where no one will recognize us . . . these no-wheres and no-times are the only home we have', the justification for the relationship easy for Harrison to accept because she *wanted* to accept it. Although Harrison was very careful with birth control, I asked her what would have happened if she had become pregnant.

'I don't know what I would have done,' she said, although given her father's lack of concern, pregnancy would, she jokes, have appealed to his narcissism. 'Another baby would have simply meant for him "more of me".' But for four years that risk of conception was ever present, along with the prospect of being caught, especially when they slept together in the home he not only shared with his second wife but also in the place where Kathryn was a hero to her little half-sister. When Harrison eventually ended the affair, her father told her she would never be able to sustain a proper relationship with a man. 'You've made your choice,' he told her. 'You've had sex with me, and no man will ever have you. You won't be able to keep the secret, and you'll always be alone.'

The finished book was accepted by one of America's top literary agents, published in 1997 by one of America's top publishers and boasted a book jacket embellished with laudatory quotes by top writers like Tobias Wolff, who said, 'Only a writer of extra-ordinary gifts could bring so much light to bear on so dark a matter. I will never forget this book.'

The advance press reviews were glowing. *Kirkus* said it was 'a mesmerizing true tale that in this talented novelist's hands takes on the mythic proportions of a Greek tragedy'.

Harrison had also shared the manuscript with her friend Andrea Dworkin, the radical feminist writer and campaigner. In her 1987 book *Intercourse*, Dworkin had written how women have learned to subdue their voices in the company of men who respond with violence. 'We lower our voices. Women whisper. Women apologise. Women shut up. Women trivialise what we know. Women shrink. Women pull back.' Dworkin warned Kathryn to 'prepare to be dragged through the mud'. But Dworkin was underestimating her friend's resolute refusal to edit the story a bit, to pull back. Harrison thought Dworkin was 'just paranoid and negative'.

But as soon as the book was published Kathryn became the 'unavoidable topic'. The reviewers were quick to condemn. The *New York Times* called the memoir 'appalling but beautifully written'. The *New Republic* said that 'just because she wrote it doesn't mean she had to publish it'. The *Wall Street Journal* said she should 'hush up'. She was nominated in *People* magazine's worst book category of 1997. But it was Jonathan Yardley at the *Washington Post* who was the most venomous, writing three separate vicious pieces about *The Kiss*. The book was 'slimy', 'repellent', 'revolting', 'self-serving hogwash' and 'shameful'. The comments that disturbed Harrison most concerned the way she wrote. He assessed the book, written in prose that, despite its sensational material, is never sensationalist, always chosen with particular care, as 'trash from first word to last, self-promotion masquerading as literature . . . chock-a-block with romance-novel clichés'. Harrison told me how much that hurt. 'I was ready to be accused of being a bad person but I was really shocked to be called a bad writer.'

Beyond the literary criticism, her personal crime was perceived as two-fold. Accused by one journalist of 'merchandising pain', by turning this 'appalling' and illegal situation into a 'commercial venture', she was guilty of absolving herself from any wrong-doing by claiming she had been powerless while under her father's spell. She was perceived to be peddling an irresponsible enthusiasm for a relationship that had damaged the lives of others, including her own young half-sister. An academic paper defined the relationship as being spun as 'an incestuous romance'. For victims of incest who told of their abuse unglossed by a thrill of secrecy, or the skill of a professional writer, Harrison had undermined the horror of that unwanted relationship. When she posed with her husband for an illustrated feature in the glossy pages of *Vogue* magazine some felt she had gone too far.

In a television interview on Charlie Rose's show on PBS on 28 April 1997, Harrison had brimmed with articulate confidence. Explaining to Rose her father's premise that 'only a woman he had created was good enough for him', Rose appeared so shocked that he seemed incapable of responding. Before transmission, a postscript was added to the taped programme to say that the *New York Observer* had finally tracked down Harrison's father even though his daughter had done everything she could to disguise his identity and whereabouts. His statement was a masterclass in denial. 'Kathryn's got a good imagination, she's a writer.'

Although Harrison had her supporters among women, women were also among her critics. Just after the book came out, the feminist, novelist and champion of motherhood Anne Roiphe, writing in in the *New York Observer*, asked, 'Why is it we like our secrets better when revealed by men? Why is female anger still not so nice?' Karen Lehrman Bloch, the writer and cultural critic, insisted on boundaries and Harrison had broken them. 'A truly liberated woman knows when to cry foul and when to keep her mouth shut.' After all, as Lehrman Bloch reminded her readers, 'up until the late 1960s good girls kept secrets'. Only with the Second Wave of feminism were women's 'intimate' stories of 'unjust laws, a sexist society, and /or deranged men considered and encouraged as an essential part of the process of levelling up the genders'.

Harrison retreated from the attention. 'People made up their minds about me before interviewing me. Some were aggressive and hostile and I became more careful and never went on tour.'

Twenty years after the affair ended, and ten years after the book came out, Harrison wrote to her father for the first time, hoping he understood what she had been trying to say. He wrote back. 'He said I had ruined his life and had screwed everything up. He said he hoped I was having fun as a writer and "I guess I'll hear from you when you next do a publicity tour".'

She is no longer in contact with him. She also wrote to his second wife to try to make some sort of atonement and received 'floods' of letters from her in return. His wife said of the affair, conducted in part in her own house, that she 'knew but didn't know. She saw it but I didn't believe it!' Only then did Kathryn realise her mother's successor had probably been complicit with her father. Appalled that after the story was in the open this second wife wanted, inexplicably, to have a relationship with the woman who had cuckolded her, Harrison stopped replying to those letters too.

The impact of Harrison's book and the notoriety she attracted remain talking points. Twenty-six years on, people sucked in their breath when I mentioned I was planning to talk to her. In an interview she gave to *Oprah* magazine in November 2014, she described her response to the critical attention she received. 'I don't care what people think about me,' she said. 'I care what people think about my work. As a young woman, I was so eager to please that I served others' happiness and even their values before my own. It didn't earn me love, but it did deliver me to a place where I had to choose between what I thought of myself and what other people did. I chose myself.'

She has no regrets. 'The attention was oppressive but I have never had any regrets that I wrote a book that made people talk and aroused really strong feelings in people, something that landed and touched people in various ways. If people understand one thing from this I hope they understand that telling the truth is good, whatever way you choose to do that . . . the truth you discover about yourself in a room with a therapist and never share with others or the truth you finally speak aloud.'

I emerged blinking into the strong autumn light of the Brooklyn streets, walking to the subway dazed by the honesty shared through the book and in that room and by the risks

Kathryn Harrison had taken, not only with the affair, but with its revelation. I thought about my grandmother Vita and her pencil-written confession in a notebook discovered after her death in 1962, hidden in that padlocked bag, and then published in 1972. My father had always argued that, as a writer, she had intended the story of a same-sex, extra-marital affair in the 1920s to be made public, even though same-sex love between women was not actually illegal. But I am no longer entirely convinced. It was possibly the best thing Vita ever wrote, perhaps because she was less self-conscious than when writing publicly. But she may not have intended to share that level of intimacy with anyone, anticipating the sort of condemnation suffered by Harrison.

CHAPTER 14

A Question of Life and Death

In contrast to the highly personal nature of secret-keeping in most of this book, there are professionals who deal with the practice every day. Alan Moses, one of Britain's most experienced and distinguished former judges, while holding to his own rule of never commenting publicly on any specific witnesses and defendants in cases in which he has been involved, gave me his professional perspective on the 'art' of deceit, truth-telling and secret-keeping.

I asked him whether he can tell whether the accused are lying.

'Not by looking at them,' he replied. 'And, as a general rule, only rarely by the way they speak. In the public place of a court, the rule is that secrets must stop being secrets,' he explained. 'With the oath that you take, you are handing over all secrets.'

However, secrets, lies, betrayal and con artists all play their part in the real-life drama of a courtroom. 'For example,' Moses continued, 'you might not want to tell the truth for a collateral reason: perhaps you have been wandering down the towpath to see a lover. Because you might not wish to admit why you were on the towpath, you might make something up. Even if you had seen someone stabbed to death on the towpath, you cannot admit it without jeopardising your own circumstances,' he said.

Mr Justice Moses was the judge in the double murder of two schoolgirls in Soham in Cambridgeshire in 2002. Before the discovery of the girls' bodies, the school caretaker Ian Huntley and his girlfriend Maxine Carr had been interviewed on television almost every day after the girls went missing, saying how well they knew the girls and insisting how much they loved them. Although it was agreed that both Carr and Huntley had lied with incredible fluency to the cameras, the trial revealed the particular emotionally manipulative skill of Maxine Carr, whose cool-headedness demonstrated an unflappable, calculated capability that outclassed her guilty boyfriend.

However, Carr's involvement in such a dreadful crime had a lasting impact on public opinion. After Moses handed Huntley a prison term of a minimum of forty years, Carr served a short sentence for perverting the course of justice by lying to the police, after which she went out into the world with the rare status of life-long anonymity for her own protection, her precarious existence dependent on secrecy.

With the lives of so many women in this book demonstrating how secrecy has been analogous with mistrust and subordination in a man's world, the experience of two women – one at the end of the twentieth century and another at the beginning of the twenty-first – exemplified the opposite: their skill of with-holding information rather than declaring it. Since 1902, two services stemming from the Secret Service Bureau had coexisted: MI6, the Secret Intelligence Service, and MI5, the Security Service, the United Kingdom's domestic counter-intelligence and security agency. MI5 summarises its responsibility as 'to protect the UK against threats to national security. Threats can range from terrorism to attempts by states to harm people in the UK and undermine our way of life.'

Up until 1992, a sequence of men had held the post of Director General of MI5, their identity never made public. Even within the office, people had once joked that you would know the boss as the man who wore dark glasses inside the building so he would not be recognised. However, women had long occu-pied senior positions within MI5 and MI6. After the end of the Second World War, Daphne Park joined MI6 and spent thirty years working in secret as one of the Service's most important and treasured intelligence officers. In 1953, Milicent Bagot, then aged forty-six, became the first female intelligence officer to become Assistant Secretary, in charge of all the Security Service's efforts against international communism. With women making up 40 per cent of the 2,000 staff at the time of Stella Rimington's appointment as DG in 1992, and several other unidentified women occupying a range of senior positions, the male mon-opoly on the top job was ready to be broken. On Rimington's retirement in 1996, another male incumbent, Stephen Lander, succeeded to the post before the position was given to Eliza Manningham-Buller in 2002.

Eliza Manningham-Buller's appointment to Director General was made as the culmination of her many years working in counter-terrorism and extensively in counter-espionage.

After spending twenty months in Washington, DC as a senior liaison officer to the US intelligence community, she returned to the UK in 1992 to head up the new Irish counter-terrorism unit. Reaching the summit of the organisation in 2002, she took up her position a year after the Twin Towers had fallen in New York, a time when civilisation itself felt under attack.

I spoke to Lady Manningham-Buller in 2024, sixteen years after she left the Security Service in 2008. Professional secret-keeping was in her genes. During the Second World War, residents in the Oxfordshire village where her mother, Lady Mary Manningham-Buller, lived knew their neighbour as a beautiful, eccentric woman who kept carrier pigeons in her loft. They did not know that she had bred and trained the pigeons to take part in top-secret missions or that she had been given a special petrol allocation which enabled her to drive to the south coast to train said pigeons to fly home to her. Dropped by parachute to agents in Germany and resistance members in occupied Europe, the birds would make their home-bound flight back to Lady Mary, carrying messages that had been strapped to their legs by the secret agents. Although Lady Mary spoke French fluently, she regarded all the messages as secret and, choosing not to read them, was unaware of their precise significance. After the war, some were revealed to have had essential strategic importance.

Switching on her mobile telephone, Lady Manningham-Buller showed me an image that her sister had found recently and had sent her the day before. On the screen was a drawing of a pigeon in a sling inside a wicker basket to which a miniature parachute was attached, the charm of the image enchanting both Lady Mary's daughter and me.

Eliza Manningham-Buller had been working as a teacher at a London girls' school in 1973 when she met someone at a drinks party who suggested she go to the Ministry of Defence for an interview. At that first interview she was told it was the role of the women to support the men. So she 'backed out', until reconsidering and joining the Service the following year. In November 1972, a group of women in the Service had taken things into their own hands and created a petition for change. 'The Revolt of the Women' had some effect on the way women were treated. But when Eliza Manningham-Buller joined the Service she knew at once that 'we were definitely a grade down from the men'. Women were not given the same responsibilities, not allowed to deal directly with human sources or to run technical operations.

'It was thought we needed to be protected,' she explained. 'There was a view that women were incapable of doing the same job as the men. They were not considered clever enough or confident enough. Their role in the Service was assumed to be temporary until they became homemakers. Not long before I joined, if you got married you had to resign because otherwise it was assumed you would not be able to resist telling your husband what you did. The culture was extraordinary, but perhaps not much different to the rest of society.'

After the Sex Discrimination Act was passed in 1975, attitudes shifted again but the process of putting a woman into the position of DG was to take a further seventeen years.

Lady Manningham-Buller described the original vetting

process for recruitment to the Service as being 'as painstaking as possible but it could not be infallible. It certainly weeded out the blabbers and the gossips and the scale of the investigation included people's school, teachers, previous employers, friends and family.' She credits two extra qualifications with giving her an early advantage. The acting she had enjoyed at Oxford helped her to maintain her equilibrium when challenged. And at school she had taken speakers classes which gave her the confidence to speak in public with authority.

We discussed the nature of trust in an organisation where lives depended on secrecy. In 1984, Oleg Gordievsky, a KGB colonel who had been working as a double agent for MI6 since 1974 and based at the Soviet Embassy in London since 1982, had seen a letter written in 1983 by an MI5 officer offering their services to Russia. Eliza Manningham-Buller was among a handful of colleagues with whom Gordievsky had shared this information, and this injection of distrust into the securest of environments, raising doubts about colleagues for whom Eliza Manningham-Buller felt such an affinity, was one of the most disturbing times of her career.

'You would get in the lift and look round and wonder.'

Those few privy to Gordievsky's information and who had their suspicions about who the traitor might be were unable to meet to discuss their theories in the office for fear any individual would get wind of the meeting. The flat owned by Eliza Manningham-Buller's mother offered a perfect leak-resistant sanctuary. Eliza Manningham-Buller did not tell her mother the purpose of these regular gatherings but she had no need to explain. Her mother, by now Lady Dilhorne (her husband had become Lord Chancellor in 1962 and had chosen the title Lord Dilhorne), with both her wartime experience and an instinctive understanding of discretion, knew that she should not enquire too deeply. Nonetheless, she offered her own form of complicit support.

'One day my elder sister rang my mother to say she was coming round, and my mother said, "You can't come today. We are having a prayer meeting." My mother was very resourceful. I mean, if she had said she had a friend coming for a cup of tea that wouldn't have worked. But nobody wants to interrupt a prayer meeting! My sister would complain to me about how religious our mother was becoming. "She's having prayer meetings every other week. Isn't it odd?" she would say to me, to which I would reply that it was indeed very odd.'

After Michael Bettaney was found to be the spy within the department, he was tried and found guilty of offences under Section 1 of the Official Secrets Act 1911. He spent the next fourteen years in prison, before his release on parole in 1998. He died of alcohol intoxication in 2018. Lady Manningham-Buller described the lasting impact on her team of having a spy in their midst. 'Being on the alert for someone who might have been a bad egg or had become one is quite hard for people to do. Even though Bettaney had brought attention to himself, joking about working for the Russians, initially people had thought it *was* a joke. People instinctively want to trust their colleagues.'

We explored the nature of trust a little further. She does not feel women are any more or less reliable than men at being trusted and is 'suspicious of gender differentiation'. And she dismissed, for example, the old cliché that excessive blinking betrays a liar. 'The ability to trust is not inbuilt. You don't trust straight off. You must allow it to accumulate.' She paused to consider her remark. 'Or perhaps you do trust straight off,' she continued, 'until your trust is damaged. You have some instincts but whether they are reliable is uncertain. People had most difficulty in believing Kim Philby was a traitor because they had trusted him.' However, in her profession 'you would never look at yourself in the mirror again if you did something that damaged the operational effectiveness of the organisation that I worked for during thirty-three years'.

The signing of the Official Secrets Act is a life-long pledge and, as she explained to the House of Lords in 2010, 'to secure freedom, within a democracy and within the law, some secrets have to remain hidden'.

'Is keeping the secret a question of life and death?' I asked.

'It is,' she confirmed. 'It is not hard to keep secrets when lives are at stake.'

Stella Rimington, Dame Eliza's predecessor but one, worked in the Service for twenty-five years, rising as a dutiful employee through the male hierarchy during the 1970s. Most women were given the minimum of responsibilities including servicing 'a safe house, equipping it with everything an agent might need for breakfast, tidying up, fulfilling the role of an undercover cleaning lady'. And this was considered progressive. Rimington dismissed as 'nonsense' the various assumptions about why women make good intelligence officers. 'Some say it is because they have orderly minds, some say that it is because they are discreet, some say it is because they are psychologically tough and better than men at keeping their own counsel.' Instead Rimington argued that it is the variety of individuals, found in both men and women, that forms the ideal composition of an organisation and that 'it is vital to have balance and common sense and an ability to relate what you are doing to ordinary life'.

Some members of the Service felt that Rimington had compromised her own reputation when, after her retirement, she published a memoir of her days in the Service. When she told the Cabinet Secretary of her plan for the book, she said she was 'bullied, threatened and cajoled in a more-in-sorrow-than-in-anger way' and left 'very shaken'. She felt she had become 'a threat to the established order'. It was made clear that some felt she had let down the establishment she had once led, and in response Rimington felt 'the sense of persecution and fear of the main character in a Kafka novel, in the grip of a bureaucracy whose ways and meaning could not be discerned'. Having gone through the process of asking for clearance for the book, she had confirmed that she would be wholly willing and cooperative about removing or changing anything to which the Security Service objected. In a fiercely argued introduction to her book, she describes how she recognised the need to preserve certain confidential details about the whereabouts and activities of individuals responsible for the protection of our country. She felt that the response to what she had written amounted to a 'wholly disproportionate fuss'. The experience was 'intimidating'. But however much she justified her decision to write the book, some people within the Service remained shocked.

A woman of a younger generation also working at the Security Service at that time eventually found the restrictions of official secrecy to be unsustainable in her private life. The agent (I will call her Chloe) had joined the counter-terrorism unit of MI5 as part of the concentrated recruitment drive after the 9/11 attacks. Having left university to sell financial products through a media agency, Chloe was looking for a more exciting job when she answered a newspaper advertisement. After an extensive vetting process lasting almost a year, Chloe, in her mid-twenties, arrived at Thames House, the MI5 building in Central London, with a strong sense, frequently reinforced by her colleagues, of her luck at being chosen for such a competitive and privileged role. While the area devoted to Russia was then occupied by just a handful of under-employed individuals who felt they had been confined to the backwater, the anti-terrorist desk was the most demanding and, by implication, rewarding department within the Secret Service. Telling her friends and family that she worked as a civil servant in the Work and Pensions office, the dullest of government departments, Chloe managed to maintain a cover story designed to rebuff any questions about what she actually did from 9 a.m. to 5 p.m. In reality, she was in the thick of it.

But Chloe was troubled by the restrictions of the double identity she was required to assume and longing to throw herself into her social life, her weekends were often consumed by her job. She was constantly on alert, feigning ignorance about current affairs that might relate to her clandestine work. Her pay cheque – her livelihood – depended on duplicity. But she often felt she was 'going crazy' and the language in the office used around the commitment she had made 'terrified' her. Her role was referred to as 'a job for life' and comments about how she would be coming to that building on the river 'forever' made her feel trapped. She described to me how eventually she could not live with the emotional see-saw, and how her life had become 'a constant search for the true alignment between who I am and what I do'. She knew that a decision to leave the Service would be riddled with consequences. As a quitter, she would be an anomaly among her peers; there would be unexplainable gaps on her CV; she would remain restricted by a lifetime's allegiance to the Official Secrets Act. But Chloe could no longer live a life of secrecy. After four and a half years she left and the sense of craziness lifted. She discovered that her memory for names and events and data became serendipitously fallible. 'If someone wanted to blackmail me for information,' she told me, with a relieved smile, 'they would get nowhere.' Since she left the Service Chloe has taken up a new career as a portrait painter; looking into the eyes of her sitters, her creative intention to make the images on her canvas reveal the truth of the person who looks back at her. There is no room for dissembling here.

CHAPTER 15

The Courage to Change

My mother was only fifty-eight when she died of liver failure in a London hospital on a damp June day in 1987. Trapped in the prison of a progressively stubborn addiction to alcohol, she had become unreachable, the damage she had done to her body finally incurable. Margaret Thatcher, leader of the Conservative Party, had been re-elected as prime minister a day or two before Philippa slipped into an irreversible coma; on her final day of consciousness she had told the doctor how pleased she was with the political news, a Tory to the very end.

By the mid-1990s I had been living a doubly secret life myself. Within a week of my mother's death, I too chose to start numbing feelings of hopelessness and inadequacy in just the same way that she had done. My sense of failure, both professionally and personally, was overwhelming. And so I too fell for the initially effective repressor of pain: alcohol. The unaffordable therapist who I had been visiting every week for two months in the anonymity of her consulting rooms in Park Avenue seemed uninterested in stories that I had hoped would entertain and distract her from the truth. As the feelings and the full extent of the facts remained unadmitted and therefore unanalysed, I would try to think of anecdotes to amuse the therapist, while excluding any mention of drink except where it might illustrate the craziness of my late mother. If I made the therapist gasp or laugh I would consider the session a success. I would navigate my way through the hour without consciously betraying any hint of how alcohol lubricated the chaos of my days. Pleased with the performance of deception, I would go home and reward myself with a stiff one. Only now do I think that she, like almost everyone else I saw on any kind of regular basis at that time, had guessed what I mistakenly thought was my own best-kept secret.

As I sank more deeply under the power of alcoholism, so my marriage frayed beyond repair. At least once a week I would wake up desperately dehydrated and mentally scrabbling for the detail of the events of the night before, attempting to decipher the notes I had scribbled for myself as an aide-memoire in anticipation of blacking out yet again. The convenient moment to quit drinking never arrived. There was always a reason to delay the decision. Christmas was coming. A visitor was arriving from England. A child's birthday party was in the calendar. A new haircut, a missed bus, toothache: each one required alcohol to enhance the pleasure or shrink the pain. In the far distance hung the certainty that I would be unable to weather the death of my father, when surely no one would begrudge me the helping hand of alcohol to get me through otherwise unbearable grief.

Sometimes the early-morning panic was followed by the blush of shame as I half-remembered where I had been and who I had been with the night before. Often I would consider whether I could experiment with just a single day of sobriety. I would manage to hold the thought intact through dressing, breakfasting and going to work. But as the effects of the night before were relieved with the hydrating help of an ice-cold can of Coca-Cola or the headache-numbing effect of frozen yogurt, a little bargaining voice would niggle its way into my thoughts. Perhaps I could just reward myself with one. Only one. I would stop at only one. But 'only one' invariably leads to the place where no number is ever enough. All the while a little beeping alert saying 'don't be caught, don't be caught' pinged at me as my consumption became increasingly furtive. Hot-water bottles were filled with vodka, window-cleaning containers were emptied out and the detergent replaced by vodka. Wellington boots with their bottle-length legs were excellent hiding places for vodka. The bookcase with the paperbacks that had already been read and need never be opened again provided the perfect concealment for a bottle of vodka. I withdrew into an existence fenced around with denial as my marriage ended and my alcoholism worked its poisonous spell. An amnesia has enveloped some of these events in an impenetrable darkness. But revelations are still being made to me today about the terrible things I said, did, did not do.

The shame around alcoholism and women contrasted vividly with the bravado around men's capacity for drink. 'The hand that rocks the cradle cannot rock the gin bottle,' an AA friend observed. 'A drunk man can be awe-inspiring; his willingness to lose control daunting and impressive to someone who runs tight circles round their lives. A drunk woman has no such charms, she's pathetic, scary because people don't know how to deal with her, the object of pity mixed with scorn and loathing.' The deception was beginning to preoccupy me, although I couldn't work out the best way to deal with it. The prospect of asking for help was always interrupted by the fear of judgement. I was a long way from the paradox that members of Alcoholics Anonymous recognise as 'the gift of desperation'.

In her Substack column *The Therapy Works*, psychotherapist Julia Samuel sums up the conclusion to this kind of deluded maze of mental negotiation. 'What if the pain of staying the same becomes more unbearable than the fear of change itself?' She encourages the addict to identify the specific fear associated with change. 'By understanding these emotions and their origins, we can gain valuable insights into our decision-making process.' For me, at the heart of it, was a fear of admitting to another person my overwhelming sense of failure, and disappointment in myself. But within the denial-stoked heat of the addictive furnace, I also began to worry that the smart, bored, Park Avenue therapist had sussed my deceit and would put an end to the sessions. I thought I would give Alcoholics Anonymous a go to prove, if only to myself, that I was ineligible for membership.

The church hall was one of those places that are hidden in plain sight all over Manhattan: tucked down the red-brick side streets of Greenwich Village, crammed between skyscrapers in Midtown, bookending the boundaries of the city and the river, teetering on the edge of the thunderous FDR Drive. Before I had even crossed the threshold I was greeted with a warmth that is rare in a busy city. 'Would you like a cup of tea?' 'Let me get you a cookie.' We might as well have been in an English vicarage. No one took off their coats in the icy room, the metal stacking chairs clanking together as I took up my place at the back, gingerly lowering myself onto the worn canvas seat. There must have been a hundred people in the room but the atmosphere felt intimate. Everyone seemed to know one another. There was a lot of laughter and hugging. No one looked remotely drunk. Just before the meeting began, someone in charge mounted the small dais and announced the members who would be celebrating their birthdays and I wondered at the coincidence of so many people being born on the same day. As each name was called, I soon realised that a sobriety rather than a natal anniversary was being marked. Two particularly exuberant, identical young women with bouncy, blonde curls and sparkling eyes approached the dais together to be given a blueberry muffin with a small lit candle sticking out of the top. The floor of the hall reverberated with the drumming of feet as the pair accepted the applause with Farrah Fawcett smiles. Still in my coat, I crept out. The waiter in the wine bar opposite asked no questions when, pulling up my hood, I ordered a double vodka and downed it in one. Slipping next door to the off-licence, I bought a very expensive bottle of wine as a sort of decoy, and then, as a pretend and unconvincing afterthought, asked the indifferent salesman to add a bottle of vodka to the bag. Making my way home, the superior but less powerful Chardonnay securely tucked into one pocket of my duffel, the knock-out vodka nestled in the other, I vowed that AA was not for me. Never again would I allow myself to experience such a display of nauseating self-congratulation. Never would I return to such a gathering of smug individuals.

In the arrogant and isolating smog of my addiction, I had failed to recognise the AA fundamental tenet that it was 'the similarities and not the differences' found in fellow human beings that would connect me to such a gathering and lead me to recovery. That simple phrase offered a wisdom that, once I'd fully understood and accepted it, would become invaluable. The shared trust, fear, shame, guilt, truth and love in those meeting rooms united us, regardless of background or circumstances. And it is this wisdom that has hummed throughout my sober life and which has helped to inform and underline this book.

In 1994 I left my husband, saddened and shaken that our marriage had not lasted, and aware that my drinking had, at least in part, been both a response to and an accelerator of its slow and sad collapse. Back in London I was now a single parent, responsible for the welfare of our two young daughters. I knew with increasing certainty that I must do something about my compulsion to drink. But I felt incapable of arresting this interminable circle of broken pledges to stop. I watched daytime television programmes accompanied by a glass of vodka, disguised by a couple of spoonfuls of orange juice so that even when drinking on my own, I reassured myself that I was not drinking neat alcohol. Something deep within me envied Oprah and her guests their courage to talk on the screen about their secrets, the programmes directed largely towards women viewers. Even though I convinced myself I was not in as hopeless a state as those in the programme, I also knew that watching their despair for entertainment was miserably, voyeuristically wrong, as well as frighteningly familiar.

I was approaching the millennium year, a time which had assumed a significance that I could not ignore. How would I celebrate that milestone without a drink? After a particularly chaotic Christmas during which I did and said things the memory of which still leave me cold with humiliation, my family intervened for the final time. After years of trying to persuade me to stop drinking, a line had been crossed. They no longer wished to discuss my behaviour. I was on my own. I knew much later that this withdrawal of support, the acting out of 'tough love', had caused my brother Adam to wonder if such a risk would be worthwhile. I owe him and my sister-in-law Sarah my eternal gratitude (and those two words are chosen with great care) for the invaluable trigger to my recovery, to my sobriety. All they asked of me was to go and get help. In a moment of acute terror, a glimpse of a future devoid of meaning, I faced the possibility that I might lose what mattered to me most. In the realisation that my children could be taken from me, I surrendered.

And yet. In January 1998, after my first day in the treatment centre, and having admitted my addiction to the group, I declared that I had no more bad secrets to tell. Just as the author Kathryn Harrison expected 'the ceiling to crack open' and a lightning bolt to destroy her when she finally told someone about her relationship with her father, the night before detonating the news of my secret drinking was one of the most fear-filled of my life. At the end of that first day I returned home, mindful that we had all been encouraged to make a list of things for which we were grateful. I had planned that beneath the 'Gratitude' heading, 'being sober' would be my first entry. But it wasn't. Because I wasn't. The power that addiction held over me was not released with ease. For the following three weeks I continued to drink. Deception still came, but not so easily. At the end of the day, I would take the tube in the opposite direction from home to seek out-of-the-way off-licences and supermarkets, paranoid that the shops near where I lived were keeping a note of my purchases and would forward a list to the treatment centre. I walked the streets feeling that at any moment I would be ambushed and revealed as a liar. Each morning I would arrive at the treatment centre with hangovers worse than I had ever experienced, terrified that my go-to cures of fizzy drinks and vodka-mopping Bath buns would give the game away.

One day in the treatment centre Terry, one of my co-patients, backed me up against the wall in the little kitchen. His breath on my face smelled of peppermint. Mine, Terry informed me, uninvited, smelled of vodka. If I continued to deceive the centre by drinking when I went home, he would report me, he said. And I would not be allowed back. And my daughters would be taken into care, he said. I might even be imprisoned for behaving irresponsibly, drunk in charge of minors. It was up to me, he said, as he left the kitchen.

I went home and finished a remaining inch of vodka. I drank the bottle of vintage champagne I had somehow managed to save for a special occasion, followed by a desperate tumbler full of cold and cough mixture with a satisfyingly heavy ethanol content. The only bottled liquid left in the house was an ancient flagon of home-made blackcurrant cordial, the sort I had not touched since I was a child. I half wondered if the contents might have fermented enough to give a little kick but the greenish mould floating on the surface was just enough to deter even me. The following morning Terry was waiting for me in the kitchen. 'Well?' was the question on his face. 'Yes' was my silent answering nod of the head. Later that day I found myself back in the kitchen with him. 'I promise you will never regret today's decision,' he told me. I tried to believe him. I wanted to believe him.

For three months I took the short tube journey to join a dozen recovering addicts for group sessions held throughout the day. The sessions were brutal, both in the honesty with which we were encouraged to share and in the manner we were licensed to challenge those reluctant to do so. I made one special friend. Aly was a single mother of two girls just like me. And she was an addict just like me. We became and have remained soulmates. Along with the alcoholics were the drug addicts, the gamblers, the sex addicts, those who struggled with anorexia, bulimia and over-eating. There were the over-spenders, including the woman whose compulsive habit of acquiring black ankle boots and hiding dozens of near-identical pairs from her husband all over her house had led to the breakdown of their marriage. There was glamour among us, too, including an actress who had become a household name in the 1980s and had been very publicly outed for her crazy, drunken behaviour and had not worked for several years.

During those weeks in treatment, I was given guidelines about how to handle a sober life. It was suggested I imagine the word 'poison' on the label of every bottle of alcohol. It was suggested I stay away from dangerous places like pubs and dangerous people who drank like me. It was suggested that on being tempted to reach for a drink I should freeze-frame myself. Just as the producer on a live radio programme operates with a ten-second delay button with which to delete profanities, I could practise giving myself time to ask if I would regret my next action. Willpower is never enough. One needs the chance to reflect on consequences. Those few seconds can keep a sober person sober.

Sometimes the head of the centre would conduct a 'psychodrama' in which we role-played a powerful influencer on our lives. I was asked to have a conversation with myself as if I was my mother. In order to do so I found myself exaggerating her 1930s plummy accent that my brother and I had mocked behind her back. But there was no laughter this time as I psyched myself up to re-enact and vocalise the disappointment she felt about the daughter who was never quite pretty enough, funny enough, feminine enough, good enough. I had carried this stuff around for years, using drink to smother the spectre of disappointing those I most wanted to impress. The psychodrama, although it made me feel deeply self-conscious, allowed me to articulate what was once taboo. For the first time I understood how behaviour, thought patterns and decisions that I had perceived to be my own had been inherited subconsciously from a mother who had never been encouraged to voice her own sense of inadequacy, never been listened to.

In 1998, three years after my return from America, Aly and I walked into another church hall, this one in London, and in speaking aloud the sentence I had feared saying for as much as two decades, I joined an extraordinary community, a fellowship that did not judge a woman who declared, 'My name is Juliet and I am an alcoholic.' In these church halls race, gender, age, politics, everything was irrelevant in the fight against addiction. The process of shared confession, recognition, revelation, amend-making, trust-restoring and creativity was transformative. If I was to meet Terry again I would tell him that his promise came true. He had given me back my life. Just for today.

One further secret troubled me: for all my passion about liberating the silenced voice, I knew that silence could at times be the wiser course, at times the empowering option. The pause button gives time to think. In the twelve-step programme, the guidelines for making amends are laid out in the ninth step, in which a sincere apology to those who have been hurt or wronged by the addict's actions is part of the route to full sobriety. But there is a caveat. The advice is to hold back 'when to do so would injure or harm others', recognising the potential risk of damage to both the harmer and the harmed. Each decision must be taken case by case. And above all I did not wish any harm to come to my children, even in the spirit of the revelation of corrosive secrets. So I hesitated about revealing to anyone that alcohol had not been the only part of my life to come to an end in the 1990s. When I left New York I finished another long association that was both illicit and harmful. I did not realise then that the affair was a corollary to the alcohol with which I dosed myself to blunt the unhappiness of a disintegrating marriage. The blurring combination of sex and drink felt far more comforting than the raw clarity of truth.

When I arrived home after the long flight to England, back from America for good, my father had left a yellow Jiffy bag beside my bed. Inside the Jiffy bag was a pre-publication proof of a novel, with the name of the man I'd just finished with in big letters on the cover. One flick through the pages left me breathless. A closer reading revealed the intimate details about our affair. The full extent of the relationship, but only from his perspective, my own truth stolen, was in danger of being revealed, albeit under the guise of fiction, not only to the reading public but to my own children and indeed to his. At the end of the book, the character based on me is killed off. Reading those pages felt like being forced to swallow swamp water, semi-recognisable but contaminated. I burned the proof and tried to put the whole betrayal out of my mind. Checking only recently what sort of attention the book received, I have found a handful of respectful reviews, but otherwise it seems to have vanished with little impact.

Years later, out of the blue, one of the man's children, Zoe, now an adult with children of her own, wrote to me. She was in the process of reaching out to many people to try to understand and clarify a whole range of events in her own past and as part of that process had wondered if I would be prepared to talk to her about my involvement with her father.

Zoe made clear that nothing I could say would be hurtful to her, that I need not feel that I must protect her and that she did not blame me for the affair. She hoped, in talking to me, to get a better handle on what was true and also a better understanding of patterns of behaviour that members of her family wouldn't discuss. Zoe was no longer talking to her parents because their level of secret-keeping had gone far beyond my relationship with her father. Initially I had written back to her saying that I did not want to rake up the past, but when I too began a therapeutic process into the puzzles of my own childhood, I understood what she was asking of me. I wrote to Zoe again to say that I was coming to America on business and if she still wanted to speak to me I would be happy to do so, hoping that our sharing of information would bring about healing.

I was sitting at a table a block away from the Rockefeller Center in Midtown Manhattan. I had been lucky to get a seat because the streets were jam-packed with tourists, office workers, shopkeepers on late lunch breaks, all glancing longingly at the little outside café area, hoping that someone would move and give up their chair. Sirens screamed, horns yelled and, from across the opposite side of the avenue, bells rang as the faintly threatening ecclesiastical shadow of St Patrick's Cathedral laid its jagged-shaped shadow across the pavement in front of me. Thirty years earlier I had sat nervously in cafés identical to this one, perhaps in this very one, waiting for a different date to appear. Then, in those long-ago days, the two of us who should have known better, committed as we were through marriage to others, had embarked on a seven-year-long affair. There is rarely any lasting fun in a secret affair. We kept the relationship going with snatched assignations at outside tables, on street corners, in trains, in hotel rooms. Using work commitments as an excuse for our absences from home, we would meet in unfamiliar parts of the city and even on trips abroad. We were harming no one if no one knew about it, we justified. And yet the harm we were doing to ourselves and risking to others could not be denied. I had seen the effect of this sort of deception on other relationships. I once knew a brother and sister, Tom and Jane. Tom was married to Jane's best friend Isobel. Jane was married to Harry, Tom's best friend. As Jane bent down to retrieve her napkin which had fallen on the floor, beneath the tablecloth she saw that the legs of her best friend Isobel and her husband Harry were entwined. Returning to her upright position she announced without a pause, 'This marriage and this friendship is over.' And they were.

I found the complexity of living a lie, trying not to stumble over the unevenness of my falsehoods, grew ever trickier to control, the deceit requiring constant vigilance, a coiled tripwire. The possibility of a spouse finding out, of being caught, removes all the thrill and replaces it with fear and guilt. These were years accompanied by blushes, hesitations, uncomfortable silences. My track-covering preparations were skimpy, my lie-concealing research inadequate. My invented excuses proved to be shams, revealing that I had no clue of the plot of a film, the decor of a restaurant, the height of a building in a city, that a train line had ceased to exist ten years earlier. During fictitious appointments, the hairdresser had clearly failed to cut my hair, the dentist to heal my toothache. And yet while I supressed the guilt, the gnawing condemnation of my own behaviour, I convinced myself that nevertheless I could keep the whole thing under wraps. Perhaps if this had all taken place a few years later, perhaps if I had given the therapy a chance, I would have had the courage to confide in someone, to ask for advice from a friend, a colleague, a professional. But I did not understand then that secrecy is like an acid, rotting and destroying judgement. But people knew. Spouses knew. And, worst of all, our children knew.

Zoe lived with her husband and children several hours from New York but she had travelled to the city to meet me at the little folding table in the shadow of St Patrick's Cathedral. Delicate silver ear-rings were just visible beneath the swing of her hair.

At first Zoe asked me for precise dates of the affair. She wanted to connect her own childhood memories and perspectives to the events of the adult world. She told me what she knew. And she and her sister had known quite a lot. They had listened in to telephone calls during which the evidence had been enough. When, in adulthood, she had asked her parents about the affair, at first they had questioned the veracity of her account. Finally admitting that something had happened between us, they minimised the truth, suggesting Zoe's suspicions were largely unfounded. All these years later she was looking for further confirmation and I was happy to give it to her.

I told her how I had been unaware that detailed notes were being taken which would then emerge in the advance copy of a thinly disguised novel waiting in its yellow Jiffy bag in my room at home. We discussed the nature of duplicity, of subterfuge, of risk, of telling lies and of 'doubleness', a frame of mind in which self-deception becomes an instinctive code of behaviour, the practice of denial when one knows in one's heart it is all so dishonest. Slowly we uncovered parallel accounts of threatening taxi rides, of manipulative behaviour, broken promises, dire consequences warned if secrets were exposed. I watched Zoe's ear-rings glinting in the sunshine on that warm October day as we slowly unearthed our mirrored experiences. Some of the details were hard to give and hard to receive. But as confidences were exchanged over the next few hours, a growing sense of relief settled between us. Sharing the truth had felt like poison being siphoned out of me. Memories were contextualised and hesitancy dissolved. We parted with an embrace before walking in separate directions, absorbed into the anonymity of the crowded streets.

Later I reflected on the risks women take in confiding in one another. I remembered how my mother had once mistakenly involved me in the practicalities of her own extra-marital affair. She too had used sex before she discovered alcohol as a way of coping with an unhappy marriage. When I was barely a teen-ager she had asked me to lie to my father about the person she had been with on a trip to London. I had been on that trip too. We had been to the cinema. We had stayed the night in her lover's house. I lied for her. I saw my father look at me, his awareness that I had conspired against him obvious in his eyes. I ran to the bathroom and threw up. And then I hated her. I had met her lover once before: he had been to our house when my father was abroad. We were still children then and he came in a car with windows that slid open and shut with the press of a button. At first raising the windows up and down had felt like fun. He told us to be careful in case we caught our fingers. And suddenly I couldn't bear him being there while my father was away. I wanted him to catch his own fingers in the moving glass. I wanted him to be punished for taking our mother away. And years later I had been inflicting the same pain, the pernicious deceit, on my children. Only with the intervening years and with the clarity of a sober mind have I understood the patterns I was repeating. An affair was as much of an escape, a mood modifier, as a glass of wine. I had entered into an addictive relationship with a man that ran in tandem with my addictive relationship with alcohol. I wonder now if the act of secrecy itself, painful and precarious as it was to maintain, was in itself an addiction. And yet despite these attempts at an explanation, I do not excuse or forgive myself. I always knew what I was doing was wrong. I wish I could go back and live those years all over again, but this time, free of deceitful behaviour.

By the end of the century, I hoped I had exhausted these addictive patterns. I hoped I had learned something about the harm that betrayal can bring, radiating beyond myself to those who do not deserve to be affected by my mistakes. But I was learning that regret of an unchangeable past is a pointless exercise. After several years spent as a single woman, a new relationship, devoid of secrets, would confirm for me how trust rather than secrecy is the element that changes everything.

PART III

My Daughters' Generation

2000–2025

CHAPTER 16

Where Are *YOU* from?

The intention to identify and challenge the status quo had felt so clear and uncomplicated for women like Rosie Boycott starting out in their adult life in the 1970s. Activism about a cause that united women arose from the growing opportunities for freedom of speech, which they used to their advantage. But at the start of the new millennium, while shared convictions of all kinds could be spread across the world with the click of a mouse or the whoosh of an email, caution was in the air. The forensic inquisition of a twenty-four-hour news cycle, an infinite number of media outlets and the increasing influence of social media platforms had not only changed the means of communication but eroded control over how information and indeed privacy was disseminated.

Big Brother was a different sort of mainstream reality-television programme that opened with the new century, and the public response which it generated, rather than demonstrating the therapeutic value of revealing secrets, came to symbolise the danger of public over-exposure.

The programme was first transmitted in England in 2000 on Channel 4 over a couple of summer months, the idea copied from the Netherlands in a format that eventually went global. The dozen or so participants, men and women who had never met each other before and had no public platform, were paid to live together, or 'gaol' together, in a purpose-built house, honeycombed with hidden television cameras, surrounded by an eighteen-foot-high fence topped with razor wire, the perimeter patrolled by thirty-five guards with dogs to keep any public intruders out. Producers hoped that despite being locked in together for several weeks, the inmates would forget the relentless night-and-day scrutiny and unwittingly expose their secrets to the nation as the television audience voted weekly to evict contestants one by one until only the winner remained. This was a psychological experiment intended to deliver an addictive and unpredictable narrative complete with characters and a plotline that would evolve with minimal editorial direction. But in 2002, in the third series, a new and sinister element entered the nightly transmissions, with the television audience slow to wonder about the wisdom of this form of exploitation of a group of vulnerable strangers.

Jade Goody, a pretty twenty-year-old dental nurse from Essex, just a few months older than my first daughter, had revealed that Jackie, her mother, had lost the use of her left arm and eye in a motorbike accident when Jade was a child. Jackie was a gay, recovering drug addict and Jade's alcoholic father had worked as a pimp and done a spell behind bars. Jade had grown up in extreme poverty. With a grandfather from the West Indies, she was of mixed-race heritage. Her education was limited. She struggled with her weight. At first the limits of Goody's education were seen as charming as the audience accepted the gaps in her knowledge and her later complaints that the media had treated her as an 'escaped goat' was received with affectionate amusement. Her lack of geographical awareness frequently tripped her up, as she wondered whether 'East Angular' was in the UK or abroad, if Jerusalem existed or was 'just in the Bible', if Rio de Janeiro was a person and whether Portugal was in Spain. But although Jade made it to the final four in the competition, the tone towards her began to change as patronising taunts made by the other contestants were woven into the game.

After a few years off-screen but not away from public attention, Jade returned to *Big Brother* with her mother, joining the celebrity edition of the programme in 2007. Jade had become monetarily savvy, determined to follow up on any commercial offer if she thought it would provide her two little boys with the material security that she had not enjoyed as a child. But after the eviction of her mother from the House, her only protector in the *Big Brother* community, Goody lost all control. Feeling under attack when advised by the sophisticated Bollywood actress Shilpa Shetty to take 'etiquette lessons', Goody hit back. Participating in racist behaviour as part of a broader, group bullying campaign, led by co-contestants Danielle Lloyd and Jo O'Meara, Jade called Shetty 'Shilpa Poppadum' behind her back, but witnessed by a national television audience.

She apologised to Shetty later, but however fiercely Goody

protested that she had not meant the remark to be racist, her defence felt implausible. Her fellow inmates, the media and public opinion all responded. Channel 4 received over 44,000 complaints against Goody, as inmates turned on inmate, making the bully into the bullied, taunting her almost to the point of collapse. Outside the compound, members of the public turned up with posters calling to 'slaughter the pig'. Newspapers referred to Goody as 'the most hated woman in Britain'. Questions about the incident were asked in the House of Commons. Her own brand of perfume was removed from the shelves in shops. In India effigies of Goody were burned in the streets.

In 2008 Goody returned to the screen yet again, this time in an attempt to make amends, as a guest on the Indian edition of the programme. But during the transmission she was informed that recent medical tests had revealed a diagnosis of cervical cancer. Although the news was given to her off camera, the scenes that were filmed in the immediate aftermath spotlit Goody's shock and terror at a moment when privacy should have been her essential right. The audience was appalled. The long process of opening up, the encouragement and compulsion to share, the self-help group's mantra that 'you are only as sick as your secrets' felt as if it had overreached itself.

On programmes where almost nothing about people's personal lives seemed taboo or indeed sacred, the boundary between privacy and entertainment appeared to have snapped. And yet when the human cost of this exposure emerged from the drama the pain was all too evident. In the months before Goody's death from cancer in 2009 aged twenty-seven, public opinion turned once again, the sympathy and admiration for the courage she

showed throughout her illness replacing the taunts. While raising awareness for cervical cancer, smashing taboos as she did so,
including about death itself, she remained devoted to the welfare
of her two sons. For some she became a hero, a role model for
survival, for refusing to conceal her secrets, whatever the cost.

Secrets and mysteries previously contained safely or corrosively
within families had started to fascinate those of all ages as
genealogy became a hot topic in television and radio, with
Extraordinary Ancestors, Antiques Ghost Show and *Who Do You
Think You Are?* all broadcast on TV and *Meet the Descendants,*
which looked at the multi-racial ancestry of modern Britain,
on radio. People appeared more curious about their history than
my generation of baby boomers, and they set about enquiring,
challenging and rejecting the behaviour patterns of the past.

The old resources of family diaries and photographs gained an
extra dimension of interest for these new generations. A Finnish
friend described to me the fearless curiosity she felt about her
father from an early age. He was a celebrated florist and there
had always been women around him.

'Whenever I saw him with them, I would wonder if there was
a bit of flirting going on,' Dee told me as she described how
from childhood onwards she would monitor his behaviour. In
about 2002, when she was ten years old, she had climbed up
to the attic at the top of their old farmhouse in the Finnish
countryside. 'The roof space was packed with old blankets, battered cardboard boxes and dreary-looking files of papers,' she
remembered. But right at the back she spotted a beautiful,
velvet photograph album, an object of luxurious and deep pink

sumptuousness, curiously free of dust. Turning the pages, Dee recognised her young father as the groom at a wedding. There was no mistaking it was her father: his distinctive way of wrinkling his eyes identified him immediately. As she turned each thick and expensive leaf, it was clear that the record of this other wedding was lacking an essential component. One half of the pair had been scissored out with meticulous care from every picture. Where was the bride?

Dee's father was casually dismissive about the evidence suggested by this curious occasion with its central missing figure. 'Yes,' he told Dee. The album was indeed the record of his own first marriage to a student. The relationship had ended ten years before he married Dee's mother. His ex-wife was no longer in touch. There had been no children. Dee should not worry.

Despite being temporarily relieved at his assurance that there were no more secrets, Dee's long-term trust in her father had been broken. With her suspicious eyes ever alert, she assumed the role of her mother's protector in a household in which secrecy felt ever present. Even when her father knew he was terminally ill with cancer he denied the severity of the illness. In his will he left instructions that his wife must never remarry. Any romances must remain secret from their daughter in order to protect Dee from feeling her father was being betrayed, his patriarchal control extending from beyond the grave.

As access to search engines opened up further research into family trees, questions were asked and answered about the identity of great- and great-great-grandparents and also about the physical and emotional health that had travelled through a family history. The British writer and journalist Helena Lee, part of the Millennial generation, found that even though she is as close as could be to her parents, persuading them to talk to her had not always been an easy task. The family custom was to circumnavigate questions, especially when they concerned the past. Helena knew some things about her family but not enough. She knew her mother, born in Malaysia, was one of seventeen children, and that her grandmother's first husband had disappeared. But the narrative then diverged: he had been kidnapped either by the Japanese or by the opposing communists. No one talked about it.

'Not losing face is a big thing in Chinese culture,' Helena said. 'If my grandmother had revealed her vulnerability at the time, she would have opened herself up to those who wanted to steal her house and to turn her out of her home.'

Helena's young parents had arrived in Britain in the 1970s as first-generation Chinese immigrants – her mother Agnes from Malaysia, her father Charles from Hong Kong. Until their daughter began to ask questions about those early days, they had never spoken to her about this time in their lives. Initially both Agnes and Charles had found work in the NHS but then Charles left to become a civil engineer. His daughter realised her father's ambition had been tempered by his lack of confidence in his standing in this new society. 'His English wasn't great,' Helena explained, 'and although he didn't see the behaviour he met as racist, he was known by his colleagues as Charlie Chan.'

Only recently did Helena find out that her parents had moved house from Hatfield to Kenton in Harrow when she was five because stones had been thrown in racist protest at their front door. Only now she is older and persistent with her enquiries have her parents admitted that the Christmas turkey they enjoyed one year had been a gift from the Irish butcher who took pity on a family unable to afford a Christmas roast. They had lived on that turkey for two weeks. As Helena's paternal grandmother had stopped talking to her son when he married Agnes, because she was from Malaysia rather than mainland China or Hong Kong, Charles had become the target of prejudice not only outside but also within his own family. Despite minimising the challenges they faced, the differences between their old and new lives, some aspects of their lost culture remained significant to her parents, a precious link to the homelands they had left so long ago. Agnes would tell her children stories of her childhood in Malaya (later incorporated to be part of Malaysia), with its 'malevolent spirits, and crocodiles', and would bring durian home from the Chinese supermarket where she worked, proud to serve her children the evil-smelling but delicious fruit. But for eight-year-old Helena, her mother's kitchen, with its noodles and exotic fruit and the strange stories of wild animals, clashed with the lifestyle for which she envied her school friends. Longing to look like her blonde-haired best friend Michelle, Helena rejected the use of chopsticks, refused to eat dim sum and chose Pizza Hut and Enid Blyton as her own gastronomic and literary favourites. Only when she had children of her own did Helena begin to question, understand and feel proud of why her parents had behaved and brought her up the way they did. Her relatively pressured academic upbringing, which meant she must work hard and read a lot, was imposed on her, she began to realise, because her mother knew 'that was the way to unlock access to everything the education system in Britain had to offer'.

Her parents' emphasis on work succeeded. 'I want to instil the value of hard work on my two young daughters,' Helena told me, 'and to make them understand that things aren't handed to them on plates. Their Chinese grandparents are just as amazing as their academic white British grandparents.'

Assumptions and questions about her heritage remain part of Helena's life. The way she looks affects the way people treat her.

'I wear my heritage on my face,' she says. 'A lot of people have an interesting heritage but people feel they can ask me the whole time *because* of the way I look. I don't think that anyone who asks me always has bad intentions. When I open the door to a postman who says, "Oh. Where are *YOU* from?" I just reply, "From this house. I am from here, my home."'

Helena has never table-thumped or appeared affronted by such reactions but she acknowledges the weariness she feels when her looks provide a way into that conversation. 'When you are asked about that one thing that makes you different it feels like you have to justify it or explain yourself.'

She applauds how the confronting and outing of racial prejudice has shifted since her parents first arrived in Britain, 'especially in literature, which is weakening the age-old shame that feeds racism'. Helena's book, *East Side Voices*, published in 2022, is a collection of illuminating essays from a wide range of contributors from the East and South-East Asian diaspora currently living in Britain. Described in the *Observer* as encompassing prejudicial attitudes involving 'crude vilification, sexualised exoticism, entitlement, self-righteous ignorance and insularity', the book also 'reaches back through centuries of colonisation, exploitation and migration and reminds us that in the sweep of human history, there is often no fixed motherland and no fixed resting place'.

Helena has read Sathnam Sanghera's children's book *Stolen History* with her eight-year-old daughter. Although she knows that 'the scenes described in Sanghera's book about the truth behind the Empire, are tough', she also feels that giving her daughter 'an awareness of the truth of the good, bad and terrible is important, even at that age'. She feels 'an extra responsibility', she says, 'because our stories are not told a lot and often pushed down'. Her determination to confront the glossing over of the past is now met with her parents' support.

'They are proud that I want to know more. They know now that if we don't dig and ask questions that things will be lost, their own history will be lost. I want to flood the plain with stories. I want the ordinary stories as well as the extraordinary ones to be out there. The funny, beautiful and ugly as well. There can't just be one story of rags to riches, social mobility and all that jazz.' The truth needs to be taken on by her children and carried into the future replacing confusion and shame with pride.

East Side Voices includes a story about how the prejudices set down when nation was pitted against nation during the Second World War have been hard to shift even up into this new century. The writer Claire Kohda, born in 1990, was aware from childhood of the stigma around her own mixed-race heritage, where opinions were held just beneath the surface, if not exactly in secret. But the concealed truth had a way of revealing itself. Kohda's paternal grandparents had been part of a wartime generation for whom 'Japanese people were represented only as an uncivilised enemy'. Claire wondered if her grandmother 'was trying to actively erase the Japanese side of me so that she could begin to accept me'. Her grandmother never mentioned her disapproval that her son had married a Japanese woman, just as she never mentioned her disappointment that he had chosen a career as an artist. But on a schoolgirl visit to her grandparents' house, sitting on the sofa with its 'floral tapestry-like upholstery, the grandfather clock making several noises, a ticking, a clocking, a whirr and a cuckoo sound', Claire was suddenly nudged to attention by her mother sitting beside her. A painting was lying on her grandmother's lap. The portrait was certainly of Claire in that it mimicked her school photograph. But, looking closer, Claire saw how the painting differed not only from the photograph but from reality. Claire's hair had been made brown rather than black, the irises of her eyes had been changed from yellow-brown to 'something much lighter', her eyebrows had been thinned and bleached and her skin was now 'porcelain-white, with a beautiful soft English-rose blush'.

As Claire's father made complimentary comments about the skill of his mother's brushstrokes, Claire stared at the picture of her which was not her. 'It was like looking into a mirror that showed just half of me; it was like looking into a mirror that showed me what, at the time, I had wanted to be, which was completely white and not Japanese at all.' For a while Claire tried to forgive, even temporarily succeeded in forgiving, what seemed like undeniable prejudice. But as she reflected on that decision, and then discovered that her grandmother had admitted she had 'deliberately' whitened her skin and in so doing 'erased my Japanese heritage on purpose', Claire became angry. The use of a paintbrush as a knife felt like 'a type of violence' which had 'removed something from me that I recognise now as being precious'. It was an act of disguised abuse, a theft at the hands of her grandmother which Claire still cannot forgive.

CHAPTER 17

And Me Too

In her book *Toxic: Women, Fame and the Noughties*, the writer Sarah Ditum describes the effect that the Third Industrial Revolution has had on women, as we turn away from the mechanical and the analogue to the digital and explode 'the distinction of "private and public" that had been more or less stable' since the nineteenth century. Ditum identifies nine women – Britney Spears, Paris Hilton, Jennifer Aniston, Amy Winehouse, Janet Jackson, Kim Kardashian, Aaliyah Haughton, Lindsay Lohan and Chyna – whose treatment at the hand of sexist culture demonstrates how lives and minds were affected or destroyed 'thanks to a peculiar mixture of new technology and old misogyny', such that 'all the wrenching forces of the digital revolution were focused through them'.

Within the space of a dozen years, Facebook (created in 2004), YouTube (2005), X (originally known as Twitter) (2006),

WhatsApp (2009), Instagram (2010), Snapchat (2011), TikTok (2016) and any number of online dating sites are fuelling connection, information, opinion, gossip, liberation and danger, their reach unprecedented and almost unregulated. In this techno world where the platforms are largely designed and managed by men, women encounter a climate of techno-chauvinism. Online harassment and misinformation encourage an anti-feminist ideology. Feminist writer Laurie Penny launched their blog *Penny Red* in 2007 with optimism and a call for the 'young left' to find 'energy, inspiration, a sense not only of the consequences of inertia but of the viscerally thrilling possibilities for change'. But later, describing their misogynistic experiences in the *Independent* in 2011, they wrote 'you come to expect it, as a woman writer, particularly if you're political. You come to expect the vitriol, the insults, the death threats. After a while, the emails and tweets and comments containing graphic fantasies of how and where and with what kitchen implements certain pseudonymous people would like to rape you cease to be shocking, and become merely a daily or weekly annoyance, something to phone your girlfriends about, seeking safety in hollow laughter.'

Emma Watson, famous from the age of ten for playing Hermione Granger in the *Harry Potter* movies, only really knew she had become 'fair game' when she turned eighteen and a photographer lay on the ground to take a photograph, his phone-camera pointed directly up her skirt. And yet he was doing nothing illegal. Ditum writes how 'women's liberation had been declared prematurely redundant'. A twenty-first-century acceleration in the underground abuse of women by men, both verbal and physical, flourished until in 2017 a screeching, flashing, red-light emergency stop sign landed on the front pages of the *New York Times* and social media was jammed with a hashtag and just two words: Me Too.

In January that year a new president had been inaugurated, a man made nationally famous through a television game show and whose private treatment of women had come under intense public scrutiny. Despite an election reached through the democratic vote, the subject of patriarchal abuse soared to the top of the conversation both in the US and internationally. In a return to the campaign methods of the 1970s, the visible and audible presence of women's bodies and voices taking part in mass marches presented a powerful opportunity for protesting against sexual assault. In January 2017 an estimated 500,000 protesters joined the Women's March in Washington, the largest one-day protest in American history. At the same time, more than two million protesters in 161 cities across the seven continents of the world marched for women's rights, racial equity, immigration reform, reproductive rights, LGBTQ rights and the protection of the environment.

But on 15 October 2017 the chorus of objections to the apprentice president was all but drowned out. The *New York Times* had recently published allegations of sexual harassment against the movie producer Harvey Weinstein when actress Alyssa Milano received a message from friend and activist Charlotte Clymer: 'If all the women who have been sexually harassed or assaulted wrote "me too" as a status, we might give people a sense of the magnitude of the problem.' Sharing this post with her followers, Milano attached her own message: 'If you've been sexually harassed or assaulted write "#metoo" as a reply to this tweet.' Within twenty-four hours the elided words complete with hashtag had been retweeted a million times and Facebook reported twelve million responses. By 2025, eighty-five countries were estimated to have joined the movement and Milano was nominated in 2017 as one of *Time* magazine's 'Silence-Breakers'.

The origins of the #MeToo movement lay further back. Born in the 1970s, New Yorker Tarana Burke had grown up in the Bronx in what she describes as 'a low-income, working-class family'. She had been assaulted and raped from childhood to teenhood. In adulthood, when working as a director of a youth camp, she had held back from admitting her own experience to a young girl who had suffered similar abuse. Burke's subsequent regret at her own reserve prompted her to think of a way to reach out to other middle-school girls where she worked. Handing out Post-it notes at the end of her class, she asked the girls to write the two words 'me too' if they had been sexually assaulted. Three-quarters of the notes carried those two words, communicating solidarity better than any others. Burke elaborated on the simplicity in an interview with CNN. 'On one side, it's a bold declarative statement that "I'm not ashamed" and "I'm not alone". On the other side, it's a statement from survivor to survivor that says, "I see you, I hear you, I understand you and I'm here for you or I get it".'

Trusted with the confidences of these young women, Burke found herself in a position reminiscent of Joan Malleson in her consulting rooms fifty years earlier or of the role that Erin Pizzey had assumed in London's Chiswick thirty years ago. 'When I first started Me Too, young people had no language to talk about this,' Burke explained. And that's something I've seen change; young people have a way to talk about it now.' In December 2017 Burke told NBC's *Today* programme, 'I could never have envisioned something that would change the world. I was just trying to change my community.'

Three years after MeToo had taken off, Black Lives Matter also aimed to address systemic injustice. In 2020 the brutality shown to George Floyd by a white policeman in Minneapolis who knelt on Floyd's neck preventing him from breathing triggered the expansion of a movement that had been founded by women in 2013 after similar racial barbarity. The movement aimed to expose and oppose police brutality, especially that shown by white officers to African Americans. But as the effect of BLM grew, the movement widened to address the widespread discrimination with which the Black community was treated throughout America as well as by other racially prejudicial societies.

I was visiting New York in the week that the *New York Times* shattered the reputation of the most powerful man in filmmaking. During the closing weeks of 2017 the Harvey Weinstein case dominated the media, the internet and conversations across the world as secrecy split at the seams. Jodi Kantor and Megan Twohey, two women reporters, had pursued allegations against Weinstein in the face of intimidating and obstructive threats from Weinstein himself and his lawyers. Like Bob Woodward and Carl Bernstein of the *Washington Post*, who had brought down the Nixon government over the 1972 Watergate scandal, these women also braved the prospect of personal harm. Their fearless enquiry exposed Weinstein's uncontrolled deployment of emotional, financial, professional and physical tactics as he used women for sexual and power kicks before blackmailing and coercing stars big and small into silence. By forcing them to sign legal conditions of their employment, he threatened to destroy their careers and even their lives if they did not comply. When he was charged with rape, sexual assault and sexual abuse conducted over a period of at least thirty years, conversations veered between euphoria at his unmasking and disgust at his despicable behaviour. Some of Weinstein's victims told how they had felt so powerless in the presence of a man who 'roared and spat' as he attacked, that they had worn two pairs of tights in order to buy themselves time to escape his advances.

Zelda Perkins, Harvey Weinstein's PA in the UK, had confronted her boss after her own new assistant was attacked by Weinstein in an attempted rape two weeks into her job. Knowing that non-disclosure agreements (NDAs) had enabled Weinstein to continue with his pattern of abuse, Perkins's focus for change became the unforeseen consequences of signing such agreements. Her organisation 'Can't Buy My Silence', which she founded in 2021 with Julie Macfarlane as 'a global campaign committed to ending the misuse of non-disclosure agreements to buy a victim's silence', was a game changer. The organisation became internationally pivotal in bringing attention to the damaging use of NDAs to cover up sexual harassment in the workplace.

I had completely buried a memory which resurfaced during that visit to New York with the breaking the #MeToo story. In

1981, when I was in my twenties and working at the publishing company in London, inspired by the example of female empowerment as demonstrated by Dory Previn and Barbara Gordon, I was given the handling of the prestigious PR campaign for a Famous American Crime Writer. I'd recently found out I was pregnant, news I had longed for but that was nevertheless accompanied by a new vulnerability, both physical and emotional. The prospect of taking this particular author to the BBC television studios in Birmingham for a live interview made me apprehensive.

Recently married for the second time, the Famous American Crime Writer had greeted me with a sweaty handshake and his eye-wandering assessment that travelled from my head to my toes. However, The FACW's new wife was to come with us, so I reassured myself that at least I would be chaperoned. The studios were abuzz that morning with the announcement of the engagement of Prince Charles to Lady Diana Spencer and I saw the FACW bristle at the failure of the distracted royalist producer to pay his distinguished American guest due attention. As the wife remained in the green room, the ego-punctured author and I took the lift up to the studio. As soon as the lift doors slid shut he pounced. Crushing me against the metal wall, the stink of stale nicotine asphyxiating, he forced my lips apart and as I felt his tongue fill my mouth I gagged. The lift doors opened. The TV interview took place. I sat on a chair at the side of the studio, barely able to watch. Shocked by the realisation that I had been unprepared for the attack and therefore unable to defend myself, I also felt a visceral maternal instinct to protect my unborn child. Back in the lift to go downstairs I stood as far from him as I could, one hand over my stomach, the other over my mouth. His wife was waiting for us.

'Your husband has just kissed me,' I said to her, adding for clarity, 'properly.' Without a word, she stood and slapped him hard across the face.

Back at the office I told no one. The example of speaking out – as shown me by those women role models whose book promotions I had also handled – deserted me. I thought maybe the attack in the lift was my fault. Or that I would not be believed. Or that I would be believed and presumed naïve. Or that I would be laughed at. But I was also angry. The FACW had behaved on the assumption that he would be safe with his assault, that a junior publicity assistant would not have the nerve to speak out and if she did he would deny everything. It did not occur to me that maybe his wife could have come to my defence. So I was angry not only with him but with myself for keeping his horrid secret and for not being able to trust another woman. On a television programme ten years later, I heard the FACW say he had a sense of what is decent and what is not, and that he considered himself a moralist for his time 'just as Tolstoy had been for his'. After his death, it was revealed that he had long used an alias to write the pornographic fiction for which he was paid through his agent in cash. #MeToo brought the whole incident flooding back.

Examples of extreme abuse by men in positions of power continued to emerge. Institutional sexual intimidation was found in governments, the media, the Church and in businesses, a landscape not of accidental silence but of collusion and exploitation. The patriarchal hierarchy remained intact in work-places and behind front doors across the world. The clamour for change in every recess where damaging gender-centric behaviour prevailed – domestic abuse, reproductive rights, sexual choice, female genital mutilation, the marginalisation and victimisation of women of colour, of class, of religion, of economic status – was still being muffled by a social structure that favoured men. In 2019 the Queen's second son Prince Andrew was interviewed on national television to talk about his relationship with the convicted paedophile Jeffrey Epstein. Even when explicitly invited by his interviewer Emily Maitlis to do so, the Prince showed no remorse for the women who had been subjected to Epstein's relentless exploitation. The #MeToo message was still en route.

Harvey Weinstein did not have the monopoly on such behaviour within his industry. In 2022 the actress Amber Heard lost her abuse case against her former husband, the movie star Johnny Depp. The couple had divorced in 2016 after a short marriage and two years later Heard wrote a piece in the *Washington Post* titled 'I spoke up against sexual violence – and faced our culture's wrath'. Depp, who was not named in the piece, nonetheless sued his ex-wife for defamation and potential loss of work. His management team knew his name had to be bleached clean if he was to continue with a lucrative career on which he and his advisers depended. Heard's mission became personal, setting out to reveal what she claimed was the horrifying extent of Depp's violence, verbal and physical. But she had misjudged her chances of success. Accused of exaggerating, inventing and lying about the evidence, Heard was charged by Depp's legal team with painting on bruises, faking photographs of her injuries and persuading witnesses to falsely corroborate Depp's violent behaviour. The well of the internet ran deep, fuelling the anti-Heard brigade as she was trolled by a legion of Depp-supporting 'bots' (fake social media accounts) as an angry woman who did not deserve to be believed. Throughout the trial, reporters ridiculed and castigated Heard, the character assassination as savage outside the courtroom as within. Characterised by the bias that sustains glamorous superstars, no matter what the evidence might say, Depp had the powerful jury of public adulation on his side. When Depp's 'Not Guilty' verdict was announced Heard issued a statement in response.

'This verdict sets back the clock to a time when a woman who spoke up and spoke out could be publicly shamed and humiliated. It sets back the idea that violence against women is to be taken seriously.'

The argument that the trial had contributed to a renewed bias against men – brought about by an unjustified, infectious epidemic of false accusations spread by women – gained traction. As a consequence, predictions were made among women that the patriarchy would close ranks against any remotely plausible allegations against men in powerful positions. Moira Donegan, writing in the *Guardian* in 2022, summed up the far-reaching impact of the Depp–Heard trial.

It is hard to shake the feeling that really, it is directed at all women – and in particular, at those of us who spoke out about gendered abuse and sexual violence during the height of the #MeToo movement. We are in a moment of virulent antifeminist backlash, and the modest gains that were made in that era are being retracted with a gleeful display of victim-blaming at a massive scale.

The case also highlighted the ways in which public attention could increasingly lead to uncontrollable trolling, a danger that became one of the twenty-first century's biggest issues for women in public life, constraining their freedoms online and in the real world and suggesting once again that keeping silent might in many cases be the safest option.

Where online 'bullying' suggests a code of behaviour learned in the playground, trolling fell into a wholly different category. The infinite capacity of the web offered no escape from the anonymous abuse, shrouding and protecting the identity of that secret abuser, with no resource available for protection once it started. Actors, media presenters and politicians were especially vulnerable. In 2019 Caroline Flack, the presenter of television's dating show *Love Island*, had tried to ignore the deluge of threatening comments that flooded her phone on a daily basis until she could no longer tolerate the demonisation. She took her own life in February 2020. She was forty years old. Three years earlier, during the 2017 General Election campaign, the Labour Shadow Home Secretary Diane Abbott received almost half the abuse directed at all women MPs on Twitter, and ten times more abuse than any other individual MP. Black and Asian female MPs were sent 35 per cent more derogatory messages than white female MPs. 'It's the volume of it which makes it so debilitating, so corrosive, and so upsetting,'

Abbott explained. 'It's the sheer volume. And the sheer level of hatred that people are showing.'

In 2021, the Walthamstow MP Stella Creasy brought her thirteen-week-old baby into the chamber of the House of Commons after she was denied maternity cover by Parliament on the basis that she was irreplaceable in a constituency which had selected her – and only her – to represent them. While in the chamber, she breastfed her son. Immediately she became fair game for those who, under the protection of anonymity, complained she was flouting the House of Commons rules. Targeted as an unfit mother by one particular troll, social services took up his baseless complaint and began to investigate the MP. Leicestershire police confirmed to Creasy that the troller was 'legally entitled to express concerns to social care' as he had expressed 'no direct verbal or physical threat'. Accusing the police of having given online trolls 'the green light to target the children of politicians', Creasy remained powerless to stop the flood of incoming messages.

Institutional protection became an unignorable pattern, as different examples kept emerging. Creasy's case was one, but new allegations directed against institutions including the BBC and the British police reflected Donegan's and Heard's concerns, including historic cases that had only just been cracked open. The BBC's 'eccentric' Jimmy Savile's catalogue of criminal depravity and his prolific abuse especially of young women, often taking place on BBC property, was only revealed after his death in 2011. Complaints by the public about the BBC lead TV newsreader Huw Edwards were not properly followed through until disclosures emerged in 2023–4 of sexual misconduct that included the possession of paedophilic images of children as young as seven and nine.

Investigation into the abuse of children had dominated headlines for many years. The shocking exposure of extensive grooming, sex trafficking and rape of 1,400 teenage girls over many decades was identified first in 2010 and involved several towns in the north of England, including Rochdale, Leeds and Bradford. Gangs of men, many of them married and with children of their own, had been sexually abusing young local girls from the 1980s up until 2013. The abuse was known to the authorities but they had done nothing to stop it. A sequence of official investigations were conducted, with the final convictions of all the men involved still incomplete some fifteen years later.

The rape and murder in London of thirty-three-year-old marketing executive Sarah Everard in 2021 by Wayne Couzens, a serving policeman, felt like an equally horrifying result of an institutional cover-up, when the murderer was known to have a record of sexual offences that had gone unpunished by the police force over twenty years. The safety of every woman walking home alone, especially in London, felt perilous, and the aggressive mishandling by the police of the Clapham Common vigil held shortly after Everard's death compounded women's anger. The often-touted phrase by senior police officials that there were occasionally 'bad apples' in the mix of an otherwise honourable institution felt reductive, disingenuous and offensive, particularly in light of what had emerged after the murder of sisters Nicole Smallman and Bibaa Henry in 2020. Images of the sisters were shared for what the sentencing judge condemned as 'cheap thrills' on a private WhatsApp chat group by the two policemen responsible for keeping watch over their bodies before the ambulance arrived. The enraged and exemplary mother of Nicole and Bibaa, Mina Smallman, called the behaviour a 'sacrilegious act'.

The revelations kept coming. In 2024 a Channel 4 documentary revealed how over several years the country's law enforcers had neglected to investigate allegations against Mohamed Al Fayed, the owner of Harrods. The father of Princess Diana's final boyfriend, a man portrayed in the Netflix series *The Crown* as a cuddly character who had made it from Coca-Cola salesman in Egypt to mega tycoon at the heart of the British establishment, had long been a serial rapist. Fayed was shown to have subjected his female staff to unrelenting sexual assault for over forty years, one of them as young as fifteen years old. The women were threatened with punitive consequences if they spoke out, including the harm that would come to their families. But fear was not the only factor that allowed this practice to continue. The television documentary investigation revealed that Fayed's crimes had gone neither undetected nor unmonitored. More than one section of the establishment, including the police, had ignored or deliberately chosen not to follow up complaints during Fayed's lifetime, dropping any cases brought by the victims after cursory investigations. His personal security team had turned away from what they knew to be the truth. Harrods executives ignored what was happening in front of their eyes. The impact on dozens if not hundreds of women was terrifying, the scale of abuse drawing comparisons with Weinstein as it became clear that MeToo had been riding a switchback, swooping and dipping between effect and fallout, hope and fear. But the fundamentals had not changed. Looking back to the height of the energy of MeToo, a time when, as Moira Donegan said, 'women refused, en masse, to keep men's secrets, or to remain silent about the truth of their own lives', a resurgence of sexism, virulent online harassment and the threat of lawsuits all emerged, aimed to compel women back into silence. A roll-call of the iconic names, figureheads of the celebrity world, who had been punished, and for whom justice appeared to have been done, was deceptive. Harvey Weinstein was put behind bars in 2020. He had been preceded in 2018 by Bill Cosby, the television actor and comedian, affectionately known as 'America's Dad', who had been convicted of 'aggravated indecent assault'. Prince Andrew had been stripped of all public roles; Jimmy Savile and Mohamed Al Fayed were dead; Huw Edwards's career was finished; a handful of policemen were in jail, some for life. But abuse could not and cannot be eradicated by the token head roll of a handful of high-profile individuals. Hiding both in and out of plain sight in communities, churches, businesses everywhere, perpetrators continued to operate with seemingly undiminished ease. And women were once again afraid to speak, colluding by default in men's undercover misogyny.

My own faith in the MeToo movement as a permanent catalyst for change was challenged again in 2023. On paper the circumstances might not have seemed serious. But after my experience with the Famous American Crime Writer years ago, I had vowed never to remain silent again about something that might affect other women. The routine check-up took place in a private clinic dedicated to the health and welfare of women. Wearing an open-fronted hospital gown, I was unaware that the male technician had locked the door behind him after showing me into a screening room. With no offer of a chaperone and not thinking clearly enough to request one, I lay down as instructed on the clinical bed. Leaning closely over my half-open gown the technician asked if I was 'ticklish, darling' as he pressed his fingers into my skin, 'feeling for the pelvic bone, darling'. Alone in the room, and after several more darlings, trapped on the bed, tensed by his proximity to my near-naked body, I became frightened. After what seemed like an interminable wait as he operated the scanning machine, he finally unlocked the door and I went straight to the female nurse in charge and reported him. An almost year-long process followed as my complaint travelled through all the correct bureaucratic channels. Although I was listened to by my understanding woman gynaecologist, my voice within the ensuing process began to *feel* unheard. Each of the events that had taken place during those alarming fifteen minutes felt minimised by the replies from the hospital's complaint system. Tickling did not seem to amount to much of a crime. They were sorry, not that he had behaved that way, but that I had *felt* he had behaved that way.

'Nothing actually *happened*?'

'No.'

I learned later that the same man had treated another woman in a similarly discomforting way and although she had not complained formally, being unconfident in the English language, the hospital authorities were aware of her allegation. In the end my complaint was examined by an independent female adjudicator. A minimal offer of financial compensation together with a

pledge to change door-locking procedures and a promise that
the technician would amend his language closed the inquiry.
The technician stayed in his job. I had been gaslit. What shocked
me most was that this response to my account had come from
a woman.

The MeToo movement threw up further complexities and questions. What if its knock-on effects included accusations and
allegations made against men who then had no recourse to any
defence, to any response at all? What if men's professional,
personal, sexual lives were disproportionately demolished? Does
a man have a right to reply? And moreover, how does his partner move on from the associated notoriety? Even if she forgives
him, will she be tarnished for doing so? Will the experience
change her too?

At around the time of the Weinstein trial I was following a
young Frenchwoman on Instagram. Grace's posts were quirky
and stylish. She would upload pictures of books she had loved
in childhood, of home-made buttermilk icing, of the Gitane-
puffing fishermen of her old neighbourhood, of herself in a
Françoise Hardy cap, on a scarlet Bardot-esque moped, mid
Beyoncé karaoke, in slippers, in love. She was cool. She and
her husband, both academics recently married, had moved
from Marseilles to Boston together to take up positions at an
American college. We had friends in Boston in common and
during a visit to the city I met her at a dinner.

Grace seemed fragile and subdued. During the course of the
evening, both she and her husband remained almost totally silent.
Grace appeared particularly dazed as she held her husband's

hand throughout the meal, tethered to him as if letting go would precipitate freefall. I knew the story behind that potentially perilous descent. Everyone at the table knew it. Many years before, Grace's husband had taken a sabbatical from his French job and spent six months teaching in a different educational establishment. A week before the dinner party he had been accused by a group of women of sexually harassing a number of colleagues during that time. An internal inquiry was under way. A month after that dinner he returned to Marseilles, bowing to what was being referred to more broadly in the US media as 'the new authority'. This powerful body was made up of women all over the United States who, carried along on the wave of #MeToo euphoria, were deemed and feared, especially by men, to be on a mission for revenge, including for historic offences.

At the dinner Grace had appeared so stunned by what was happening that I could not see how either of them would survive without the wrath of the accusers severely affecting her as well, no matter how lacking in evidence some of the accusers were. Protestations that 'there are always two sides to a story' were not going to stand a chance in the backwash of #MeToo. But I was wrong about Grace. Several years later I met her again. She explained to me how her decision to remain silent at the time, even at a private dinner party, gave her the paradoxical power she needed. I had not realised when I first met her that she had deliberately been 'armouring up', secretly empowered by the knowledge that she could *choose* whether to reveal or to withhold her own state of distress, and in so doing retain power and dignity. Her apparent vulnerability at that time was tactical. She reminded me of the American first lady, Eleanor

Roosevelt's saying that 'a woman is like a teabag. You don't know her strength until she is in hot water.'

Grace had been taught how to 'armour up' by her American mother. Having grown up in California, Grace's mother moved to New York in the 1970s, 'exchanging her trans-continental bus ticket for a switchblade and using her thumb to hitch a ride. My mother was a tough cookie.' She told her daughter how, when travelling on the subway, she would find some space away from an aggressor, face the open carriage and yell 'Pervert' twice at the top of her voice. For a second-generation tough cookie, after the initial period of shock, stabilised by that self-imposed silence, Grace began speaking openly about what had happened. Lancing the vicarious shame that might have otherwise engulfed her, she encouraged her husband to do the same.

Neither of them has escaped unscathed even though the whispers that clung to him have gradually faded to near-silence. For Grace, the recovery has also been gradual. She has reined back her spontaneity, her exuberance. Her clothes are more muted. She no longer jumps up and grabs the hand of a male friend and pulls him onto the dance floor. Whereas she was once 'so sure of myself', she is wary of displaying 'unselfconscious seduction' and of alienating other women. 'Only at home can I lose my inhibition,' she says. 'Home is my sanctuary.'

The #MeToo backlash was directed against the very technology that had enabled the spread of the movement, the techno-chauvinism that had existed at the launch of many of the social media platforms and showed no sign of abating. Statistics said that women, from graduate age upwards, were being excluded from reaching strategic and planning positions in the techno-logical industry. Back in 2012, concerned by the patriarchal monopoly on the design of the major technological platforms, lawyer and activist Reshma Saujani set out to give young female scientists a voice in computer science classrooms by founding Girls Who Code. Her successful enterprise attracted the support of bastions of male power, including Google and Microsoft. However, it was not success but failure in a man's world that had brought Saujani such resolve. She was brought up in sub-urban Chicago after her parents, originally from Gujarat, were expelled from Uganda by Idi Amin in 1973 and sought refuge in America. Having worked in New York City's public advocate department and on Hillary Clinton's 2008 presidential cam-paign, in 2009 Reshma became the first Indian-American woman to run for Congress. In 2012 her own 'failure' to be elected to Congress at the age of thirty-three came close to defeating her. She found herself buying into the common female response of 'being so terrified of not doing everything perfectly that we tamp down our dreams and narrow our world'. Instead, she founded Girls Who Code. A year later, her determination was reflected in the TED Talk 'We Should All Be Feminists' given by Chimamanda Ngozi Adichie and later quoted in part by Beyoncé in her hit song 'Flawless'. As Adichie said: 'We teach girls to shrink themselves, to make themselves smaller. We say to girls, you can have ambition, but not too much. You should aim to be successful, but not too successful.'

On the recommendation of my daughters, I watched the May 2023 YouTube recording of Reshma Saujani's inspirational address to the graduating students at Smith College in which she urged the overturning of the silencing by speaking out. Urging her audience to 'make your argument' and 'lead your movement', her talk culminated in a call to arms to go out into the world and 'feel the freedom'. The Smith faculty is gathered behind Saujani at the lectern. They are smiling, respectful, clearly proud to have landed such a star at this important ceremony. The lens switches to the audience, where the expressions of the young women are exuberant. Saujani is speaking their language. These women are successors to Smith's game-changing graduate Betty Friedan. Saujani tells them a story about Victorian chauvinism. Women who dared to get on a bicycle without the permission of their husbands were warned they would develop the clenched jaw and bulging eyes of 'bicycle face'. This terrible, paralysing affliction was caused by 'over-exertion, the upright position on the wheel, and the unconscious effort to maintain a balance', and symptoms included 'the beginning of dark shadows under the eyes' and 'an expression of weariness'. Doctors cautioned that the condition might result in exhaustion, insomnia, heart palpitations, headaches and depression. Worse was the suggestion of moral chaos. The president of the Women's Rescue League declared bicycling to be 'the foremost evil of the age'. Bicycling was becoming 'a mighty influence against the Lord's day as a day of rest and worship'. Saujani's address was greeted not only with hilarity but also with respect for a point well made. There would be no imposter syndrome, no giving in to prohibitions that might curtail freedom of movement or speech for these graduates as they made their way into the world, armed with Saujani's rallying call.

When I met Saujani for breakfast in the Chelsea Hotel in

downtown Manhattan she was dressed in school-drop-off Lycra but her energy was as electrifying as when, cloaked in sub fusc, she had faced her audience of graduates-to-be. Over a shared fruit platter, water for her and tea for me, we explored the costs and benefits of silence. 'Women feel like we are making progress and then we take ten steps back. And we are feeling exhausted by the process.' But there is a difference, she said, between being 'quietly powerful and being silent. Silence is not good. But quiet power is.'

In the meeting rooms, office spaces and community groups that she visits on a weekly basis around the country, Saujani repeats again and again to her audiences of women her belief that 'when you are vulnerable you are powerful'. She remembers how the entire point of it all seemed lost once again when in 2016 'Hillary didn't get in'. In Saujani's book *Brave, Not Perfect*, she acknowledged that 'being afraid to take risks, to use our voice to take a stand or ask for what we want, even to make mistakes, leads to a lot of disappointment and regret'. And yet she learned that power through vulnerability will arrive 'when women attain a certain status or get to a certain age'. She learned that 'part of being strong is NOT sitting with your own feelings because if you do that, the whole thing can come crashing down'. Instead of waiting for the moment to 'exercise your rage', a moment that may never come, she focused on her growing conviction that she could make changes *outside* the formal political structure. 'I said fuck it. I don't care any more' and changed direction.

Saujani's organisations are designed to give women a voice, movements, she says, 'which have proved that a group of women can have an idea and make it work'. Girls Who Code targets industries which do not trust women with technical know-how. Her second campaign is to fight for payment for women 'who do not wish to become president'. It is a successor to American activist Selma James's 1972 campaign Wages for Housework, in which James argued that the state should compensate women for their unwaged, full-time management of the home. Saujani was inspired by 'conversations that generations preceding me have been having for ages. Two-thirds of American men believe someone should stay at home and take care of the kids and guess who that is?'

The cause erupted with particular impact during the Covid pandemic, as women continued to carry the domestic load despite their husbands working with them from home. The inequality became impossible to ignore. In January 2021 Saujani made a call to action. Her advertisements in the *New York Times* and *Washington Post* demanded government backing for the payment of women through her Marshall Plan for Moms, which would give financial relief to home-bound mothers, as well as those in the workforce. Moms First, which emerged from that movement, is now a full-fledged non-profit that works to change the experience of motherhood in America by focusing on, among other things, winning affordable child care, paid family leave and equal pay.

Saujani believes there is 'a reason why Barbie, Beyoncé and Taylor Swift are so high on the radar now', their unifying voices and reach across the generations, even those at the earlier end of Generation Alpha (those born after 2010), convincing her that 'women WANT to come together'. But despite the supporting voices of global fictional characters and universal pop icons, Saujani is aware of the strength of that challenge. The women's *movement* can sometimes feel *stationary*, especially when the vehicle, perhaps something as basic as a bicycle, suddenly brakes. On the re-election in 2024 of Donald Trump as US president and the defeat of the democratic candidate Kamala Harris, Saujani delivered a rallying cry. 'Do not fall into the trap of blaming Kamala,' she said. 'Don't fall into the trap of believing that we lost because we had an imperfect woman running an imperfect campaign. We fell for that con in 2016. Let's not fall for that con again. This is all about power: the "uncomfortability" that men and women feel about women having power – the power to have control over her body, her voice, her mind, her money.' Saujani ended on a triumphant note.

'I don't know about you. But I am not going back. WE are not going back.'

CHAPTER 18

Who Am I?

With the ever-surging technological tide, information that was once unknown, hard to find or only featured in out-of-date reference books is now instantly available. The gender of an unborn child no longer requires any guesswork. The health, mental and physical, of a child in utero can be monitored with almost total accuracy. And in 2006, a biotech company in California began selling relatively inexpensive genetic testing kits online, no questions asked, which would unlock the mysteries of identity.

Through simple laboratory analysis of a sample of saliva, 23andMe, a game-changing kit, available to buy on the internet, offered to reveal the hidden secrets of identity. Named by *Time* magazine in 2008 as 'the invention of the year', the process would analyse data that could alert a family to the risks of inherited diseases such as cancer and heart deficiencies and bring health options to millions of parents and their children. During the past two decades, women and men of all ages who have armed themselves with this new tool seek answers not only for health reasons but also out of simple curiosity about the make-up of their ancestors. My own generation has been inspired by the younger to look into mysteries we had assumed we would never solve, which is what happened when Mary Taylor's daughter encouraged her mother to send off her own saliva sample.

Mary, now in her seventies, lives in a thatched cottage, once a shepherd's dwelling, set back from a country lane behind a small wrought-iron gate. In spring the daffodil-scattered garden is the sort that appears in advertisements for the olde-worlde charm of England. As we sat beneath low beams at the kitchen table she told me her story, her recall cinematic and unfaltering, from the earliest flickerings of childhood awareness

Mary was born on 9 November 1949 in St Giles' Hospital in Camberwell, London, which abutted an imposing circular Victorian tower that once housed a workhouse. After three weeks her mother disappeared and for the next six years Mary lived in Hammersmith, in an establishment run by the Sisters of Nazareth, a strict order of nuns who cared for 350 orphans. Starved by the limited rations at mealtimes, Mary would secretly forage for moss and earth in the convent's small garden, avoiding the watchful and threatening eye of the lanky gardener, a rare adult male presence in the community. Punishment rather than care and concern hovered in every corner, whether for breaking an arm when somersaulting off the bed or when Mary wet herself, stuffing her damp knickers beneath her mattress to avoid detection. Puzzled why nuns who did not drink alcohol kept

Toby jugs lined up on a shelf, she was also bewildered by the inescapable but baffling teaching of the Catholic Church. After an older girl had swallowed the bread at Holy Communion, Mary asked her to stick out her tongue. Transubstantiation, flesh made real, surely meant that the bread would be transformed into a doll-size figure of a man? The Catholic teaching was to live an honest life but she felt she could never be honest if her surroundings were so contradictory and when she did not even know the truth about herself. 'I cried every single night. Desperate for a brother or sister, all I really wanted was a photograph of my mother. Over and over again I would ask myself, "Who am I?"'

In 1956 the lawyer who arranged Mary's legal adoption asked Mary how she wanted to be known. Somehow she could not remember what she had been called in the orphanage, or even if she'd been addressed by a number rather than a name. When offered the choice of Mary or Theresa she chose both, in alphabetical order. Mary Theresa's new parents, Ambrose and Susan King, were an elderly couple, Edwardians born just after the turn of the century when motor cars were in their infancy. Ambrose King was a distinguished physician specialising in the treatment of venereal disease, popularly known as 'the disease of gentlemen's lavatories'. He travelled far and wide for the World Health Organization, setting up research centres in far-off countries. Ambrose and Susan, both committed Roman Catholics, a religion to which she had converted, had been married in 1931. When she was a girl, Susan had held an ambition to be a ballet dancer, and indeed Susan and Ambrose both became such elegant ballroom dancers that the floor of the Savoy ballroom would clear completely, as other couples watched the Kings foxtrot in admiration and envy. But Susan had grown too tall. Disappointment affected her spirits. As a wife she knew she was an afterthought: everyone wanted to speak to Ambrose, who was so popular, so articulate. But their inability to conceive a child lay not with Susan but with her husband, and Ambrose was determined to make a childless wife happy, to give her a sense of purpose, to calm her agitation and perhaps, above all, to dissipate his sense of personal failure and guilt.

Ambrose arranged the adoption, but even at her young age, Mary sensed that for Susan, a woman in her fifties in the 1950s, 'life was over' and Mary had never stood a chance. A photograph shows that Susan could easily have been mistaken for the grand-mother of this sickly child who arrived on her doorstep suffering from chilblains, fleas, ring worm and warts. Mary knew she 'was just not the answer' to poor Susan's sense of hopelessness.

The Kings lived and worked in London's smart medical district near Regent's Park. There was little privacy. A spare bedroom acted as the consulting room for Ambrose's private practice, while his patients used the family sitting room as a waiting room. The patient files and medical library were kept in a bookcase in Mary's bedroom, with Susan, the practice sec-retary, bustling in and out to retrieve information. Although she was a good enough cook Susan had no idea what to give an undernourished child. Never seen outside or in without a hat or a cigarette, Mary's adopted mother would lean over the sink preparing potatoes and let the ash drop from her mouth to mingle with the peelings. A creamy trifle left over from an adult dinner party, generously laced with sherry, was served up again the following day to a reluctant Mary for lunch. Instructed to sit at the table until she had eaten it, and loathing the taste, Mary waited till Susan left the room before pushing up the window and depositing the sickly pudding on the heads of the passers-by in Portland Place below.

Despite her lack of intimacy with Susan, Mary was ever aware of the advanced age of her new parents. She dreaded the thought that, 'they will die and then what will happen to me?' Having heard about a deathly poison in tobacco, whenever Susan fell asleep after lunch with a cigarette hanging from her lips, Mary would hold a needle with all the steadiness she could muster and prick holes to interrupt the lethal flow of tar. She knew about the contingency plan. In the event of the Kings' death, Mary would be placed under the care of Cardinal Heenan, her adopted father's great friend, a severe, bespectacled cleric who lived in the precincts of Westminster Cathedral. She knew she belonged to no one. She felt like a 'mongrel dog'. Only when she was sent away aged seven to board at St Leonards-Mayfield School in Sussex did she begin to feel a little 'normal'. Having been deprived of the company of children of her own age, she at last found herself among girls with whom she formed life-long friendships.

During the summer months, the Kings would spend the weekends and the holidays at the cottage where I had come to talk to Mary. From the kitchen I could see the large garden with its lovely views over the sweep of the South Downs stretching outside the black-painted door. All those years ago, breakfast had never been enough for a child so hurt by scarcity. 'I would go out there,' she remembered, gesturing to the black door, 'and secretly cram fistfuls of earth into my mouth, and swallow clumps of moss that I pulled off the wall. I could not get enough of it. The feeling of pulling the moss was magic. And I loved the taste of it.' In her untethered existence she sought to 'earth herself', to connect herself to the ground, to root herself in something ancient, to belong to this cottage that she was growing to love, to belong when she had never belonged anywhere before.

Unlike his wife, Ambrose had felt an instant warmth for his new charge, his sense of humour charming her. His face lit up whenever he saw her, and he would sit with her at the garden door and painstakingly remove the lice from her hair. It was the first adult kindness ever shown to her. It would be another forty years before he allowed himself to criticise the Catholic nuns who had once been responsible for her. 'You weren't very well looked after,' he finally acknowledged in his nineties, 'and if you had received the care you deserved there you would have been much happier.'

In 1983, seven years after the passing of the Adoption Act that entitled a child to search for their birth mother, Mary received her full birth certificate. She held the document out to me, the cream-coloured form with its sticking-plaster-pink type in which every word mattered. Here was the name of Mary's mother who had left her in St Giles' Hospital thirty-four years earlier.

Maureen Kerrigan, a café cook of 182 Westmoreland Road, SE17.

But the space allocated for the father's name and occupation had been obscured by a heavy black horizontal line. Determined to follow the trail to its conclusion, Mary consulted the archives in Somerset House and found an address on her mother's marriage certificate to a Peter South. She planned to take Maureen a letter asking two questions. One of Mary's daughters was a diagnosed coeliac. Was there any history of gluten intolerance in Mary's birth family? And secondly, could Maureen tell Mary the name of her father? Arriving at the block of flats named on the marriage certificate, there was no answer to Mary's knock but on pushing the envelope through the letterbox, Mary heard a woman coming down the stairs.

'Oh yes, I know Maureen,' she said. 'She's a school dinner lady over there,' pointing to a building just behind the flats. 'She's probably there now.' Mary went round the corner, through the front door of the school, found the dining room, and saw that lunch was over. A couple of women were clearing the tables.

'Could you point me in the direction of Maureen South?' Mary asked.

'Yes. She's over there.' And there she was.

'She was my height,' Mary told me, 'and she had dark, curly hair whereas mine was straight. She had' – pausing to find the right expression – 'middle-aged spread. She wore a pinafore over trousers and a blouse.' But Mary barely took in the clothing 'because my dearest dream had been to see her face. And I saw that her bottom row of teeth crossed over one another just as my daughter Nathalie's teeth had once done before she had them straightened.'

Standing in the school dining room, the smell of cabbage and potato in the air, listening to the clatter of cutlery returned to drawers, Mary spoke to her mother for the first time.

'This is going to be a bit of a shock. I am your daughter.'

Across the table from me, Mary paused.

'She was not pleased, this mother of mine,' Mary continued eventually. 'I remember her reply. "I dreaded the day you would find me."'

Afterwards, the two women spoke a couple of times on the telephone and then Maureen changed her number. Mary never received an answer to her letter. They never met again.

I asked Mary if she had forgiven Maureen.

'I don't think forgiveness ever crossed my mind,' she replied. 'Life was so different then. I have no feeling for her, but I have a great sadness. She took away my Irish heritage and she took away my childhood and she took away the brothers and sisters that I longed for.'

The entire encounter remained Mary's secret. Her daughters had always believed Mary to be the Kings' child, and knew nothing of the circumstances of their mother's birth, of her search for Maureen, of the missing name of their birth grandfather. Neither of her daughters were close to Ambrose and Susan and, protective of her adoptive parents, Mary did not want her children to reject them even further. So she held on to her secret until one day her daughter Catherine unwittingly helped to solve the final piece of Mary's puzzle. She gave her mother, who was then approaching her seventieth birthday, the greatest gift of her life. In 2019 Catherine had taken a DNA test, out of sheer curiosity, and was puzzled when her results flagged up the names of American cousins that she had never heard of. Catherine began to communicate with these new relations until a very brief message arrived across the Atlantic from 'Cousin Kevin' specifically addressed to Mary. Catherine showed the one line to her astonished mother: 'I know who your father is.'

As a child Mary had longed for siblings of her own. After a flurry of transatlantic communications Mary learned that dreams come true, that miracles happen, that prayers are answered, that clichés can be specific – and that her father had provided her with no fewer than four American half-sisters. After what became Mary's single-minded and intensive investigation, she discovered that a half-brother had been occupying the same flat in which she had originally hoped to find her mother. Although the flat had been sold, a friendly local estate agent gave her the information she needed. Not long afterwards, a corner booth in Dirty Dicks pub in Liverpool Street in London rocked with the laughter of yet more siblings. For the first time Mary met her three half-brothers and half-sister, the children of her mother's marriage to Peter South. The interlocking pieces had slotted into place. Learning from the brothers that Maureen had died eighteen months earlier aged eighty-six, Mary asked them about her mother's life as a professional cook, her occupation given on Mary's birth certificate. 'A cook ?!' The siblings had been brought up on Spam and chips.

Mary has one photograph of her father, Michael McGrail. One of twelve children, he had been working on a building site in Camberwell in 1949, saving money to travel to New York to make his fortune, and had probably dropped into Maureen's café on a tea break. One thing led to another, and in turn led to Mary. I looked at the picture. A man of exceptional good looks beamed from a black-and-white photograph, his eyes glistening with laughter. He seemed to say he was embracing life, opportunity, openness. He reminded me instantly of the woman opposite me, a woman who could only be this man's daughter.

Michael died in New Jersey in 1986, probably unaware of Mary's existence. Susan King died in 1992, aged eighty-six like Maureen, but Ambrose survived her for another eight years. During his widowerhood, Ambrose and Mary grew ever closer. She knew that he had loved her from the moment she had come into his life nearly half a century earlier. He knew that the cottage in which she had spent those first days of freedom meant as much to her as any relationship. He had ensured that on his death in 2000, aged 98, the cottage would become hers. As we walked outside, Mary showed me round the place where she told me she had found 'peace at last', the beauty of her garden the result of her own imaginative and careful nurturing of the very soil which she had once consumed and to which she knew she at last belonged.

Instead of bringing resolution and joy as it did for Mary Taylor, secret-busting, twenty-first-century science can also demolish previously unchallenged certainties and deliver shattering news. In a pretty village not far from my own, a composed young woman sat facing me, pushing her long blonde fringe away from her eyes as she spoke, the better to give me her full concentration. We were talking about infertility, medical breakthroughs, adoption, death, fear and truth. Of course we were talking about secrets too, and also betrayal. For all the scientific advances that have reduced stigma and the need for secrecy, fertility remains a minefield. Thomasina Whitehead was in her forties by the time she realised the extent to which she had been caught up in the reflected shame of the inability to conceive naturally.

In his futuristic novel *Brave New World*, set in 2540 but published in 1932, in the years when the Nazi threat and the idealisation of an Aryan ruling class were growing ever stronger, Aldous Huxley imagined a world in which babies are created and grown in factories, infertility is irrelevant and sex is no longer necessary for procreation. But genetic engineering became a reality far sooner, with the birth in Britain of Louise Brown in 1978, in the reductive, clinical language of the time, the world's first 'test tube' baby. The birth was a game changer and Brown remains proud of her notoriety and 'passionate about breaking the silence on all things fertility and ending the taboo about getting help for fertility issues or being born through scientific means'. But if the hopes of some couples struggling with conception were realised with in vitro fertilisation (IVF), this option remains beyond the budgets of many. Before the law changed in 1990 to include further regulation, an alternative, affordable solution was offered without questions being asked. Clinics in prestigious Harley Street offered couples life-changing, life-giving 'donations' – sperm wrapped in euphemism – provided mainly by medical students and guaranteed by the clinic, so the children conceived in this way were guaranteed to come from 'intelligent stock'. These sperm donors, untested for any possible hereditary illness, received a small fee for delivering the magic solution. Their role, in exchange for cash payment, was to make sure the clinic's supply of samples, its 'wank-bank', remained in credit.

This resulted in what Jenny Kleeman in the *Guardian* called 'a wild west for doctors who made grand promises to people who were desperate, secretive and ashamed'. Clinics assured their customers that the students could provide donations no more than three times to prevent 'consanguinity' (siblings having children together without being aware of their genetic relationship) but the lack of regulations meant that the possibility of a donor child having a relationship with a 'dibbling' (a donor sibling) remained a risk.

In the early 1970s, Thomasina's parents, Mr and Mrs Whitehead, married. They were in their twenties and in the prime of life. They longed to complete their happiness with a child, but after ten years, the couple had still not become pregnant, and the prospect of childlessness seemed to them to sentence their marriage to a future of emptiness. The Whiteheads made an appointment with a Harley Street fertility clinic run by a woman whose white laboratory coat and horn-rimmed spectacles commanded authority. After the 'exchange' had taken place, the name of the donor was not revealed to the Whiteheads, and neither was the donor informed of the identity of the recipients. As was customary with most couples, the clinic advised the Whiteheads that it would be better if any child conceived by this process was never told the truth. That sort of revelation could disrupt the harmony of future relationships.

As a child, Thomasina already knew about the significance of this kind of secret as she'd grown up aware of the distressing circumstances of her mother's adoption. Not only had Mrs Whitehead's birth mother died within a year of giving up her baby but her elderly adoptive mother had died soon afterwards, leaving the baby to be raised by a strict Victorian grandmother. Without any records available, Mrs Whitehead believed the identity of her father would be denied her for ever. Mr Whitehead had embarked on the search for his wife's missing father on her behalf but when he died in 2015, Thomasina decided to take up her mother's cause by taking a DNA test to see if that might give any clues. When the emailed print-out arrived detailing her DNA results she could not make sense of the information. There was no trace of her father's ancestry, his Yorkshire-based family associated for centuries with the same farming village. Instead, Thomasina was presented with a 50 per cent connection to an Italian company director living in the south of England with extensive family connections in Canada and the northern United States. Surely there was a mistake? But no, Ancestry.com reassured Thomasina on the telephone, errors in the DNA testing were almost unheard of.

By now Thomasina's mother was in the early stages of dementia. But after a few days of shock and indecision, Thomasina finally went to Mrs Whitehead with the laboratory results. The older woman began to weep, her memory about events so long ago as clear as daylight. Yes. There had been a donor who had supplied the donation 'for beer money', the triviality of the phrase especially difficult for Thomasina to hear. She had longed to be told that there had been some sort of intimacy, a romantic affair that had resulted in her creation. Instead, for more than forty years Mrs Whitehead had protected first the dignity and now the memory of her husband and their inability to conceive without help. Only now did she reveal how angry and ashamed she was to have been put through such a humiliating procedure. She wanted Thomasina to know how difficult it had been for them to live through all those years with the fear of being found out, about the shock Mrs Whitehouse was now experiencing at their secret being unmasked and also at the thought of how mortified her husband would have been at this revelation. But she wanted Thomasina to understand that the victim of the story was not Thomasina but Mrs Whitehead herself.

Knowing that not knowing who her own father was had caused her mother a lifetime of uncertainty and distress, Thomasina could hardly believe that her parents had somehow cheated her out of her own truth. Half of Thomasina's identity had vanished with the testing of a single swab of saliva, while at the same time opening the possibility that she was part of a mass-produced line of half-siblings, a cog in a production line. With the help of sympathetic friends when the investigative process felt too overwhelming, too daunting, she found out that the donor, the Italian company director, lived within driving distance of her house. For the Whiteheads he had given life to a dream. He was a worker of miracles. But he also represented a source of shame, never to be revisited. Thomasina tried to contact him through Ancestry.com.

'I know this must be a huge shock,' she wrote to him through their website.

For a couple of months there was no response. 'It was like a dating app,' she told me. 'All the time I was wondering if he had seen the message. Would he get in touch?' Still there was silence.

But one day she logged on to the site, still expecting nothing. And there, clearly posted on his page, was a meticulously detailed family tree going back, astonishingly, to AD 60. Here were the names of ancestors who, centuries ago, had ruled kingdoms, were commemorated in statues and in portraits hung on the walls of cathedrals and castles. Branches of the family had emigrated to Quebec and Montreal. Occasionally a lone twig from the tree had travelled its fragile way across oceans towards Australia. And then one night the family tree vanished from the site. Thomasina was baffled. Had the family map been put up to give her the basic information but afterwards communication was to cease? And then, with the help of techno-wizard friends, in the recesses of the web, she found a photograph. Here was no God-figure, no mystical, mythical person behind the anonymous creative act that had resulted in the gift of her life. Here was a flesh-and-blood individual, smiling into a camera, dressed in a dinner jacket, his arms extended around a daughter and a son, Thomasina's half-sister and half-brother. All of Thomasina's life she had felt something was missing, that her parents loved one another, or perhaps included one another, more than they included or loved Thomasina. The recognition that Thomasina belonged in the most visceral way to these people in the photograph, that they were her true family, was overwhelming. She had the donor's address, her father's address. She could go and knock on his door any time.

'I don't know where to go with this now. I would like to know how many mannerisms and behaviour traits I share with him and his family,' Thomasina told me. She is conscious that adoption stories can have more hopeful endings, 'at least they may have had something of a relationship to start with but these donor stories don't generally end with a happy ever after'.

She has stopped herself from taking matters any further. 'I worry about the impact on his wife, who might not know he had done this, or on his children, who probably have no idea what their father did in his youth. I feel the burden of responsibility:

they are the innocent parties and in a way he is too. He was a twenty-five-year-old with his life ahead of him, earning his "beer money", not thinking that in future years he would be meeting a surprise daughter in her forties.'

Even though Thomasina has decided against any further communication with the donor, she feels she is 'in limbo', while admitting that she hopes one day, somehow, her dream will come true and that she will meet the man 'who gave me life'.

I wondered if the prophecy feared by Thomasina's parents had itself come true. 'Has the knowledge of the donor affected your love for the father that brought you up? Do you feel differently about him?'

'No,' she replied. 'I love him no less.'

As I was leaving, Thomasina gave me her upbringing-father's first name. It could have been no other. The man who had longed for a child of his own, had bound his daughter as closely as possible to himself by giving her part of his own identity. Thomas and Thomasina had been joined in every way he could conceive of, except conception.

CHAPTER 19

The Last Word

Perhaps the biggest secret that we continue to keep from ourselves and try to protect our children from is that the narrative of human life must end somewhere, as all stories do. Two new generations are rising beneath me as I reach the precarious top slot and the ultimate vulnerability is hard to accept, for the individual as well as for those close to her.

The Victorian protocol was to celebrate death. The Queen of that age had made black-drenched mourning fashionable on the death of her husband Albert in 1861. Victorians believed that the custom of propping up the dead body as part of the surviving family group provided the opportunity for a touching final photographic portrait which, propped on the country's mantelpieces, became an integral part of the Victorian grieving process. But after the decision not to repatriate the dead from the battlefields of the First World War, funerals and graves were suddenly made impossible and as the reality of death became less visible, death itself became shrouded by taboo. In my lifetime the secrecy that has surrounded illness and death persists, masked in cliché and genteel euphemism.

In our family, as in so many, death was rarely openly discussed, but often treated as a failure in both a psychological as well as a physical sense. From a male perspective, females were presumed to have a heightened sensitivity and delicacy of temperament and needed to be especially 'protected' or insulated from the facts of illness and death, even their own. In my childhood, the convention was to omit, fudge or even lie about the truth of a patient's terminal illness if it was considered too distressing for the sufferer to know about. The novelist Susan Hill has described how her mother (born in 1909) was of a generation for whom the word 'cancer' was as toxic as the illness itself. So, when Mrs Hill was told by her surgeon in the 1970s that she had 'ulcers in the back passage' she was spared the reality of a fatal diagnosis of bowel and rectal cancer. With this secret kept safely from her, she lived another three years until someone mentioned the word cancer by mistake and she was dead within weeks. My mother's final days were hazed in a blur of platitudes. 'While there is life there is hope,' my stepfather told a friend as his wife lay in hospital in a coma with irreversible liver damage. While the dying sometimes wish to be told their prognosis, the decision is unique to each individual. Writing from her own experience, the journalist Rachel Cooke commented, 'Some people may well find it helpful to talk publicly about illness: doing so gives them a sense of control and support. But not everyone feels like this and, for those who don't, the pressure to speak of intimate things is invasive: an incursion we disdain at the best of times, let alone the worst.' Cooke remembers her granny weeping as she described the agony of not being able to tell her rapidly fading sister that she was dying of breast cancer, when obeying the doctor's advice to observe discretion. My own grandmother, on suspecting she had fallen terminally ill while away on holiday with my grandfather, kept the severity of her symptoms from him until their return home. Even the most determinedly open of women can be pushed back by the barrier of admitting life-limiting illness. Letty Cottin Pogrebin had admitted her abortion in the pages of the *New York Times* but in 2009 when confronted with the news that she may have a malignant brain tumour she kept the potential diagnosis secret until she found out that the tumour was benign. In many Jewish families cancer was as much of a 'shanda' as divorce or infidelity, all three suggesting that one possessed some shameful flaw or inadequacy. Nora Ephron, the American feminist and author of books and films including *When Harry Met Sally* and *Sleepless in Seattle*, which defined the power of truth telling, and for whom 'everything is copy', had a similar response to her own illness. Her death in New York in June 2012 from acute myeloid leukaemia leading to pneumonia was a shock. She had told almost no one that she was ill, even her closest friends. Some thought that rather than the fear of death, the loss of control and the possibility of losing writing and directing jobs might have prompted her to keep her impending mortality secret.

Diana Athill, publisher, memoirist, born in 1917, dented the stigma of advanced maturity in her nineties when writing about the emotional and physical actuality of old age. She credited the philosopher Montaigne with her approach of taking 'a short time every day thinking about death, thus getting used to its inevitability and coming to understand that something inevitable is natural'. She described how in the old people's home in which she spent her final years she would discuss the approaching inevitability with her co-residents. 'As a result of this openness, I think that most of the people here would consider it foolish to be frightened of being dead.'

The boundary that divides privacy and secrecy around illness and death is nebulous and confusing. The poet bell hooks defines her understanding of where that boundary lies, applying her thoughts not just to death but to life. 'Open, honest, truth-telling individuals value privacy. We all need spaces where we can be alone with thoughts and feelings – where we can experience healthy psychological autonomy and can choose to share when we want to. Keeping secrets is usually about power, about hiding and concealing information.' The dilemma around this boundary is especially evident in the admission of illness suffered by those in public life. People feel they have the right to know everything about celebrities, including any medical diagnosis. If the royal family falls into the celebrity category, the precise details of the myeloma suffered by the ninety-six-year-old Queen in 2022 remained concealed even on her death certificate, which stated that the ending of her long reign was due to 'old age'. Respect for her privacy held. But just over a year later, sections of the media demanded more information from a family still hoping to keep their private lives private. A few months after King Charles was crowned in 2023 the double

diagnosis of cancer for himself and the Princess of Wales dominated world news. Both individuals felt bound to reveal their
illnesses in order to face off the insistent questioning. The King's
greater age made him less of a focus than his much younger
daughter-in-law, whose circumstances, as the mother of three
small children, added a particular poignancy to the news. While
King Charles underwent his cancer treatment with minimal
intrusion from either the conventional or social media, the
Princess's condition dominated every conceivable news outlet.
Issuing a sequence of televised solo statements and a soft-focus
film towards the end of her medical treatment, she successfully
headed off the frenzy of conspiracy theories, satisfying public
curiosity with these carefully timed updates, while simultaneously retaining the precise details of her condition as private
information.

If the Princess of Wales found it challenging to manage her
own narrative, even with access to the very best PR advice, death
brings the ultimate loss of control over personal truth for everyone. A secret may well be buried during a lifetime but however
many layers of concealment and denial have been piled on top,
it is unlikely to remain in place after death. Since 2020 a Danish
television programme, *The Last Word*, has given well-known individuals the opportunity to anticipate any inaccurate or invented
post-mortem revelations by recording their own valedictory
notices, frankly and finally, by talking to the programme's sensitive, charismatic host Mikael Bertelsen, on the understanding
that the programme will not be released until after their death.
With the title of the show implying that the guest will triumph
by having the final say, the interviewer and interviewee sit alone

in large, black leather armchairs in a dimly lit studio, the recording made with remotely controlled equipment. At the end of the session, Bertelsen leaves the room and the celebrity remains behind, speaking their very last words direct to camera, looking straight into the eyes of the viewer.

During the transmission of one of these ghostly programmes, Lise Norgaard, a much-respected Danish journalist, writer of fiction and TV drama, and veteran feminist, shocked her huge post-mortem audience with her revelations. Filmed a couple of years before she died in 2023 aged 105, and in a hoarse but intelligible voice, Norgaard revealed why she had chosen to break up her family of four children in the 1950s. She had suffered from physical abuse by her husband. She spoke about how 'a slap in her face' had been the last straw. For a long time she had seen no way out of the marriage but the slap made her 'think clearly'. And so she left him. She had never told anyone before, not wishing to be seen as a victim. Norgaard explained to Bertelsen that she 'was conscious of leaving behind a kind of manual for the women of the future with her own experiences and advice on how to make yourself free and independent'.

A few years ago, a friend of my age wrote to me to say she did not wish the news that she was dying to be a secret. She had just been diagnosed with terminal, small cell, lung cancer, was planning her funeral and all her greatest friends were to be invited. There would be a delicious tea with every variety of cake and sandwich, bowls of her favourite red and black jelly babies and a chocolate fountain for the children. Everyone would be given a song sheet to join in the singing. And there would be a guest of honour: Christina herself. The attached invitation stated the occasion to be a celebration of 'This Glorious Life'. Did I feel up to saying 'a word or two', she wanted to know? I accepted the invitation without a moment's hesitation.

And so it was on bonfire day – I remember, remember that 5th of November – that I stood in front of a half-glowing, half-tear-stained group including Christina's husband Mark, her children Kate and Edward, and a big gathering of her family and her friends as I addressed directly the woman whose life we had come not to mourn but to celebrate. At the beginning of the party the guests had been apprehensive. How would we cope with such a conspicuous leave-taking? How would she cope with the finality of the moment? But when Christina arrived, we needed no reminder that we were gathered there because she had told us that she wanted to see our faces one last time and because we loved her. Christina sat in a chair, shawled and shimmering, as her grandchildren draped themselves over her lap, and her daughter, son and husband wrapped their arms around her. The only evidence of her condition lay in the little phial of morphine that she held undisguised, unashamed, contrasting with the flutes of champagne in the hands of her guests, as I joined her family's affirmations of love, in describing why I had 'fallen in friendship with Christina'. She was not going to rage against the dying of the light but rather *use* that remaining brightness to illuminate the amazingness of living. I was spellbound by her gaiety and by her calm. Life within death. As we walked out into the garden to watch the sky turn psychedelic, cosmic, rockets zipping into the darkness of the evening, banks of starlit memory were forming for us all.

And yet despite Christina's shining example, I still try not to think about the prospect of endings. Just as the process of birth involves a dilation of space that allows entry to the world, so the approach of death demands a retraction. The changes of the ageing process are also as destabilising as adolescence, a transitional process equally baffling. A shrinking of height and a thinning of hair arrive alongside the narrowing of opportunities to run, skip and dance with the energy that characterises youth – hard to ignore, but even harder to admit.

Having duped myself into feeling eternal, I fell. The fall itself was not exactly an age thing, I told myself: I had no fragile bones or weak ankles, nor was I prone to dizzy spells or unable to balance. Surely my trip was the sort that could happen at any age? An accident or failure to concentrate rather than a weakening of limb or eyesight? But I could tell that however I might spin it to myself, I had joined the statistics. A third of adults over the age of sixty-five fall every year. That figure rises to half in the over-eighty age group. The fall pulled me out of denial, but it left me with a knowledge that felt as destabilising as when I was pretending I wasn't drinking myself to death, bringing with it the suspicion that I was now living in the 'after' with the good stuff all confined to the 'before'. But I did not confess these thoughts. I thought that by voicing them, they might come true. I was changed. I was not the grandmother, mother, wife, sister, friend, person that I had been. As the writer Hanif Kureishi so simply and beautifully put it in a tweet after his catastrophic fall in

2022, a year after mine, 'I once had a full and enjoyable life, and then one day I had an accident, and that life was over.' Kureishi described how Masha in Chekhov's *The Seagull* is in 'mourning' for her life, a sentiment that resonated with him 'as a piece of music can'. I understood exactly what he meant.

It happened to me like this. It was Sunday 28 November 2021. We were having some friends to Sunday lunch. The smell of roast chicken (as ever) was filling the kitchen. It was one of those longed-for November days when the low sun was slanting through the window, the light landing on the glasses on the table set for lunch and making them zing. My brother and sister-in-law were coming too. As they appeared at the kitchen door I was holding a saucepanful of carrots in boiling water and tripped on a rug. As I stretched towards the sink to avoid spilling the boiling water over myself, I felt my spine bend in a sort of Nureyev twist, a split-second corkscrew, convinced I had heard the snap as I crashed onto the stone floor. My sister-in-law moved fast, her training many years ago as a GP surfacing instinctively. She grabbed a bucket, filled it from the tap before drenching me, fully clothed, in freezing water. 'Do you think you can get to the bath? Can you get there right now? Freezing water is the best thing for burns.' But it was not the burn that worried me: I was completely unable to move. There was just one thing over which I felt I had control. I could scream. I remembered an organist on the radio saying that a humble piano does not hold the power to make a room move. As the kitchen seemed to spin around me, I screamed like an organ. As soon as each scream ended I knew what I could do next, the only thing I could do. I could scream again. And I did. Many, many times. Lying drenched in buckets of cold water, making as much sound as I could, screaming from deep within my lungs, screaming for survival.

My brother had rung 999 for an ambulance and moved a kitchen chair near to me. His proximity radiated concern. I stayed face down on the floor, my face in the water, my body immobile. Angela, our physio friend from the village, dashed over to check if my back was broken. My husband Charlie had brought a sunlounger mattress from the hut in the garden, uncoiling it from a bin bag. No one had anticipated that it would find a use in the depths of a grey, November day. I could smell the damp mustiness as Charlie stretched it out onto the hard floor before Angela rolled me onto it. She asked if I could wiggle my toes. To my surprise all ten responded. Everyone said I was going to be okay. Three hours later, with no sign of an ambulance arriving during that pandemic-stretched weekend, I made my way slowly upstairs to bed, making sure I took each step with geriatric caution.

Two days later I went to the cinema with my best friend Rachel to see a movie starring Lady Gaga. Rachel drove. The film was brilliant. We laughed. I was fine. Two days after that the pain began. What to compare it to? Childbirth is the obvious one but this was different. Less identifiable. Even deeper within the depths of me. In early 2024, the therapist Julia Samuel fell on a skiing holiday and broke her shoulder, badly triggering a reaction which affected her face, a semi-paralysis caused by an extreme form of shingles. That March she told *The Times*, 'The minute I was told I had the diagnosis I felt like I walked through the door of health to illness. I lost myself.' She explained how she felt 'grey and inchoate whereas normally I feel springy and energetic and upright. I really felt the fragility of life. I kept thinking of my former self, and wanting to get back to her.' Her words summed up what I felt too. But I did not have Julia's courage to admit it.

Over the next week kind medical friends came by and suggested over-the-counter painkillers, suggested increasing the recommended dose by just a little, suggested lying on one side, suggested hot-water bottles. Suggested, suggested. I could barely listen. For the next few months, I found myself withdrawing. I did not read, talk, meet anyone, laugh, watch television, listen to music, leave the house to go into the garden or write my diary. I spent entire days failing to change out of my pyjamas. I was careless of myself. I caught my finger so deeply on a kitchen knife that it bled for eight hours. Exhaustion swamped me. I had to sit down after standing up for more than a minute or two. I relived the fall on an hourly basis. I couldn't manage the easiest of practical tasks. Instead of using kindling to light a fire, I struck the match to an entire box of petrol-impregnated blocks almost igniting the whole chimney. I tried to disguise my inability to bounce my grandchildren on my knee. I burst into tears at the sight of a beautiful dawn. The beauty of the world became intolerable.

The only thing that eased the pain was an almost scalding bath. As the pain intensified fiercely at night I took baths as hot as I could tolerate, submerged in the water until it began to cool, heaving myself out, and running another as soon as the pain became so bad again that I could not bear it. In the meantime, I paced the spare room, hoping I could keep the urge to cry out loud to a level that would not wake my sleeping husband next door. As I paced I mourned my past life, convinced that everything had changed for ever and that I was facing a limiting existence. Every organ in my body felt as if it had been shaken and rearranged. And there was another dimension to this fear. Many years ago, I had almost abandoned my children in childhood. Alcohol had almost taken precedence over my wish for survival not just for me but for them. Unlike last time, these circumstances were involuntary but I felt as if I was once again on the brink of abandoning those I loved most and this time I felt powerless to change the outcome. My then eight-year-old granddaughter Imogen wrote to me. I had been unable to join her and her brother at the Christmas pantomime. 'I don't like you being hurt,' Imo wrote. 'Are you badly hurt? When are you going to get better?' She sent me a drawing of an unhappy face and on the reverse of the paper handwritten phrases were enclosed within multicoloured felt-pen hearts: 'you are brilliant'; 'you are the best'; 'you are lovely', as if by telling me those things she could reassure herself that I was still the person she had known all her life. I wanted to be well, if only for Imo.

The first glimmer of help came with a diagnosis: I had experienced a blunt trauma. That is to say I had not outwardly damaged myself but the force of the fall had been similar to that of a massive car accident. The impact had reached deep into my body and twisted and shaken ligaments and muscles, the bruising and tearing enough to cause almost intolerable pain. The cure was time. I would have to be patient. And I would have to trust. And when I did, professional help listened to me. Katie, an NHS paramedic of exceptional patience and concern, sorted out the strongest of painkillers. Liz, a cranial therapist of singular empathy, released my blocked circulation through her miraculous laying on of hands. And I discovered Professor Webborn, an expert in muscular injury, who had looked after the Paralympic competitors and whose clinic was just twenty minutes away from my house. And then one day I started writing my diary again after a three-month lapse. Here was a place in which I could confide my secrets without facing an audience who might be sceptical about the extent of the despair I had felt. My diary was a way out of isolation, a release from fear. The act of writing things down centred me, restored my sense of control. And slowly the burning corroding fear of endings began to dissipate. I would not die. Not yet, anyway.

Talking and writing about my fall reminded me of how Diana Athill, older than my mother by just a decade, had challenged her generation's reserve by writing so beautifully about the imminence of death. Christina will forever remain the hero of my own age by setting an example of how a final goodbye need not be one of despair. And I saw courage in death demonstrated by the generation that follows mine, too, in Dame Deborah James, whose bowel cancer was never allowed to be a secret. Diagnosed in 2016, she was just thirty-five years old, married with a son Hugo and a daughter Eloise aged eight and six. For the next six years Deborah set out to raise awareness of one of the most stigmatised forms of the illness, known by Deborah with irreverent irony as her 'glam cancer'. Without an iota of shame, she laughed, teased, TikTok-danced and charmed her way through her remaining years, raising huge sums for research into the disease. Journalists stretched for descriptions to do justice to a 'force of nature' who had existed with such 'unbelievable tenacity'. Loved for her 'sparkly, sweary, taboo-busting fun', Deborah was for *The Times* writer Alice Thompson 'the bravest woman I have ever interviewed'. Taking positive advantage of social media, Deborah used every form of communication, proving that when steered with altruistic energy, it can turn the world around. Her blog, initially written for her friends, attracted millions and her star quality made her patron for the UK's leading bowel cancer charity. She headed up the 'Never too Young' campaign, posted daily on her Instagram account, wrote a weekly online column for the *Sun*, shared the BBC's weekly podcast *You, Me and the Big C* with two women friends also living with cancer and published a bestseller, *F***You Cancer*. On the day she died, 28 June 2022, the contributions to her Bowel Babe fund soared by the hour. After her death the NHS reported a ten-time increase in those checking out early symptoms of bowel cancer. In her final weeks, when even the indefatigable Deborah James had acknowledged that further treatment would not win her any more time, she had been visited at her parents' home by Prince William, who toasted her in champagne in her parents' sunny garden as he awarded her a damehood.

CHAPTER 20

Shame Must Change Sides

In 2023 the first of a series of annual seminars called 'Truth Tellers' took place. Organised by Tina Brown in memory and celebration of her husband Harold Evans who died in 2020, the theme of the conference emulated Evans's work by showing how journalists can give a voice to those who have none and the courage required of them to do so. Evans was the giant of British twentieth-century investigative journalists and a champion for women's rights. As editor of the *Northern Echo* in the 1960s, he had fought successfully for regular screening for cervical cancer and in 1968, as editor of *The Sunday Times*, he began working on exposing the thalidomide scandal. The drug prescribed for pregnant women in the late 1950s and early 1960s as a sedative and to counteract morning sickness had been licensed for use without being put through a fully rigorous testing process. As a result, 2,000 babies in Britain and about

10,000 world-wide, across forty-six countries, were born with severe physical defects, with half of them failing to survive longer than a few months. Evans not only revealed the background and extent of such disastrous negligence, but lobbied ceaselessly for compensation for all of those affected by the tragedy.

Some of the contributors at the Truth Tellers conference were men. In the opening session, the *Guardian*'s Nick Davies, who had exposed the 2006 phone-hacking scandal behind the murder of schoolgirl Milly Dowler, set the agenda for the day when he declared that 'for journalists, silence is not an option'. Every half-hour or so another luminary took to the stage to describe the work done in investigating wrong-doing across the world. Here were Bob Woodward and Carl Bernstein, the journalists who blew open the Watergate cover-up. Here was Don McCullin, the celebrated photojournalist whose work had long brought home the reality of both war and peace. Here was Jesse Armstrong, creative genius behind the 2018 super-hit television series *Succession*, getting beneath the skin of his satirical character Logan Roy, assumed to be inspired by newspaper titan Rupert Murdoch.

But what struck me most was the courage and selflessness of purpose of the many young women who appeared in the hall or who were live-beamed from around the world onto the large screens in front of us. Questioned about whether they put their own growing families before or after the cause they were covering, several of them, many of them young mothers, paused before answering. One struggled to hold her voice steady as she described seeing a cross stuck into the scattering of earth that barely covered the body of a child that had been killed in the war in Ukraine. Another risked her life while investigating the Mexican drug cartels and their associated slave labour, sexual exploitation and governmental corruption. Conversations about monsters of abuse like Harvey Weinstein and the misogynistic attitude and lewd language used by President Donald Trump when boasting of taking advantage of women cropped up throughout the day.

The conference left me in no doubt that women, despite the fear of retribution, remain on a mission to expose, expose, expose. A year after the conference ended I met a young Jamaican poet on a visit to England from her home in America. Talking to me about her book *How to Say Babylon*, which uncovered the story of her Jamaican upbringing, Safiya Sinclair explained how she now handles the consequences of that act of exposure. Born in 1984 within the Rastafarian community of Montego Bay, Sinclair grew up throttled by religious patriarchy which brought her to 'the knife-edge of her existence'. Her father Djani was convinced that the Ethiopian emperor, Haile Selassie, had been the Black Messiah. As a reggae musician born in 1962, Djani earned his guitar-playing income from gigs in the tourist hotels where 'Babylon' thrived – the corrupting, empire-drenched Western world that Djani deplored. 'At twenty-six his thick beard and riverine dreadlocks gave him the wizened look of an augur whose tea leaves only foretold catastrophe.' With its loathed figureheads including President Bush, Prime Minister Margaret Thatcher and those who lived in 'Foreign', including the British queen, Babylon represented for the Rastafari 'the government that had outlawed them, the police that had pummelled and killed them'.

At first the darkness of the control exerted by her father over her entire family, including her younger brother but especially over Safiya, her mother and her two younger sisters, felt engulfing. Until the age of five she lived in a small Jamaican hamlet on the white sand of the endless beaches, many of them owned by 'the white enslavers', whose predecessors had stolen Jamaicans' freedom and who had left behind their unforgettable, unforgivable legacy. In the beginning, in *her* beginning, as music filled the salt air, Sinclair never doubted, never questioned, whether her country had given her all the blessings she could ask for, recording those memories in language as richly beautiful as the natural world she inhabited. Male jurisdiction dominated Sinclair's story. Sleeping with 'one watchful eye on my purity and one hand on his black machete' and with a 'gaze that could overcloud the sun', Djani's extreme interpretation of the Rasta ethos controlled every aspect of family life. Fish, meat, dairy, alcohol and tobacco were all banned, as were trousers and the revealing of any flesh. Above all, hair must always be covered, never brushed and never cut. As money became scarcer and Safiya and her siblings were moved into smaller and smaller houses, so the parameters of their existence shrank. Her father's Rastafarian rules felt like the potential control of her soul and even her mind, a concept as chilling as any I had ever heard. Sinclair explained how 'it felt that so much of myself did not belong to me. It was not an existence that could continue that way. Nobody wants to live with every aspect of their lives under the control of another. The secret parts of yourself don't belong to yourself. When I lived in my father's house there was no part of me that belonged to me. Even my thoughts. Even my desires and dreams, he wanted to control those as well, and those are the parts of ourselves that should be ours only.'

As the Rastafarian religion had only been adopted by a small section of the community in Montego Bay, Sinclair's outsiderishness caught her and her siblings in the full spectral beam of oddity at her school of just thirty-five students. Her fellow classmates included a couple of rich white Jamaicans and the children of American and Canadian expats.

'It was nearly impossible for me to hide, even when I longed to disappear,' she told me. Safiya's dreadlocks 'announced me dramatically wherever I went'. Desperate for inclusion, she struggled in 'a strange bubble of alienation', mocked by other pupils for her unfashionable clothes, rejected by yearned-for friends.

Her mother was her salvation; her passion for books showed her daughter that no rules could obliterate the liberating power of words. 'A wild wonder' of a mother, when she introduced her children to the Romantic poets such as the eighteenth-century British poet William Blake, she ignited Safiya's literary 'sense of wonder' and showed her 'a way to heaven within hell's despair'. As Safiya's hair grew to mirror the 'curtain of vines', the phrase she used to describe her father's own hair, any transgression would trigger fury and punishment. But when Safiya was instructed by a teacher, as cruelly culpable as the students, to scrub the ineradicable henna pattern from her hands, 'fear had finally given way to fire' and she had at last reached the point of defiance. With a self-inflicted wound made by a rusty nail, and deepened by the use of a forbidden pair of scissors, the 'seedling of a voice' began to rebel. But one weapon resisted confiscation: the writing of poetry, the one thing over which her father had no wish to claim ownership.

'My father knew I had it,'Sinclair explained, 'but I don't think he knew what poetry could actually become or do in the world. That was because his connection to his own art had never really blossomed the way he wanted. So, all he wished to give me was a cautionary tale: if you become a poet you might be living a failed ideal of what you want your life to be.' Sinclair's secret from him was her unshakeable certainty that if she gave herself up to becoming a real poet she would not fail. She would soar.

Thirty years later, after her mother had separated from her father and made her home in America, Safiya also left home.

I wondered if the process of writing had taught her the benefits of self-analysis.

'No. I wouldn't have called the memoir self-therapy,' she says. 'It was something I just had to do. It felt like a passion. I was driven to do this.' But although she did not classify her writing as therapy, it became therapeutic and restorative. Early on with her very first poems she knew that 'the more that I wrote the more confident I felt in myself. Writing gave me strength and confidence on the page that I hadn't felt before in the world. So I kept doing it.' She would write about her family, about her mother's mother who died an early death. 'My father said to me, "Why are you digging up the past, why can you not let it be?" And I thought, "I want to know and her story deserves to be told. The people who came before us deserve to have someone bear witness to their words and deeds and to say their lives mattered." And that is why I write, the driving force of why I write.'

There was an additional trigger for writing the memoir. When Safiya was at college in the United States she heard that her only brother and his wife were to become the parents of a baby who would be Sinclair's niece, the first girl of a new generation.

'It felt so crucial to me to write this story once I knew my niece, Cataleya, was coming. I felt then it was absolutely necessary because I began to be concerned about what kind of a life she would have. And what kind of life the next generation of women in my family would have. I thought if there is anything I can do to change this traumatic cycle of violence and change the things that had happened to my sisters and mother and all the women that had come before us by writing the story, not just to make sure that my niece knew about our history and our lives but that I could give her an idea of the possibilities, that the future was hers for the making.'

Although Safiya and her brother had fallen out over his urging her to forgive their father, the first thing she did when she heard the news about his daughter was to break the silence by calling to talk about the impending arrival.

'However long the silence between us had lasted, it went right from my mind. I thought about what kind of family dynamic she was going to be born into and I thought whatever I could do to heal that fissure I would do it. Writing the book was an extension of that.'

I asked her if she would still have written the book if her brother's expected baby had been a boy. She hesitates but only for a moment. 'I would have wanted to reach out to my brother.

But there was something different about thinking about this little girl being born in Montego Bay, the same place as me.'

Safiya Sinclair had come to London as one of six authors shortlisted for the inaugural Women's Prize for Non-Fiction. On my way to meet her, the rain was running fast through the gullies of the Piccadilly streets and even though it was mid-summer I had left the muddy fields at home wearing a sweater and ankle boots. Sinclair's shoes were pointed and delicate. Her leather jacket was slung across her shoulders like an off-duty model. Nothing on paper connected us. We did not share an age, a race, a religion, a country or a culture. And yet I knew that when I first read her memoir I recognised so many feelings that I too had felt my way through, oceans and decades away as a teenager growing up in the south of England. The body shame, the ostracising at school, the patriarchal and confidence-eroding attitude that dictated how my mother and I were to behave, all of these things were part of my emotional inheritance too. And there were other links: womanhood, daughterhood and the love of poetry.

Safiya understands why my generation, her mother's generation, might be alarmed by the prospect of a return to a state of secrecy when we had hoped we had made more progress than that. However, she sees the focus of activism shifting in the generation below her from gender equality to the climate crisis. Safiya wonders, 'what kind of world we are giving the next generation and the one below that? Will there be breathable air? Will there be a world?' Finally, I asked about her mother's response to her daughter's breakaway life.

They are unquestioningly as close as a mother and daughter

could be. Her mother often attends Safiya's speaking events and they text and FaceTime one another multiple times a day.

'She is proud of me,' Safiya told me, the simplicity of the sentence deceptive. Her mother's words mean the world to her. Words, written and spoken, have changed everything for them both.

It was impossible to forget that women living under gender-repressive regimes were not only forced by law to stay silent, their mouths, on occasion, concealed from public view, or that they simultaneously depended on secret-keeping as a means of survival. But in September 2022 twenty-two-year-old Mahsa Amini demonstrated the fearlessness and defiance which hopes to change what feels like an intractable law requiring women to exist in an undercover life extinguishing identity. Amini had been travelling from Iran's western province of Kurdistan with her family to visit relations in the capital, Tehran. She was wearing 'an inappropriate' hijab, failing to cover her hair as required since the Iranian Revolution in 1979, a ruling strengthened in 2022 by the fierce enforcement of the 'Hijab and Chastity' law. Amini was arrested for flouting that law and ferociously beaten up in an enclosed van by the 'morality' police, before being transferred to hospital in a state of collapse. Her subsequent death from catastrophic wounds to the head united millions of Iranian women for whom marches in solidarity took place in Athens, Berlin, Brussels, Istanbul, Madrid, New York, Paris, London and Melbourne. The red heat of anger triggered by Amini's violent death triggered a united battle cry against the suppression of women's freedom. Hope for change must not be eliminated. Hope must and can survive.

Two years later the campaign to overthrow another despotic regime was reignited in Afghanistan. In August 2024 the Taliban issued a ruling, 'Commanding the Right and Forbidding the Wrong', which detailed 114 pages of new restrictions on women's lives. The following month a journalist from Afghanistan, writing under a pseudonym in *The Sunday Times,* described the shattering impact the directive was having on her own family and on all women living under a regime in which 'women's voices are now deemed instruments of vice'. In 2024 the Human Rights Council reported on a dictatorship it found to be 'an institutionalised system of discrimination, segregation, disrespect for human dignity and exclusion of women and girls'.

Women were forbidden from working in public places or from deriving any source of income from employment in government offices or hospitals, reducing families to breadline poverty. Public speaking was banned as was singing or reading aloud, 'even in our own homes'. Colour was drained from their lives and bodies, as the wearing of the black uniform that covered every inch of their bodies was further enforced by the morality police. Women were told to lower their voices when in public prayer so they should not be heard by other women. And in the winter of 2024, even the training of midwives and nurses was suddenly abolished. *The Sunday Times* journalist admitted to having 'no hope left', in an existence which is barely an existence. 'No woman here has a life. It's just survival.'

As women's lives continue to go backwards as well as forwards, with AI and data theft compromising the sense of self, is it any longer possible to trace the steady line of progress that seemed so promising to my generation? In 2012 a chain of American online pharmacies that had been tracking customers' buying habits noticed that one customer was ordering vitamins and other products that suggested she was in the middle stages of pregnancy. When these purchases triggered unsolicited offers for baby products, the customer's innocent father noticed the unusual traffic arriving in his own email inbox as well, and telephoned the pharmacy to complain. 'She's still in high school,' he cried, exasperated by their intrusion, 'and you're sending her coupons for baby clothes and cribs?' A follow-up conversation with his young daughter revealed the digital world knew more than he did: he was soon to be a grandfather. When a computer is privy to more information than one's nearest relations, you might wonder if your secrets will ever be your own again.

In America, the reversal in 2022 of its landmark 1973 abortion laws, Roe v. Wade, instantly brought into question the country's foundational narrative of progressive liberalisation. When the US Supreme Court made a decision in the Dobbs v. Jackson case to remove the constitutional right to abortion in the USA, fourteen states recriminalised the majority of abortions, with a further four strictly limiting options. The removal of choice over women's reproductive rights and replacing it with the imposed requirement to continue with a pregnancy, no matter what the individual woman desired, was a further landmark viewed by millions across the world as shockingly regressive. Joan Malleson fought specifically for the right to a legal abortion for a British rape victim in the 1930s. Nearly a century later, that fight was now being enacted in Idaho, a state with some of the country's most stringent anti-abortion laws.

In 2022 a ten-year-old child rape victim, six weeks pregnant and ineligible for an abortion in her own state, was forced to travel to Indiana for the procedure. In the eighteen months after the reversal of Roe v. Wade, an estimated 65,000 victims with rape-related pregnancies were unable to access a termination in their home state. In an interview in June 2022 with the *Financial Times*, Democrat Hillary Clinton warned that one state – 'and this is hard even to speak about' – was on the point of requiring a woman 'to get the permission of her rapist before aborting. Others plan to criminalise women who have the procedure in states where it is legal.'

Roe v. Wade became one of the central issues in the Democratic Party's campaign in the 2024 American election. The electoral ballot papers of ten traditionally Democrat-supporting states included the option to vote for amendments to the Supreme Court ruling which would allow the right to choose to end a pregnancy. Huge numbers of voters in all ten states chose to tick the amendment possibility, but less often the box below containing the name of the Democratic candidate. As the law in the remaining states still forced women to relinquish control over their bodies to governmental regulation, the challenge to a previously held right of democracy meant that half the population would be making potential choices undercover and illegally.

Gloria Steinem remained vocally optimistic of a Democratic win up until the eve of the vote. Her optimism felt well sourced. On election day a rumour went around that thousands of women who had previously voted Republican in deference to their husbands were mounting a secret rebellion and marking the ballot paper with a cross for the Democratic candidate. A video funded by the Democratic Party, voiced by the actor Julia Roberts and released shortly before election day, encouraged this rebellion. Kamala Harris was a better choice than a man who believed he was entitled to 'grab' women 'by the pussy'. In the advertisement women were seen winking at one another as they left the voting booth, the conspiratorial voice-over whispering, 'No one needs to know who you're voting for.' A reporter for Fox News, the Republican-supporting TV network, said that such treachery would be tantamount to marital infidelity. But the predicted female vote for Harris never materialised. Women were not cheating on their husbands, or aligning themselves with a whispering campaign as the only way to get themselves heard. Discussing the arc of women's progress over her own sixty years of activism, Steinem said she had learned 'the lessons of defeat are more important than passing victory'. But a very senior BBC journalist texted three words to me on the morning after the election. She wrote 'men are winning'.

When data fuels algorithms, it licenses a commodification of intimacy where each post made by an 'influencer' is rewarded not only by 'likes', an addictive enough dopamine hit that requires constant feeding, but by money. Pain pays. Secrets are trade. I have considered this dilemma myself as one among many who has used social media accounts to post information or join the commentary on a range of taboo subjects from addiction to incest to financial crisis, to illness, to crime, to relationship breakdown, infertility, miscarriage, infertility, abortion and death. Have we created a culture in which secrets only matter, only hold value, when you tell them, when you commercialise them? With disclosure comes the inability to retreat and with that inability comes the loss of control. Having encouraged ourselves to reveal all, should we now be contemplating whether things would be safer if the lid was slammed shut again? Those things that my mother's generation had not dared to speak about became for my generation the things we *must* no longer repress. But are our daughters and granddaughters now being obliged to return underground to a place where openness will once again be curtailed by caution and fear?

In her 2022 BBC Reith Lecture, one of four speakers to address the subject of 'freedom', Chimamanda Ngozi Adichie, Nigerian writer and author of *Purple Hibiscus*, *Half of a Yellow Sun* and *Americanah*, challenged the new climate of repression, speaking up for 'freedom of speech'. She argued passionately against the censorship of subjects considered unsayable in a misogyny-drenched planet. She addressed the tyranny and repercussions of online abuse. 'One cannot help but wonder in this epidemic of self-censorship, what are we losing and what have we lost? We are all familiar with stories of people who have said or written something and then faced a terrible online backlash. There is a difference between valid criticism, which should be part of free expression, and this kind of backlash.' Having grown up in a country where a brutal political regime was spoken about 'in whispers' for fear of reprisal, she had direct experience of the consequences of outing the truth. And yet truth of all sorts must be expressed, she says, if 'the death knell of literary and other cultural production' is to be interrupted. Those who do not agree with what is said do not have the right to close an argument down: that is the right to which a dictatorship lays claim.

Adichie focused her lecture more specifically on the cultural fallout of being silenced, a template for those who no longer wish to choose to cower in secrecy rather than risk condemnation. 'We all need free speech,' she said. 'Free speech is indeed a tool of the powerful, but it is also crucially the language of the powerless. The courageous protests by Iranian women, the ENDSARS protest in Nigeria, where young people rallied against police brutality, the Arab Spring: all wielded speech. Dissent is impossible without the freedom of speech.'

The feminist writer Laura Bates's Everyday Sexism Project, founded in 2012, continues to provide an invaluable website where women of all ages can express their experiences and anxieties around misogyny anonymously. But in her post-#MeToo book *Fix the System, Not the Women*, Bates talks about how 'it is extraordinary, really, that we live in a society that has managed to pull off the most incredible feat of silencing. A society in which almost all women have these long trailing lists of stories, yet where many of us still feel utterly alone in them . . . it makes it much more difficult to see your experiences as part of a systemic problem. And, if you can't see the system, you can't fight it.' And if you can't see it, you can't speak about it. By allowing a problem to be ignored, accepted and normalised, it becomes invisible and therefore silenced, secretive and dangerous.

Voices continue to resist the fear associated with revealing difficult and painful truths. At the end of 2024 the multiple rape trial in France of the husband – and fifty-one other attackers – of Gisèle Pelicot dominated headlines all over the world.

Dominique Pelicot was discovered to have filmed many dozens of men who, over ten years, he had lured to his marital home to join him in raping his drugged and unconscious wife. Having waived her right to anonymity, and allowed the public and the press into the courtroom, Gisèle Pelicot took the depravity of her assailants out of the secrecy of a marital bedroom and exposed it to the world. She did so, she said, because 'shame must change sides'. She was acting on behalf of the 'unrecognised victims whose stories often remain in the shadows'. As one of Gisèle Pelicot's lawyers Antoine Camus said, she had chosen 'to go beyond the darkness of her story to find meaning in it'. She became an immediate feminist icon.

Reshma Saujani was among the international community of women who responded in horror to Gisèle Pelicot's tale of trauma, aghast to read about the multiple acts of violation, humbled by her courage to speak out. 'In a moment where so many of us as women are feeling like we've lost our voices,' Saujani posted on Instagram the day after the end of the trial, 'Pelicot is a heroic example of taking your power back.'

The police had also shown the Pelicots' daughter Caroline Darian two photographs they had found in her father's files. In the pictures she was in a state of undress that strongly suggested she too had been abused and possibly raped by her own much-loved and trusted father, also when Darian was unconscious. Dominique Pelicot denied the charge but his daughter did not believe him. Darian, child of both victim and perpetrator, insisted her father was 'not sick' but 'dangerous'. A brave and disturbing BBC conversation in January 2025 with Emma Barnett 'forced us as a society to hear the details of what happened to this family'. Emma Barnett, whose journalistic and feminist commitment to giving women their voice means she has witnessed the profoundest of revelations, called it an interview that had 'burrowed itself deep into my soul and psyche'. Gisèle Pelicot is my age and Caroline Darian is from the same generation as my own daughters. Here were fearless truth tellers, corrosive secret exploders like no others. Audre Lorde's words echoed through the years: 'That visibility which makes us most vulnerable is that which also is the source of our greatest strength.'

Another final, perfectly timed, younger voice, arguing her case for not keeping anxieties secret reached me just as we turned the corner into the second quarter of the century. Addressing an audience of one, my now eleven-year-old granddaughter Imogen, on hearing I was laid low with the kind of bug that arrives with the damp, leafless skies of early January, sent me a video message. Intuitively aware that I was worrying, Imogen's message was a rallying call, a healing cry, describing the futility of letting worry of any kind fester in isolation. She was learning by heart a monologue for a drama competition and it was important to her that I listened. Carefully. 'For all the problems in the world, human kind is astonishingly good at finding solutions,' she began, reciting from memory from the wonderful Scottish playwright Douglas Maxwell's *At First I Was Afraid (I Was Petrified!)*.

'So we need our worriers not to remain in our bedrooms but to be out in the street, making suggestions, volunteering, putting our hands up, ignoring the haters, climbing to the very top of the wall and screaming at the top of our lungs.' She ended with her own words, speaking to me directly now, not screaming but in a conspiratorial whisper. 'Can you be brave? Can you inspire?'

There will always be times when human beings *choose* to escape to the attic under the slope of the eaves, to a place where it is possible to guard those soul-nurturing secrets that we do not wish to admit or explain to anyone. Intervals of self-imposed silence, a withdrawal into the life of the mind, remain essential sources of creativity. Moments when, between the acts, the imaginative process is at its most powerfully active. Meditative practice, the longing for a garden shed, a bench in an allotment, even a bathroom with a lock on the door, all offer mental and physical spaces which promise the opportunity of a secret, private existence away from the turmoil of life. In her semi-autobiographical novel *Sexing the Cherry*, Jeanette Winterson wonders if we *all* live on two levels, 'the ideal outer life and the inner imaginative life where we keep our secrets?' Virginia Woolf urges us to 'escape a little from the common sitting room' to a room of one's own if we are to flourish. I, too, cherish the times when I can withdraw completely, seeking out my own form of secrecy in an attic space of both place and mind, by retreating to the sanctuary of a magical wood near where I live.

But it is through the collective power of sharing and listening and supporting others that change and reassurance in solidarity is reached. A woman in labour in the sixteenth century would surround herself with the friends who she considered as close, sometimes closer than siblings. They were known as 'God-sibbs'. With semantic drift the expression contracted into 'gossips', and lost its original message of support, but those gatherings were not unlike the networks of women of the 1970s who came together in each other's homes, lifting the social restrictions on discussing bodies, sex, relationships, frustrations, anger, sources of shame and fear and joy, and who offered a refuge to those in need. Once a year my daughter and her closest friends from university travel from widely scattered homes to meet in the height of summer when the light lingers longest, before the moon appears at its brightest, gathering just as woman have done for millennia, talking through the night, overheard by no one except a low-flying owl or an inquisitive ghost. They draw strength from admissions of fragility. They confide and they listen, nourished by the balance offered by that exchange. Protected by the quietness, the agenda set only by themselves, these are occasions precious in their rarity and in their intimacy, in which unfiltered honesty is predicated on trust, a chance to dissolve the taboos that insist on secrecy and look at them in another way. Can shame, for example, be an emotion from which positivity can emerge? The writer Zadie Smith suggested in 2018 (at the Louisiana Literature festival in Denmark) that feeling shame, despite shame getting 'a bad rap these days', the 'shame of being vulnerable', could instead be a 'productive thing' and a valuable 'corrective on certain kinds of behaviour'. Can guilt lead to forgiveness? Can indifference or jealousy lead to compassion and pride? Can doubt lead to trust beneath the light of the moon?

As I have been writing this book I have been conscious of threading my way cautiously through the gaps in my own experience. Reminding myself again and again of the importance of open-mindedness, of listening properly, of other perspectives, of being proved wrong in long-held assumptions, has led to some of the most intense and revealing conversations I've ever had. They have changed the way I see the world and also myself. All the while I have kept in my mind the image of my mother. Of course it is never possible to completely know another human being, perhaps especially a parent. But I have come to feel that in the act of writing, thinking, forgiving, that a new and profoundly revealing conversation with her has been happening in these pages. Time has brought knowledge. It has dislodged secrets and, on occasion, replaced them with understanding. Her death did not bury all those uncertainties, all those unspoken words. Instead, they have emerged through the prism of reflection and imagination, aided by conversations with many other women from different generations. As time dissolves and allows my mother and me to confide in one another at last, to share our secrets woman to woman, I am newly conscious of how trust and truth, those essential companions, can both protect and liberate us and those we love.

Acknowledgements

Hoping to be trusted with the keeping of secrets is one thing, but asking whether those secrets can be included in a published book is quite another. I have been moved and honoured by the trust shown me by everyone, anonymous or not, who allowed the inclusion of their precious and secret stories in this book, among them Charles and Hugo Anson, Helena and Elena Bonham Carter, Rosie Boycott, Eliza Manningham-Buller, Jo Fairley, Ann Godoff, Pamela Gordon, Elizabeth Harkins, Kathryn Harrison, Susan Hill, Kate Howells, Rebecca and Caroline John, Helena Lee, Nigel Leigh, Caroline Llewellyn, Edward and James Macmillan-Scott, Natalie Meddings, Alan Moses, Erin Pizzey, Letty Cottin Pogrebin, Dee Rouse, Reshma Saujani, Safiya Sinclair, Augustus Skidelsky and Mary Taylor.

*

My love and thanks also to those treasured loyalists who have listened, asked, answered, encouraged, confided in and uplifted me as this narrative slowly unfolded. My wonderful Sils, David O'Rorke and Miles Johnson. And my friends Rachel Wyndham, Julia Samuel, Aly Van Den Berg, Arthur Parkinson, Fiona Lansdowne, Belinda Giles, Anne Goldrach, Clover Stroud, Joanna Scanlan, Angharad Wood, Philip Norman, Gaby Tana, Virginia Nicholson, India Knight, Liz Bussey, Leila Farzad, Sarah Solemani, Tom Grant, June Chichester.

And thank you also in so many various but indispensable ways to Gemma Arterton, Clare Asquith, Francis Baldwin, Sarah Bourke-Borrowes, Kildare Bourke-Borrowes, Susan Boyd, Tina Brown, Linda Clifford, Rachel Cooke, Oriole Cullen, David Dimbleby, Elizabeth Easton, Debbie Exley, Amanda Foreman, Lesley and Chris Goodchild, Dorte Heurlin, Juliet Hughes-Hallett, Kelly Jessiman, Kim Jones, Michelle Kane, Rebecca Lemonius, Sarah Lucas, Sarah Lyall, Chloe MacArthur, Naomi Mantin, Harriet Maxwell, Ysenda Maxtone Graham, Molly Nicolson, Rosie Nicolson, Vanessa Nicolson, Nicci Obholzer, Cate Olson, Jane Dunn Ostler, Caroline Parish, Jemma Paterson, Hugh Penfold, Melissa Perkins, Norah Perkins, Roland Philipps, Justine Picardie, John Preston, Sigrid Rausing, Sarah Raven, Robert Sackville-West, Nash Robbins, Leonie Shearing, Elisa Segrave, Anthony Seldon, Farrah Storr, Jo Thompson, Sasha Lee Wulfsohn, Deborah Young and Klara Zak.

Katie Mair at the Wellcome Collection and the ever-resourceful staff at the London Library, especially Claire Berliner, have helped provide me with words written and spoken that form the backbone of the book.

Elizabeth Day's support has been unflaggingly generous throughout, even before I had written a word.

Hannah Dawson gave me insights, ideas and comments beyond anything I could have dared wish for.

Thank you so much to Alison Tulett, Mireille Harper and Nicola Evans for your meticulously professional and sensitive guidance. Thank you also to Rebecca Gradinger and Madison Hernick at UTA for always believing in this book.

Thank you, Lizzie Milne, for being amazing in so many ways.

Clare Conville is the agent a writer dreams of, forever cheering, encouraging, guiding and making an author's longed-for aspirations a reality.

Clara Farmer, Asia Choudhry, Molly Slight, Rowena Skelton-Wallace and Anna Redman Aylward at Chatto & Windus are unparalleled suggesters, fixers and enthusers. Thanks too to the expert proofreader, Jane Howard and ace indexer, Chris Bell.

Thank you from an indebted author to Becky Hardie, my friend, interpreter of thoughts, flawless adviser and the most infallible, patient, perceptive publisher in the business.

The book came out of a conversation and a cup of tea with William Nicholson one summer's day at the Charleston literary festival a few years ago. His friendship, sensibility and sensitivity around the elusive, indefinable subject of women and secrecy made instant and inspirational sense.

Adam was the first person with whom I shared the gestation of this idea, his advice was, as always, invaluable.

Acknowledgements

Gigi, Gabriel, Gus and Orly light up my life. And Imo (LLHA) has shown me and voiced for me the courage, creativity and strength of a new generation who refuse to be silenced.

The biggest loving thank-you to a Beloved Husband, whose staying power, while sharing a marriage with an all-consuming book, has never wavered.

Above all, this is a book that could not have happened without my daughters, Clemmie and Flora. The wisdom and inspiration of their voices ripple through these pages. It is no secret from me that unconditional love, both given and received, is really all that matters.

Spring 2025

Bibliography

Introduction

The Secret Life of Secrets: *How Our Inner Worlds Shape Well-being, Relationships, and Who We Are*, Michael Slepian; Robinson 2022

The Penguin Book of Feminist Writing, Hannah Dawson (ed.); Penguin Classics 2021

When I Dare to Be Powerful, Audre Lorde; Penguin Books 2020

Scolds Bridle: https://www.bbc.co.uk/ahistoryoftheworld/objects/

Chapter 1

The Hare with Amber Eyes, Edmund de Waal; Chatto & Windus 2010

Giving Up the Ghost: A Memoir, Hilary Mantel; HarperCollins 2013

No More Secrets: *My Part in Codebreaking at Bletchley Park and the Pentagon*, Betty Webb; Mardle Books 2023

The Last Secret Agent, Pippa Latour with Jude Dobson;
    Monoray 2024
Mother was a Black Shirt; BBC Radio 4, 4 January 2010
'The Younger Generation', *Time* magazine; 5 November 1951
*East Side Voices: Essays Celebrating East and Southeast Asian
    Identity in Britain*, Helena Lee (ed.); Sceptre 2022
Conversation with JN and Pam Leigh, 2008

Chapter 2

Out and About (1949*)*, *I Know a Story* (1949), *I Went Walking*
    (1949), *Here We Go* (1949), *Off to Play* (1949*)*, *Through the
    Garden Gate* (1951) and *Once upon a Time* (1951). Janet and
    John Series; James Nisbet and Co
https://www.timegoesby.net/weblog/2020/07/a-tgb-reader-story-
    ladies-of-the-silent-generation.html with Elizabeth A. Rogers
Young Again with Kirsty Young and Gloria Steinem; BBC
    Radio 4, 29 October 2024
BBC News Channel Online Magazine on Katharine
    Whitehorn; 17 January 2005
*Working Class Cultures in Britain 1890–1960 Gender, Class and
    Ethnicity*, Joanna Bourke; Routledge 1994
Jennifer Worth in the *Guardian*, 6 January 2005
More About the Sex Factor in Marriage, Dr Helen Wright;
    Williams & Norgate 1959
Married Love, Marie Stopes; AC Fifield 1918
Thinking about Marriage, J. H. Wallis; Penguin 1963
The Mother's Welfare Clinic pamphlet by Dr Mary Macauley,
    Obstetrician and Gynaecologist, Senior Clinical Research
    Associate, Centre for Maternal and Newborn Health,
    Liverpool School Tropical Medicine
Any Wife or Any Husband, Joan Malleson; Heinemann 1951
Wellcome Foundation https://wellcomecollection.org/
    collections, (CC BY 4.0),Date:1936-1951Reference: SA/
    EUG/C.222 SA/FPA/SR22/14 and SA/FPA/SR22/16

Discovering the family of Miles Malleson 1888–1969, Andrew Malleson; unpublished genealogy, 2012, available at the WL and Google Books

' "You Can't Dismiss that as Being Less Happy, You See it is Different", Sexual Counselling in 1950s England', Caroline Rusterholz, *Modern British History*, Volume 30, Issue 3, September 2019, pages 375–398

Conversation with JN and Oriole Cullen, Victoria & Albert Museum, 2003

Note: The Abortion Act was not passed in Britain until 1967, although the Soviet Union revoked Stalin's 1936 ban on the procedure and re-legalised abortion in 1955. American estimates for illegal abortions in the United States in the 1950s and '60s had ranged from 200,000 to 1.2 million a year. In 1967 Colorado was the first American state to decriminalise abortion in most cases, followed by California and North Carolina and New York in 1970. Three years later the Roe v. Wade case resulted in the Supreme Court ruling in which women from all fifty states were granted access to abortion in the first trimester.

Chapter 3

Merle: A biography of Merle Oberon, Charles Higham and Roy Moseley; New English Library 1983

How We Lived Then: A History of Everyday Life During the Second World War: History of Everyday Life During the Second World War, Norman Longmate; Pimlico 2002

Britain's 'Brown Babies': The Stories of Children Born to Black GIs and White Women in the Second World War, Lucy Bland; Manchester University Press 2019

Notice Me! A Barnardo Child's Scrapbook of Memories: 1946 to 1961, Suzi Hamilton; Melrose Books 2012

Doreen and Andrew, *24 Hours In A&F*; Channel 4, July 2018

Conversation with JN and Natalie Meddings, 2024

Chapter 4

Guardian, 27 February 2020
Dagmar Wilson obituary, *New York Times;* 23 January 2011
Sunday Times interview by David Walsh with Billie Jean King;
    9 December 2007
Portrait of a Marriage, Vita Sackville-West and Nigel Nicolson;
    Weidenfeld & Nicolson 1973
Dawn, A Charleston Legend, Dawn Langley Simmons; Wyrick
    and Company 1994
*Wicked Charleston, Volume 2: Prostitutes, Politics and
    Prohibition*, Mark R. Jones; The History Press 2006
Conversation with JN and Dawn Langley Simmons, 1994

Chapter 5

*Terms and Conditions: Life in Girls' Boarding Schools,
    1939–1979*, Ysenda Maxtone Graham; Slightly Foxed 2016
A Very Private School, Charles Spencer; William Collins 2024
Conversation with JN and Augusta Hope, 2024

Chapter 6

Casper John, Rebecca John; HarperCollins 1987
Thinking the Plant: The Watercolour Drawings of Rebecca John,
    Rebecca John; Pimpernel Press 2020
Conversation with JN and Caroline and Rebecca John, 2023

Chapter 7

The Millstone, Margaret Drabble; Weidenfeld & Nicolson 1965
Sisterhood Is Powerful, Robin Morgan; Random House 1970
Talking to Myself, Anna Raeburn; Elm Tree Books 1984
Pool of Light: The Autobiography of a Punjabi Agony Aunt, Kailash
    Puri and Eleanor Nesbitt; Sussex Academic Press 2013

'In Remembrance: Kailash Puri', Eleanor Nesbitt, *Journal of Sikh & Punjab Studies*, Volume 24, Numbers 1 & 2, Spring–Fall 2017

Midnight Baby: An Autobiography, Dory Previn; Elm Tree Books 1977

I'm Dancing as Fast as I Can, Barbara Gordon; Bantam Books New York 1979

'Squeezed like Sardines in Suburbia', *Guardian*; 19 February 1960

'Sisters under the Coat', Katharine Whitehorn, *Observer*; 29 December 1963

Chapter 8

The Secret Life of Bob Hope, Arthur Marx; Robson Books 2003

The Feminine Mystique, Betty Friedan; W. W. Norton 1963

Scream Quietly or the Neighbours Will Hear, Erin Pizzey; Penguin Books 1974

Infernal Child: A Memoir, Erin Pizzey; Victor Gollancz 1978

This Way to the Revolution: A Memoir, Erin Pizzey; Peter Owen 2011

Conversation with JN and Erin Pizzey, 2024

Note: Marital or spousal rape was criminalised in 1991 in the UK and incorporated into the Sexual Offences Act 2003 and made illegal in 1993 in most states in the USA.

Chapter 9

Spare Rib Reader: 100 issues of Women's Liberation, Marsha Rowe (ed.); Penguin Books 1982

A Nice Girl Like Me, Rosie Boycott; Chatto & Windus 1984

Daring to Hope: My Life in the 1970s, Sheila Rowbotham; Verso 2021

Feminism Is for Everybody: Passionate Politics, bell hooks; South End 2000

The Female Eunuch, Germaine Greer; Harper Perennial 2020

Sexual Politics, Kate Millett; University Illinois Press 2000

The Second Sex, Simone de Beauvoir; Vintage Classics 2015
Shanda: A Memoir of Shame and Secrecy, Letty Cottin Pogrebin;
    Post Hill Press 2022
Fenwomen: A Portrait of Women in an English Village, Mary
    Chamberlain; Virago-Quartet 1975
Women's History Review, Volume 31, Issue 7, 2022
Family Secrets with Dani Shapiro https://podcasts.apple.com/
    gb/podcast/family-secrets
Conversation with JN and Rosie Boycott, 2023
Conversation with JN and Letty Cottin Pogrebin, 2024

Chapter 10

Betty Parsons obituary, *Independent*; 15 February 2012
https://www.gla.ac.uk/schools/humanities/research/history
    research/researchprojects/housingandwellbeing/castlemilk/
Shuggie Bain, Douglas Stuart; Picador 2020
Discover magazine, Issue 47; Winter 2022
Vogue interview with Douglas Stuart; December 2020
Conversation with JN and Fiona Gem, 2023, 2024

Chapter 11

Oprah, Celebrity and Formations of Self, Sherryl Wilson;
    Palgrave Macmillan 2003
Forbidden Britain: Our Secret Past 1900–1960, Steve
    Humphries and Pamela Gordon; BBC Books 1994
Conversation with JN and Pamela Gordon, 2023

Chapter 12

https://www.oprah.com/spirit/what-oprah-knows-for-sure-
    communication
The Microcosm, Maureen Duffy; Hutchinson 1966

From the Closet to the Screen: Women at the Gateways Club 1945–85, Jill Gardiner; Pandora Press 2003
The Last Party: Studio 54, Disco & the Culture of the Night, Anthony Haden-Guest; William Morrow 1997
American Psycho, Bret Easton Ellis; Simon & Schuster 1991
Morbidity and Mortality Weekly Report, the Center for Disease Control (CDC) 1983
Steve Rubell's Archive of Studio 54: Private Collection
Conversation with JN and Ann Godoff, 2023

Chapter 13

Time magazine; 7 October 1991
The Courage to Heal, Laura Davis; Vermilion 2002
Incest, Anaïs Nin; Peter Owen 1993
Intercourse, Andrea Dworkin; The Free Press 1987
The Kiss: A Memoir, Kathryn Harrison; Random House 1997
Conversation with JN and Kathryn Harrison, 2023

Chapter 14

Open Secret: The Autobiography of the Former Director-General of MI5, Stella Rimington; Hutchinson 2001
The Spy and the Traitor: The Greatest Espionage Story of the Cold War, Ben Macintyre: Viking 2018
Conversation with JN and Alan Moses, 2024
Conversation with JN and Eliza Manningham-Buller, 2024
Conversation with JN and Chloe, 2024

Chapter 15

The Therapy Works, Substack by Julia Samuel; 25 March 2024
Alcoholics Anonymous: The Big Book; Hazelden 4th revised edition 2002

Twelve Steps and Twelve Traditions; Alcoholics Anonymous
World Services 1991
Conversation with JN and Zoe, 2023

Chapter 16

*East Side Voices: Essays Celebrating East and Southeast Asian
Identity in Britain*, Helena Lee (ed.); Sceptre 2022
Conversation with JN and Dee Rouse, 2024
Conversation with JN and Helena Lee, 2024

Chapter 17

Toxic: Women, Fame and the Noughties, Sarah Ditum; Fleet 2023
'A Woman's Opinion is the Mini-skirt of the Internet', Laurie
Penny, *Independent*; 4 November 2011
Independent on Diane Abbott; 24 September 2017
Christian Intelligencer; September 1985
Brave, Not Perfect, Reshma Saujani; Crown 2019
Girls Who Code: Learn to Code and Change the World, Reshma
Saujani; Virgin Books 2017
Conversation with JN and Reshma Saujani, 2023

Chapter 18

Jenny Kleeman, *Guardian*, 25 September 2021
Conversation with JN and Mary Taylor, 2023
Conversation with JN and Thomasina, 2024

Chapter 19

Somewhere Towards the End: A Memoir, Diana Athill; Granta
2008
Alive, Alive Oh! And Other Things that Matter, Diana Athill;
Granta 2015

Tweet on X (formerly known as Twitter) by Hanif Kureishi;
9 September 2023
Rachel Cooke, *Observer*; 24 March 2024
All About Love: New Visions, bell hooks; William Morrow 1999

Chapter 20

How to Say Babylon: A Jamaican Memoir, Safiya Sinclair; 4th
Estate 2024
'How Target Figured Out a Teen Girl Was Pregnant before Her
Father Did', Kashmir Hill; *Forbes* magazine, 16 February
2012
We Should All Be Feminists, Chimamanda Ngozi Adichie; 4th
Estate HarperCollins 2014
A Feminist Manifesto in Fifteen Suggestions, Chimamanda Ngozi
Adichie; 4th Estate HarperCollins 2017
Everyday Sexism, Laura Bates; Simon & Schuster 2014
Fix the System, Not the Women, Laura Bates; Simon & Schuster
2023
*I'll Never Call him Dad Again: Turning our Family Trauma of
Chemical Submission into a Collective Fight*, Caroline Darian;
Leap 2024
Passage reproduced by kind permission of Douglas Maxwell
from *At First I Was Afraid (I Was Petrified!)*, Douglas
Maxwell, *Positive Stories for Negative Times*, Volume Two;
Methuen Drama 2021
Sexing the Cherry, Jeanette Winterson; Vintage 1990
Conversation with JN and Safiya Sinclair, 2024
Conversation with JN and Imogen, 2021, 2024

Social History

*Sinners? Scroungers? Saints? Unmarried Motherhood in
Twentieth-Century England*, Pat Thane and Tanya Evans;
Oxford University Press 2012

Modernity Britain, Volumes One and Two, David Kynaston;
  Bloomsbury 2009 and 2014
*Family Secrets: Living with Shame from the Victorians to the
  Present Day*, Deborah Cohen; Viking 2013
*Sex, Race and Class: The Perspective of Winning: A Selection of
  Writings 1952–2011*, Selma James; PM Press 2012
Men Explain Things to Me, Rebecca Solnit; Granta 2014
The Mother of All Questions, Rebecca Solnit; Granta 2017
British Culture and Society in the 1970s: The Lost Decade,
  Laurel Forster and Sue Harper (eds.); Cambridge Scholars
  Publishing 2010
*All the Rage: Power, Pain, Pleasure: Stories from the Frontline of
  Beauty 1860–1960*, Virginia Nicholson; Virago 2024
Difficult Women: A History of Feminism in 11 Fights, Helen
  Lewis; Vintage 2020

Relationships

Fifty Shades of Feminism, Lisa Appignanesi, Rachel Holmes and
  Susie Orbach (eds.); Virago 2013
The Captive Wife: Conflicts of Housebound Mothers, Hannah
  Gavron; Routledge 1966
Thinking about Marriage, J. H. Wallis; Penguin Books 1963
The Patriarchs: How Men Came to Rule, Angela Saini;
  4th Estate 2024
Why Be Happy When You Could be Normal?, Jeanette Winterson;
  Vintage 2011

Voices

The Secret Garden, Frances Hodgson Burnett; Vintage 2012
Forbidden Notebook, Alba de Cespedes, first published in 1953
  by Mondadori, reissued in 2023 by Pushkin Press
The Years, Annie Ernaux; Fitzcarraldo editions 2022 (plus all
  her other books)

Orlando, Virginia Woolf; The Hogarth Press 1928
Heartburn, Nora Ephron; Virago Modern Classics 2008
I Feel Bad About My Neck: And Other Thoughts on Being a Woman, Nora Ephron; Doubleday 2020
Friendaholic: Confessions of a Friendship Addict, Elizabeth Day; 4th Estate 2023
Grief Works: Stories of Life, Death and Surviving, Julia Samuel; Penguin Random House 2017
This Too Shall Pass: Stories of Change, Crisis and Hopeful Beginnings, Julia Samuel; Penguin Random House 2020
Every Family Has a Story: How we Inherit Love and Loss, Julia Samuel; Penguin Random House 2022
Good Girls: A Story and Study of Anorexia, Hadley Freeman; 4th Estate 2023

Podcasts

How to Fail with Elizabeth Day
Laid Bare with Dami Olonisakin, Shakira Scott and Shani Jamilah
Where Should we Begin? with Esther Perel
Agony Aunties with Julia, Emily and Sophie Samuel

Substacks

These are some of the Substacks I have followed and which have all prompted information, ideas, debate, points of reference, research, inspiration and delight.

Trying by Emma Barnett
Home by India Knight
The Kureishi Chronicles by Hanif Kureishi
Tending to Things by Clemmie Macmillan-Scott
No Holds Barred by Arthur Parkinson
Things Worth Knowing by Farrah Storr
On The Way Life Feels by Clover Stroud

Index